Internationalism
and Its Betrayal

Contradictions of Modernity

Edited by Craig Calhoun
University of North Carolina at Chapel Hill

The modern era has been uniquely productive of theory. Some theory claimed uniformity despite human differences or unilinear progress in the face of catastrophic changes. Other theory was informed more deeply by the complexities of history and recognition of cultural specificity. This series seeks to further the latter approach by publishing books that explore the problems of theorizing the modern in its manifold and sometimes contradictory forms and that examine the specific locations of theory within the modern.

Internationalism and Its Betrayal

Micheline R. Ishay

Foreword by Craig Calhoun

Contradictions of Modernity, Volume 2

 University of Minnesota Press
Minneapolis
London

Published by the University of Minnesota Press
111 Third Avenue South, Suite 290, Minneapolis, MN 55401-2520
Printed in the United States of America on acid-free paper

Library of Congress Cataloging-in-Publication Data
Ishay, Micheline.
    Internationalism and its betrayal / Micheline R. Ishay ; foreword
by Craig Calhoun.
        p.   cm. — (Contradictions of modernity ; v. 2)
    Includes bibliographical references and index.
    ISBN 0-8166-2469-0. — ISBN 0-8166-2470-4
    1. Internationalism — History.   2. Nationalism — History.
I. Title. II. Series.
JC362.I73   1995
320.5'4 — dc20   94–30647

The University of Minnesota is an equal-opportunity educator and employer.

*To Edmond, Sheila, Nathalie,
and Carlangelo*

Contents

Part II
Internationalism and the French Revolution: Kant, Paine, and Robespierre

Part III
*The Rise of Nationalism and the Counter-Enlightenment:
Burke, de Maistre, and Fichte*

Foreword

Craig Calhoun

Nationalism appears to most analysts either as an all but primordial inheritance or as a basic and constitutive feature of the modern era. Those who study it are only somewhat less likely to naturalize it than those who preach it. Nationalism — the discourse of national identity, the primacy of national interests, the very notion that there are clearly bounded sociocultural units called nations — seems always already-there in contemporary political theory. Analysts occasionally worry about the justice of various regimes of immigration and citizenship, or of international wars, but democratic theory, especially in its liberal, individualist variants, has little capacity to offer an internal answer to why democracy should end at the borders of any polity. Rather, it borrows tacitly from nationalist thought the idea that political communities have self-evident prepolitical identities that can be invoked to ground questions of legitimacy.

Because nationalism appears as always already in place, and often as quasi-natural, internationalism is commonly explored as the problem of going beyond nationalism. The normalcy of the nation is granted, and with it the idea that modernity had to be structured in terms of nation-states, and then the possibilities of reducing the power of nation-states or creating new, broader frameworks for political cooperation are considered. These are important, indeed vital concerns, but we get off on the wrong foot in addressing them if we fail to see that nationalism did not simply precede as a yet-untried possibility of internationalism. Rather, as Micheline Ishay shows in *Internationalism and Its Betrayal*, the primacy of the nation in political theory grew alongside the production of an international politics organized in terms of nation-states, and in rejection of earlier "internationalist" theories and programs.

Not least of all, the premodern notion of Christendom as a broadly inclusive and internally diverse sociopolitical counterpart to the universal religion offered an internationalist inheritance to early modern thinkers. Many, including Vico and Grotius, sought to build on the foundations of this notion of Christendom, expanding it into the basis for a new world vision that would address newly significant problems of war and commerce. This project lived on to inform later thinkers like Rousseau, despite their generally more ambiguous relationship to the church.

Abandoning Christendom, for the most part, the Enlightenment nonetheless celebrated internationalism, now reconceived in a new secular universalism that was at least conceptually global. Much early nationalist thought grew within the Enlightenment, but as a universalistic notion of solidarity and citizenship, sometimes complemented by the bounded universalism of patriotism. It was linked more closely to the conception of rights of the politically unified people against the monarch than to clashes among peoples. For this reason (although Kant perhaps remains the paradigmatic Enlightenment philosopher) the Enlightenment is closely linked in political thought with the French and American revolutions. Paine and Robespierre are thus appropriate foci for Ishay's exploration.

It was primarily after Napoleon transformed his early ostensible commitment to Enlightenment universalism into a more conventional attempt at power politics and empire-building that the dominant accounts of nationalism began to stress the particularistic rights of specific ethnically or historically constituted nations against more general projects of Continental or global unification. This shift was also driven by the Romantic reaction to Enlightenment rationalism and the growing emphasis on organic understandings of social solidarity and primordial identities. Perhaps no version of this process makes the shift clearer than Fichte's gradual transformation from the most loyal of Kant's disciples into an increasingly Romantic apostle of German national identity for whom the globally universalistic project of a perpetual peace gave way before the primacy of the project of national unification. In other settings, Burke and de Maistre gave distinct but related accounts of the importance of gradual historical constitution of collective identity in opposition to revolutionary attempts at the whole-sale reconstitution of collectivities.

The betrayal of internationalism did not come entirely from with-out, however. As Ishay argues, earlier liberal political theory incor-porated implicit particularisms, even where it was ostensibly and intentionally internationalist. The tension between notions such as universal human rights and nationalism was played out significantly within liberal theory, not only between liberal (or Enlightenment) theory and other putative forces of darkness.

Ishay's account of these phases in the development and transfor-mation of internationalist thought focuses on key individual political theorists. It offers both a new context in which to read canonical theorists and an important indication of the connection between the conventional history of political thought and a thread in its develop-ment that is commonly left obscure. Although this is a work of more abstract political theory, Ishay is concerned to see theory developing within the social and political history of the early modern era, and specifically to see the tensions between internationalism and nation-alism, universalism and particularism, working themselves out in clear phases. Indeed, that Ishay concludes her book with a consideration of Hegel is no accident. Hegel attempted perhaps the greatest synthe-sis of liberal universalism and nationalism, Romanticism, and other more particularistic perspectives. He also contended that philosophy amounted to "the epoch comprehended in thought." Ishay explores the difficulties of Hegel's proposed synthesis of universalism and par-ticularism, but shares the attempt to comprehend epochs by key mani-festations of their philosophical thought. In this sense, *International-ism and Its Betrayal* is very much a work of political theory, albeit historically informed, not an attempt to explore the many and some-times conflicting currents of political and cultural contention within each period that did not issue in enduring works of philosophy.

But this is also a study that bears on significant practical concerns of the contemporary era. Crises from Bosnia to Rwanda have brought nationalism to the forefront of thought in the 1990s. Though aca-demic analysts rushed to offer explanations, few were altogether sat-isfying. These genocidal civil wars and other conflicts of the era seemed not to have been caused simply by ancient ethnic hatreds, *ressenti-*

ment, delayed state-building, late entrance into the capitalist world system, or any of the other factors offered as master explanations by academic theorists. Social scientists underestimated the extent to which manipulation by certain elites and formal political leaders like Slobodan Milosevic brought to powerful life half-dormant nationalisms. They also underestimated the extent to which regimes like that of the U.S.S.R. helped to create later nationalist conflicts by simultaneously institutionalizing national identities they formally declared to be of declining importance and massively relocating populations in ways that reinforced the salience of national identities. And most social scientists underestimated the extent to which the rhetoric of nationalism had been enshrined in an international discourse that made it appear both normal and legitimating for a host of projects.

If the academic discourse about nationalism was problematic, the public discourse of political leaders and diplomats was even more impoverished. The reduction of nationalist conflicts to mere continuations of ancient ethnic hatreds (as, for example, in U.S. Secretary of State Warren Christopher's analysis of the Bosnian conflict) was shockingly simplistic. Unsurprisingly, it was also very self-serving, for such an account suggested that international actors could do little beyond limiting the supply of arms and sponsoring humanitarian relief efforts. Faced with nationalism, most of the international community threw up its hands, despairing of what it saw as a disastrous inheritance for which it neither shared responsibility nor had the resources for constructive action.

Yet in both Bosnia and Rwanda, international actions were directly productive of nationalist conflict. The ways in which the international political and diplomatic elites handled the post-1989 crisis of East European communism undermined relatively stable political systems like that of Yugoslavia and reduced the possibilities for peaceful transition. Encouraging the secession of Slovenia and Croatia (partly because they presented themselves in the internationally approved rhetoric of primordial ethnic nations rather than the more confusing Bosnian claim to be a multinational republic) left both a rump Yugoslavia dominated by Serbia and a widespread sense among Serbs that they had better act fast and violently rather than count on benefiting from any peaceful transition. Likewise, Rwanda was a relatively stable and well-governed country prior to 1988. It had a long-standing history of ethnic oppression, and colonial powers had fanned the flames of Hutu/Tutsi conflict. But there was peace and growing national integration until the collapse of coffee prices in the international market produced an economic crisis. As is its wont, the International Monetary Fund stepped in with advice: export more (even though the net effect of this will be to drive down global commodity prices further) and implement "structural adjustment" policies to ensure a maximally private market, minimal state subsidies, and long-run security for international creditors. The effect was a domestic economic collapse, a rapid rise in food prices combined with unemployment, and a country ripe for the imprecations of nationalist demagogues. In both cases, the problem of internationalism does not just arise with questions about universal human rights and possible humanitarian interventions, but is constitutive of the very crises themselves in ways not unrelated to the blind spots of liberal individualism.

The problem is not just that international diplomats and multilateral agencies mishandled two specific situations: the entire international framework for understanding nationalism and related conflicts is deeply flawed. Among other things, it systematically obscures such international influences on the production of domestic, putatively entirely ethnic, struggles. It also leaves well-intentioned international actors with no good way of grasping their connection to the genocides and nationalist wars that have marred—but systematically marked—the twentieth century. Not only do these appear often as premodern inheritances, and therefore disconnected from their genuinely modern and even contemporary sources, but they appear as fundamentally separate from the institutions and discourse of the respectable international community. Diplomats and analysts fail to see the connection between the structuring of the international community as a world system of putative nation-states, of making adaptation to the rhetoric of nationalism a condition for entrance into the United Nations, and the pernicious forms of nationalism they decry. Not only they but many of the rest of us fail to reflect on the ironic nationalism reproduced in asking whether intervention in genocidal wars is or is not a part of the compelling national interest of the United States or any other country.

At the intellectual heart of these difficulties lies the tendency to see nationalism as a problem to be explained on its own, to be endured until it fades away with the last of various "old orders," and to be cleared up before internationalism can work. *Internationalism and Its Betrayal* helps us see how this tendency leads us to misunderstand both nationalism and internationalism. In particular, we fail to see that nationalism is not a discursive formation clearly prior to internationalism, but rather that internationalist projects shaped the way early political theorists addressed the expansion of markets, the breakup of empires, and other transformations of the early modern era. This bears directly on how we think today about the questions of international responsibility in the face of nationalist violence and about the practicality of internationalist projects. Knowing the extent to which modern nationalism did not simply precede the project of internationalism but involved its betrayal should give us a more critical view of conventional political discourse and a greater sense of the possibilities open to us. So should knowing that the betrayal was not simply an arbitrary act of later generations but a development rooted in the internal tensions of liberal political thought.

Preface

*After many revolutions, with all their transforming effects, the
highest purpose of nature, a universal cosmopolitan existence, will
at last be realized as the matrix within which all the original
capacities of human existence may develop.*[1]   —Immanuel Kant

Kant eloquently warned in his treatise *Perpetual Peace* that the ultimate alternative to a lasting internationalist peace was the vast grave-
yard of the human race—a possibility that has not disappeared in
our fragile "New World Order." To explain the ephemeral appeal of
internationalist projects, as espoused by liberal (and later by socialist) thinkers,[2] it is important to understand how internationalism developed during its formative period. Such an analysis may help to lay
the foundation for a durable approach to international peace, based
on equality and social justice.

Internationalism is typically understood as being diametrically
opposed to nationalism. It is commonly perceived as an ideology that
stresses universal justice and political rights regardless of national,
ethnic, or religious origins, whereas nationalism places primary emphasis on the nation, its culture and particularist interests, as opposed to
those of other nations or supranational groups. A survey of the literature on nationalism shows that scholars have treated this issue in
isolation from internationalism. In this respect, it will suffice to mention the work on nationalism by Hans Kohn, Carlton Hayes, Elie

Kedourie, Anthony Smith, Eric Hobsbawm, Benedict Anderson, Ernest Gellner, Julia Kristeva, and Liah Greenfeld.[3] Yet it is essential to recognize how the appearance of internationalist initiatives coincided with the periodic resurgence of nationalist ideologies. This does not imply that internationalism is either the "cause" or the "effect" of nationalism, but rather that the acute manifestation of one has invited what might be considered the dialectical response of the other.

Internationalism and nationalism (defined at length in the Introduction) have been intertwined throughout history. The internationalism of the French revolutionaries followed the particularism of feudal monarchs after the disintegration of Christendom. Likewise, the internationalist spirit emanating from the Paris Commune in 1871 succeeded the birth of nationalism after the Napoleonic Wars. The internationalist visions of the Russian Revolution and the League of Nations responded to the nationalist fever of World War I. Similarly, the establishment of the United Nations was predated by the bloody chauvinism of World War II. Finally, nationalism has risen in this fin de siècle from the ashes of Soviet and East European Communism.

By examining the nature of internationalism and nationalism in their early manifestations, I hope to shed new theoretical light on our understanding of liberalism in general.[4] Most of the contemporary literature on liberalism (and socialism for that matter) considers the notion of citizenship and moral virtue on the domestic or communitarian level rather than on the international stage.[5] Focusing mainly on the national or communal realm, scholars have explicitly or implicitly embraced an ill-conceived alternative to nationalism, a liberal or socialist version of global solidarity uninformed by nationalism.

The liberal and socialist challenge to Eurocentric perspectives, rightly developed against conservatives' claims of Western supremacy over the Third World, has further contributed to the intellectual paralysis regarding the question of universal morality. The lack of a universal framework of reference has created an open field for the development of cultural and political relativism. This relativist attitude is also reflected in international politics by liberals' reluctance to criticize the internal and cultural values of other states, for the sake of fostering stable international cooperation. The absence of a consistent democratic commitment in global affairs might well also have been responsible for the difficulty in implementing a new liberal world order, announced after the fall of the Berlin Wall.[6] Instead, the collapse of the Eastern bloc has left a political and intellectual vacuum that has been dangerously filled by a new tide of nationalism.

To develop a coherent democratic internationalist position in the new global context, one must understand the original patterns of its failure. This book will try to capture how Western liberalism discloses at its early stage an ambiguous and schizophrenic character that oscillates between particularist interests and a worldwide politics of compassion. Indeed, the history of liberalism is characterized by its attempt to unify these conflicting drives; it involves the attempt to espouse humanist ideals while maintaining a particular class and national perspective.

Acknowledgments

This book would not have been possible without the comments and suggestions of various individuals. I would like to thank Stephen Bronner for being a shrewd critic, a wonderful teacher, and a loyal friend without whom this book would not have seen the light; Benjamin Barber for challenging my way of thinking; W. Carey McWilliams's support and stimulating mind; and Zeev Sternhell's guidance in the fascinating study of nationalism.

I am particularly indebted to John Vail for having read the manuscript more than once, for his constructive criticism, and for his loyal friendship; to David Goldfischer for his steady support, cautious editing, and warm collegiality; to Michael Forman for his comments, technical help, and camaraderie; to Gill Kent for her proofreading; to William Daniels, Michèle Pietrowski, and Kristen Bornhorst for their diligent assistance; to David Thorstad for his attentive copyediting; and to my editors Craig Calhoun and Lisa Freeman for their valuable suggestions.

In addition, I would like to thank many friends, colleagues, and students for their help or suggestions: Mary Caponegro, Manisha Desai, Alan Gilbert, Ruth Heim, Grant Holly, Paul Kan, Giorgio Mariani, Daniel Madorsky, Avner Offer, Jim Orsini, T. Regan, F. Peter Wagner, and Robert W. Williams.

The political strength and emotional sensitivity of my internationalist friend Lillian Fahrat remain a source of inspiration. The friendship, political commitment, and encouragement of Tony Crowley will not be forgotten, nor will the penetrating insights of Rhoda Singer.

I owe a special thanks to Carlangelo Liverani for shedding a scientific and methodical light on my work, for his patience, and most important, for his emotional support.

Finally, I would like to thank my family, Edmond Ishay, Sheila Bazini, Nathalie Ishay, Udi Shapir, and Tal Ishay-Shapir, who provided me with the internationalist and emotional background to realize this project.

Introduction

What Is the Meaning of Internationalism?

Internationalism is defined in this book as a process sui generis rather than a static concept, shaped and transformed by progressive thinkers and historical events. "Progressive" refers here to actions and ideas that challenge the status quo in pursuit of altruistic ends. Although internationalism is evolving, common characteristics can be identified throughout history. Unlike the realist paradigm in international relations, which conceives the global arena as a system of relationships between monolithic states, internationalism has to be understood in broader terms, as philosophical guidelines describing social relations between and within states. Internationalism assumes a dynamic between the global and the domestic social arrangement. It is thus the historical record of progressive events and thoughts clustered around philosophical, political, and global perspectives.

Furthermore, unlike the realist paradigm, which focuses on economic, military, or any other instrumental links between nations, internationalism includes both an instrumental *and* a normative view of social and global unity. By instrumentalism (or particularism), I refer to all kinds of formal relationships guided by self-interest such as commerce or conquest; whereas by normative (or universalism), I mean all types of social relationships inspired by ethical and political rights applied equally to all people. The instrumental and the normative character of internationalism each predominated in different periods. During the seventeenth century, for instance, internationalism was conceptualized both globally and domestically mainly in instrumental and mercantilist terms. In the eighteenth century, internationalism acquired a normative attribute with the development of republicanism—a belief that maintained that political and economic rights, as legislated by representative institutions, could be maintained domestically only when these rights were extended to the global system. Yet the failure to propagate these rights on the global level led to the decline of internationalism and the subsequent rise of nationalism, that is, to an instrumental and ethnic perspective on the nation.

Scholars on nationalism such as Hobsbawm, Gellner, Greenfeld, and Anderson generally agree that cultural, ethnic, or religious claims are integral elements of nationalism.[1] They have identified in different ways various types of nationalism, ranging from more universal attitudes aroused by the nation-state to the most exclusionary sentiments. Gellner identified, in the same nationalist rubric, eighteenth-century "universal spirit" and Mussolini's political *sacro egoismo*.[2] Greenfeld includes in her definition of nationalism both eighteenth-century universalist views of the nation and a "particularist" attachment over the nation.[3] Unlike Greenfeld and Gellner, Anderson and Hobsbawm argue that universal patriotism should not be confused with nineteenth-century nationalism: the one promotes popular sovereignty while the other celebrates cultural loyalty.[4] Despite these distinctions, none of these scholars offer a systematic analysis of the dynamic between nationalism and internationalism, showing how nationalism is an intrinsic part of internationalism.

In this book, I propose to explain nationalism as the product of the breakup of republican internationalism. The concept of national identity, which evolves into nationalism, is discussed as fundamentally entwined with internationalism. Like internationalism, nationalism is understood as a historical process, which emerged as a result of the tension within internationalism, and later in reaction to the betrayal of the principle of universal and political solidarity. Nationalism is shaped in diametrical opposition to internationalism: citizens' rights are superseded by cultural rights, representative regimes by a strong national unit, and individuals' rights by national interest. Since the idea of the nation and therefore of nationalism is encompassed in the notion of internationalism, this book focuses on the latter broader concept. Such attention may provide a new framework of reference for understanding the reasons for the failure of internationalism.

It is important to note that the concept of internationalism often has been associated with mid-nineteenth-century socialism rather than with eighteenth-century liberalism. Despite their ideological differences, both liberals of the eighteenth century and socialists of the nineteenth century developed a worldview that aimed to replace authoritarian and unrepresentative regimes domestically and globally; both developed a global perspective of solidarity based on secularism and democratic institutions; and both identified a particular class as the natural advocate of internationalism.

Yet the growing cleavage between political and economic rights, global and domestic political aspirations, led to the downfall of "democratic" or "republican" internationalism. Napoleon Bonaparte's and Joseph Stalin's practical nationalism betrayed the democratic internationalist forces of their respective revolutionary countries. Bonaparte's internationalist claims were an attempt to veil both domestic authoritarianism and France's expansionist policy throughout Europe, whereas Stalin's internationalism was a mere disguise for Russia's internal dictatorship and domination in Eastern Europe.

The discussion of internationalization has been revived by social scientists during the second half of the twentieth century. Karl Deutsch emphasized the development of a global communication network; Robert Keohane and Joseph Nye described the growth of telecommunications, transnational organizations, multinational banks, and multinational organizations; Immanuel Wallerstein and Andre Gunder Frank focused on the increasing structural interdependency created by world capitalism.[5] Yet, by focusing on a formal definition of the globalization of world politics, the realist, structuralist, and dependency paradigms—whether from the right or the left—have emphasized the mechanistic and instrumental nature of globalization rather than the qualitative and normative aspects of global relationships.

To resurrect such aspects, it is therefore important to evaluate the global order in relation to the development of democratic political and economic arrangements. Formalist systems of belief, such as realism, behaviorism, structuralism, and dependency theory, neither provide the space to understand the reasons for the failure of democratic internationalism nor allow the theoretical room to explore the ways in which "democratic internationalism" could be sustained. Before positing a viable democratic internationalism — a task within the spirit, but not within the scope, of this book — it is important to trace the roots of internationalism to its origins in the Enlightenment.

I shall thus briefly distinguish internationalism from two other concepts commonly used in the literature of the Enlightenment: cosmopolitanism and universalism. Cosmopolitanism was inextricably associated with Greek and Roman antiquity. It stressed an individualist and a secular sense of solidarity with the rest of humankind. Socrates, for example, derived the idea of citizenship from the Athenian polis and applied it to the world at large. Later on, Roman cosmopolitans — Cicero from provincial Tuscany, Seneca from Cordova in Iberia, Epictetus of Hierapolis in Phrygia, Plutarch from Greece — preached a collective spirit designed to transcend the disintegrative impact of polytheism in the huge empire in which they lived. Inspired by Socrates, they proclaimed their "world citizenship" as the ideal of all erudite and virtuous men.[6]

Cosmopolitanism of the Roman sort naturally excluded unpropertied individuals, *proletarii,* and slaves from political participation in the res publica. In fact, the citizenry of Rome was defined mainly as the property-holding classes. This ideal of citizenship allowed the aristocracy to consolidate its power by excluding the rest of the population from political responsibility. This discriminatory domestic policy would later have repercussions on Roman foreign policy. The particularist ambitions of the imperialist Roman oligarchy indeed gradually spurred rebellions of peasants and slaves, contributing to the weakening of the cosmopolitan spirit of the empire, which finally collapsed under external threats.[7]

The erosion of cosmopolitanism during the last days of the Roman Empire was met with the universalist claims of early Christianity. The Roman pontiff, universal bishop and ambassador of God on earth, stood as a symbol of a great supranational and supernatural society; it was a new cosmopolis with Latin as its worldwide lingua franca and a revealed orthodoxy as its corporate and universal frame of reference. Cosmopolitanism may have originally stressed the solidarity between the individual and humanity; now, however, this connection could occur only through the mediation of the church.

The universalism preached by the church in the global sphere served also to link organically each member of the domestic social body and to solidify new political arrangements. John of Salisbury identified the clergy as the soul of the body, the king as the head, the council as the heart, officials and soldiers as the hands, farmers as the feet.[8] Boniface VII declared in the *Unam Sanctum* (1302) that temporal power should be subordinated to the spiritual power of the universal church, while Dante, in the *Divine Comedy*, celebrated a universal religion of the human species and a single polity for all individuals under the tutelage of the emperor.

Despite its universalist intentions, the church was beset with divisiveness from its inception. The schism between Western and Eastern Catholicism, confessional antagonisms toward Jews and Muslims, and the gradual stratification of the church seriously impeded the growth of a universalist spirit. In addition, the universal love propagated by the church never meant global or domestic political equality among its members. For the majority of the population throughout the Middle Ages, universal felicity remained a purely theoretical and spiritual ideal, whereas for feudal leaders and bishops it was expressed in material reward: wealth monopoly, tithe and tax exemptions, and special prerogatives for public office. By promising universal happiness in the kingdom of God in compensation for people's earthly poverty, the clergy shielded the feudal system from potential usurpers of power. This global illusion of universalism perpetuated in the domestic sphere the wide economic disparity and privilege differences between the aristocracy and the rest of the population.

An individualist and intellectual climate propitious to the cosmopolitan attitude was slowly revived during the Renaissance and gained a further impetus through the Enlightenment. The discovery of the "New World," the expansion of trade, the rise of the bourgeoisie, and startling technological advances ignited a cosmological intellectual curiosity that stimulated the individual's sympathy for the rest of humanity. At the same time, with the growth of the nation-state and mercantilism, a new global perspective, internationalism, premised on a new form of national allegiance, was developed during the Reformation against both the Catholic res publica's jurisdiction over a wide *imperium* and its false vision of universal happiness.

Internationalism was both global and national in character. In its first phase, it began to be associated with the increased self-awareness of mercantilists seeking global solidarity and freedom from the Catholic commonwealth. Such achievements were, however, mainly contingent upon the formation of strong national units able to acquire more wealth and develop further commercial transactions. Internationalism was thus understood in terms of natural and economic rights. It was applicable to individuals both within and between states, compatible with the spirit of free enterprise, able to free the realm of knowledge from Christian tutelage and to expand the property rights of the mercantilist class.

This new internationalist ideology reached a second phase of maturity when the bourgeoisie, allied with the *petit peuple* in opposition to the feudal state, added to the economic meaning of internationalism a normative vision of global and domestic unity. "Republican" or "democratic" internationalism was now aiming at political equality and economic opportunity for all individuals within and across nations. Political philosophers such as Paine, Kant, and others maintained the importance of establishing republican and representative institutions throughout the world in order to develop commerce and mitigate wars. The extension of political and economic rights to sections of the Third Estate, however, threatened the economic superiority of the bourgeoisie. The French Revolution indicated the progress of internationalism, yet also unveiled its contradiction. The tension between the political and economic realms in the domestic sphere undermined the collective spirit of the Third Estate and aborted its further development in the global sphere.

The third phase of internationalist solidarity occurred after 1794. It served national aspirations and was limited to the political and economic interests of the Thermidorian bourgeoisie, later consolidated by Napoleon's regime. However, the unfulfilled internationalist pretensions of Bonaparte's Continental System, like those that underlined Stalin's Soviet empire, stirred up nationalist discontents throughout Europe. Internationalist solidarity was eclipsed by the rise of nationalist resentments and the politics of national interest — or rather, the pursuit of national interest was perceived as ultimately promoting international welfare. The history of the nineteenth century illustrates that the principles of justice, as espoused by the French Revolution, could not be reconciled with the capitalist order. Thus understood, democratic or republican internationalism remained a futile theoretical abstraction.

In short, cosmopolitanism, as it originated during antiquity, was a secular and psychological attitude, derived from the individual in the polis and extended to the rest of humanity. Universalism, by contrast, signified a formal outlook, which linked each individual in the community through the medium of the church. The new internationalist vision maintained elements of both cosmopolitanism and universalism and was gradually appropriated by the rising middle class, as the late nineteenth-century internationalism found its most fervent champions in the working class.

The internationalist vision as espoused by seventeenth-century mercantilists preserved the secular and individualist sentiment of cooperation derived from cosmopolitanism. It no longer supported a feudal agrarian form of production, but instead endorsed individual freedom and instrumental exchange in the marketplace. Internationalism during the eighteenth century also maintained the communal and organic character of universalism. It was, however, no longer identified with the hierarchical order of the church or by any supernatural force, but by individuals' gradual subscription to the rule of natural law, universal reason, and the republican state.

Method and Structure

As we have seen, changing conceptions of internationalism can be divided historically into three phases. The first covers the origins of internationalism from the disintegration of the Catholic commonwealth; the second examines the contradictions of internationalism as it matured throughout the French Revolution; the third analyzes the reasons for internationalism's downfall, which coincided with the rise of nationalism engendered by Napoleon's conquests.

For each historical phase, I have selected significant political thinkers whose writings critically reflect both their cultural and historical context and the contradictions of internationalism. Vico, Grotius, and Rousseau, whose works cover either the progress of the Reformation or the prerevolutionary period, are discussed in Part I; Kant, Paine, and Robespierre, who defined internationalist thinking during the French Revolution, are examined in Part II; Burke, Fichte, and de Maistre exemplify the rise of romanticism and nationalism, discussed in Part III. The Conclusion explores the contribution of Hegel, who incorporated the ideas of the Enlightenment and the new ideas of romantic nationalism.

Each phase of internationalism will be discussed in terms of its significance for three realms of human activity: the philosophical, the political (political society or the state),[9] and the global. It is important to point out that this is not a study covering the extensive ideas of Grotius, Vico, Rousseau, and others, but rather a thematic explanation of internationalism and nationalism, as interwoven historical processes, through the lenses of key thinkers. Before investigating the political thinkers' respective vision of internationalism and later nationalism, I should explain the criteria used for the selection of the thinkers. Why are these thinkers chosen as representative and not others? Why are they classified in three different periods?

After all, a great number of progressive political thinkers — as well less progressive thinkers for the postrevolutionary period — could have been chosen for this project. It was important to maintain a representative sample of progressive political thinkers from various areas of Europe to illustrate the European character of internationalist ideology. Without implying some definitive judgment regarding the importance of one European thinker over another, the pool was narrowed to select thinkers whose intellectual or political contributions have been widely recognized.

Moreover, each thinker was selected in terms of his relationship to critical events that generally influenced intellectual works published during these periods. These historical criteria assume that such events not only shaped the political, economic, and cultural character of the European societies but also inspired new intellectual visions across the Continent. These events were clustered around three historical turning points that had major repercussions on European politics: the Reformation, the French Revolution, and the establishment of Napoleon's empire.

The writings of the selected political thinkers have thus not been treated in strictly textual fashion, which often privileges an ahistorical interpretation, but rather within their respective socioeconomic and cultural contexts. By underplaying the social background of those who advocated universalism and cosmopolitanism, important critics

of the Enlightenment were unable to explain the shift from internationalism to nationalism.[10] Their analyses remained, in other words,
static or descriptive. Although intellectual works are not crudely determined by the historical context in which they arose, a historical
study must, in the words of Lucien Goldmann, "connect the conscious intention of the actors of history to the *objective* meaning of
their behavior and actions,"[11] for the transformation of internationalism can only reflect the interplay between ideas and events. The
following sections outline the evolution of internationalism as a product of the dialogue between ideas and contexts, and of the interplay
between philosophy, political society, and global affairs, within each
of the three historical phases. Given the summary nature of this Introduction, the similarity rather than the difference between the thinkers
of each phase will be emphasized.

Phase 1

The first phase of internationalism grew out of the fragmenting and
unifying tensions of the sixteenth century. Successive events gradually dismembered Catholic unity: the Protestants' attempt to replace
the Catholic church led to prolonged religious wars; the rationalist
postulates of the scientific revolution defied the revealed assumptions of the church; and the development of autonomous mercantile
nation-states in Europe challenged the centralizing impetus of Catholic
doctrine. These rapid changes hastened the decay of feudal society,
which broke progressively into small nuclei, into independent
spheres of human activities polarized between the supernatural and
the natural kingdom, the private and the public realm, domestic and
international politics. The disintegration of Christendom and feudalism created a space for the development of towns, in which a rising
bourgeoisie succeeded in strengthening itself through economic transactions, outside the jurisdiction of the church and the landowning
aristocracy.

The international nature of these erosive events created the conditions for the emergence of alternative forms of universalist unity.
To surmount the fragmentation of the Catholic church, a new form
of collective solidarity was sought by the emerging bourgeoisie. In
the quest for new patterns of international cooperation, the thinkers
of the ascending mercantilist class strove to retain the compartmen-

talized features of the decomposing feudal society that had created room for their own growth. Through the marketplace, and no longer under the aegis of the church, internationalism emphasized the instrumental needs of individuals distinct from their race, locality, and creed. The universal and particular aspects of this new ideology reverberated on various levels of human expression: in philosophy, political society, and the global order.

In the philosophical realm, Thomas Aquinas's distinction between divine and natural law was developed by Reformation and Enlightenment followers. Luther and Calvin argued that God's law and wisdom were revealed to individual reason in the process of working with nature.[12] Divine law and revelation had proven elusive and divisive concepts during the sixteenth-century religious wars. René Descartes's *Discourse on Method*, Pufendorf's *De officio hominis et civis juxta legem naturalem,* and Francis Bacon's *Novum Organum* shaped the new intellectual climate, which gradually replaced divine law with natural law and the universal principle of reason.[13] By focusing on earthly happiness rather than the supernatural, they shifted the focus of attention from universalism to internationalism. In the spirit of the Reformation, a new collective vision was elaborated to enhance both the individualist aspect of God's material reward and the universal accessibility of these terrestrial benefits.

The particular and universal character of the developing internationalist vision was also formulated in political society and at the global level. Endeavoring to develop a universal legal code for international transactions, the new middle class employed the nation-state to advance its particular interests by demanding national subsidies and monopolies in foreign trade and the restriction of foreign imports. Hobbes and Locke conceived civil society as a social contract integrating the interests of individuals with the rule of law.[14] The state provided the space for individuals to acquire property and to exchange it freely, without tariffs. The institutions of the state were expected to uphold the needs of property owners by enforcing contracts between individuals according to universal principles of reason, and by establishing tariff barriers against foreign competitors.

On the global level, Gentili, Vattel, and von Wolff announced the future world as a large platform where people would be united by common interest, by contractual and legal arrangements.[15] The new international forum was envisioned as the instrumental outcome of private and public contracts. As a worldwide network of mutual interests, trade and commerce would reduce conflicts and thereby promote peace according to a seemingly natural law. Along with the rising bourgeoisie, these various thinkers rejected the idea of a world government or an international federation to secure the universality of natural rights, fearing that a centralized authority, reminiscent of the Holy Roman Empire, would curtail individual liberties and the competitive interests of mercantilist nation-states. In the global sphere, mercantilists thus endorsed a world vision stressing legal arrangements in the global sphere that would allow them, if needed, to protect their interests behind protective barriers at the national level. This instrumental internationalist vision was thus predicated on particularism. Indeed, this particularism would prove decisive.

The particularist and contractual character of internationalism during its first phase of national development is best exemplified by three political thinkers. Hugo Grotius (1583–1645), Giambattista Vico (1668–1744), and Jean-Jacques Rousseau (1712–78). Although the thinking of these writers cannot be reduced to their social background, one should not ignore the evident linkage between their bourgeois upbringing and their later worldviews. Hugo Grotius, the son of the Dutch burgomaster of Delft and curator of Leiden University, became a jurist and scholar. His work *On the Law of War and Peace,* one of the great contributions to legal theory, emphasized the need for international legal arrangements in a period of religious wars. Giambattista Vico, son of a poor Neapolitan bookseller, became a scholar and philosopher of cultural history and law, and was well known during his lifetime among Italian legal thinkers. His *Scienza Nuova* depicted cyclical patterns of national development. Jean-Jacques Rousseau, son of a Geneva watchmaker, became one of the greatest intellectual influences on the French Revolution. In the *Social Contract,* he brought together the international perspective of Grotius with Vico's national focus, and expressed the internal contradiction of the prerevolutionary bourgeoisie, oscillating between internationalist and nationalist concerns.

At the philosophical level, their criticism of the universalism of the Catholic church was not expressed in one and the same unreserved voice. Grotius and Rousseau, both Protestants, denounced the abuses of the church: its universalist rhetoric and its inability to administer a large territory by appealing to a single truth. Despite Vico's proclaimed allegiance to the Catholic church, his *Scienza Nuova* was affected by the Reformation. His split of the *verum* from the *certum,* God's reason and human reason, was analogous to the philosophical division between the supernatural and the natural in Grotius and Rousseau, and exemplified the growing chasm between the holy and secular spheres. By referring to natural law as the new standard of reference, these thinkers progressively swept revelation aside as the criterion of truth. By appealing to nature, the creative realm of the Almighty, they made God's wisdom evident to the thinking individual. By expelling God from history, they enabled individuals to determine their own destiny. They created a space for the bourgeoisie to develop an identity, the spirit of free enterprise, and the quest for new forms of association.

Grotius, Vico, and Rousseau argued that the domestic agenda would best be served by a national contract among individuals. Their emphasis on the nation reflected its growing development, its autonomy from Christendom, the centralization of feudal provinces and principalities, and the mercantilist orientation of internationalism. Grotius explained that individuals, allied by necessity, mutual exchange, trade interest, and legal contracts, would be inclined to secure the free flow of commodities and to promote peace and harmony. These activities, he argued, heralded the highest stage of civilization. His optimistic views reflected the intellectual, artistic, and commercial blooming of the Netherlands. To keep alive intellectual energy, peaceful harmony, and commercial adventures, he, along with Dutch mercantilists, also advocated the integration of the Low Countries, divided by religious wars, into one strong nation that would protect individuals from foreign competition and wars. Grotius perceived monarchy to be the best type of government to undertake such a unifying and protective mission.

Vico, for his part, believed that an enlightened monarchy would unite the Italian principalities in such a way as to both activate and protect their declining commerce. Although he agreed with Grotius about the importance of contractual arrangements to consolidate human associations, he devoted more attention to the way in which such social and legal cooperation could degenerate into chaos. The grandeur and decadence of the Roman Empire and of the "Golden Age" of the Italian Renaissance strongly influenced his cyclical analysis of the nation-state.

Rousseau, however, saw this matter differently. His perspective on the nation-state, reflecting in part the ideas of the petite bourgeoisie[16] at a later stage of its historical development, differed from that of his predecessors. His *Social Contract* was more than the "sum of individuals' instrumental interests" imposed by an external authority. The universal content of the contract alone constituted the raison d'être of the state precisely because it alone would protect the fundamental rights of the citizenry—voting rights, political participation, and private property rights. A monarchy, by its very nature, could not represent the *volonté générale* of the people. The democratic urge became more pressing. Rousseau indeed anticipated the frustration of the revolutionary Third Estate, as well as its longing for political and economic power.

On the global level, these three thinkers sought universal peace in a hostile world, while keeping the nation's autonomy intact. Bearing in mind the fierce struggles that had led to the disintegration of the Catholic commonwealth, a centralized federation of states could only be regarded as an alarming idea; in addition, a centralized body could obstruct the further development of private trade. Therefore, Grotius could only advise monarchs to temper the excess of abuses during war, and to be guided by the laws of nature, or the laws of nations, in order to secure commerce and peaceful relations between states. Vico did not extend his analysis to the international system in the same vein as Grotius. By treating the nation-state as the cornerstone of his investigation, in fact, Vico implicitly provided the theoretical incentives for the nineteenth-century nationalist Carbonari to reestablish Italy's prestige in the community of nations. His analysis of the cyclical evolution of nations, in *Del corso che fanno le nazioni*,[17] was an attempt to articulate the historical conditions for universal peace and stability.

Rousseau did not disguise his skepticism concerning the viability of a world government.[18] He considered that self-sufficient, independent republican states alone were capable of establishing global harmony. Rousseau's ideal of state isolation was unsuitable, however, for a world that was extending its commercial links between nations. Caught between two contradictory forces, his thinking, no less than that of his two precursors, exemplifies the initial tension of the prospective internationalist ideal—promoting, on the one hand, an instrumental, universal harmony and encouraging, on the other hand, the development of a protectionist national unity. How could peace prevail without a world authority entrusted with the capacity to penalize the violence of transgressing nations? This question remained unanswered.

Phase 2

Nevertheless, toward the end of the eighteenth century the universalist character of internationalism gained further ground. Commerce and trade relationships were indeed no longer a satisfactory justification for civil associations. The colonial conquests undertaken by leading European countries — England, France, Holland — throughout the eighteenth century and the republican legacy of the American Revolution paved the road for the changing character of internationalism. Yet, although the bourgeoisie had increased its wealth substantially as a result of these expansionist policies, it was no longer satisfied with its political status. Despite the progress of mercantilism and worldwide trade, political and civil structures remained backward. In order to remain competitive in the global scene, to alleviate the burden of the tithe, and to suppress the censorship of the church, merchants, peasants, scientists, and intellectuals found it crucial to renovate the political establishment, and thereby to expand their control in the political and religious spheres, which had remained in the hands of the aristocracy and the clergy.

In France, the rigid system of political privilege encouraged all the components of the Third Estate, which included everyone but the aristocracy and the clergy, to ally themselves against the old regime. In his famous pamphlet *Qu'est-ce que le Tiers État?*, the Abbé de Sieyès appealed to the Third Estate's unity against aristocratic privileges.[19] This alliance contributed to the further development of the universalist and organic aspect of internationalism. This worldview was now based on a secular ethics and the extension of political rights, and opposed to the particularism and arbitrariness of both revelation and the system of political privileges. Internationalism, then, became the growing self-awareness of a group seeking in economic, political, and ethical terms (instrumentally and normatively) a new form of collective justice within and between nations against the ancien régime.

Internationalism gradually moved toward its second phase to reach a new level of maturity during the mid-eighteenth century. Discussions about political, economic, and religious freedom guaranteed to everyone everywhere were held throughout Europe. Deism represented the new philosophical approach. In France, Voltaire, Diderot, and d'Alembert rejected revealed truth.[20] In Germany, Lessing and Forster deplored prejudices and ignorance perpetuated by the church;[21] in England, Wollaston celebrated the development of a new natural religion.[22] Despite their contextual and personal differences, they all called for a new intellectual climate that elevated deism, a universal secular religion. They also appealed to the speculative rather than to the formalistic and passive reasoning of individuals—as espoused by the church. Internationalism, now sanctified by the new cult of reason, propagated social values and altruistic duties, and asserted egalitarian solidarity among people of the Third Estate, within and between states.

During the French Revolution, internationalism was also envisioned in political society as a large organic version of Rousseau's *Social Contract*. In the eyes of Jacobins such as Marat and Saint Just, the social contract was more than the "sum of individuals' instrumental interest" as depicted by Hobbes and Locke.[23] The "general will" was now understood as an "inalienable" and "indivisible" political entity premised on political and economic justice. This organic vision of the social contract provided the Third Estate with a perspective that could transcend its particularist interest. The 1789 *Declaration of the Rights of Man and Citizen* formalized these new aspirations.

Nevertheless, the attempt to reconcile civil society (or, in a strict sense, the realm of private property interactions) with republican institutions, endorsing equal political rights, created insoluble contradictions for the further development of liberal internationalism. Aspiring to unite these various spheres of interests into one front against absolutism, revolutionaries from the enlightened aristocracy and the Gironde provided the popular classes a channel through which they could further their political demands (i.e., male voting rights) and, ironically, could threaten the economic preeminence of the affluent classes. Lafayette, Vergniaud, and others gradually realized that the full extension of political rights to all sections of society impeded the progress of capitalism and, more importantly, middle-class interests.[24]

With the advent of the French Revolution, the *patrie* was also perceived as the lighthouse from which internationalist ideas would radiate globally. Patriotic feelings, deriving from the republican state, were used to exalt the social bonds between citizens throughout the world. Contrary to nationalism, which praised the superiority of one national cultural grouping over another, patriotism justified the raison d'être of the republican state according to universal political and economic rights of citizens regardless of their countries of origin—yet not regardless of their race and sex. Despite the increased political participation of women in the public sector and the abolition of slavery during the period of the revolutionary government, women and blacks still did not enjoy the same legal rights as their white male compatriots.

Notwithstanding the white brotherly qualification of internationalism, a strategic question remained: how to extend these republican ideals abroad to secure global peace. Would the French *patrie* become the civil and political model for other nations to follow as the American model was for the French? Or were wars still necessary to promulgate democratic principles and abolish absolutism? Jacobin patriots entertained the idea that the progress of republican institutions required the development of capitalist society. For a great number of revolutionary thinkers—such as Lanjuinais, Mirabeau, and Danton—commerce, trade, and mutual interests would ineluctably promote political justice and perhaps pave the way for an international federation.[25]

These ideas were in conformity with Adam Smith's theory of laissez-faire. In the *Wealth of Nations*, the Scottish economist maintained that growing commerce and political freedom, unhampered by governmental interference, would mutually reinforce each other while advancing global welfare.[26] Yet, in response to the threatening advances of foreign troops and the internal spread of the counterrevolution, the development of a coercive state apparatus was seen as necessary to save and expand the Revolution. Overwhelmed by events, relying sometimes on Smith's "invisible hand" and other times on the interventionist state apparatus, revolutionaries failed to formulate a clear strategy for the way internationalism should progress across borders. The late eighteenth century embodied the tension of bourgeois consciousness torn between humanistic commitment deployed against the ancien régime and self-interest. J. A. Pocock has aptly commented that the social thought of the eighteenth century can be envisaged as a single momentous quarrel, oscillating between the worldwide compassion of Roman patriotism and the particularism of private investors.[27]

Three political thinkers from different countries—Immanuel Kant (1724–1804), Thomas Paine (1737–1809), and Maximilien Robespierre (1758–94)—exemplify the universalist and particularist tensions within internationalism during the period of the French Revolution. Immanuel Kant, son of a Prussian saddler, became a professor at Königsberg and a philosopher known internationally in intellectual and literati circles. He symbolized the age of the Aufklärung, and was a strong advocate in Germany of the French Revolution. His *Perpetual Peace* was one of the most ethically daring internationalist projects formulated in his time. Thomas Paine, son of an English corset maker, became a pamphleteer and writer during the American and French Revolutions. In *The Rights of Man,* he fervently pledged his commitment to world citizenship, and enthusiastically defended the French Revolution and the spread of republican ideals. Maximilien Robespierre, son of a French lawyer, himself became a lawyer. He played a leading political role during the revolutionary government and was a major advocate of the sans-culottes against the affluent bourgeoisie. A controversial figure during the period of the terror, Robespierre was known for his speeches condemning the discrepancy of wealth within the Third Estate, the exclusion of non-property owners from voting and civic rights, and slavery in the colonies.

The writings of these political thinkers illustrate the maturity of internationalism, defined both in instrumental and normative terms. They reflected as well the collective spirit of all sections of the Third Estate—united to achieve moral, political, and economic transformations of the feudal society—and at the same time its internal divisions.

It was in the name of universal reason and internationalism that Kant, Paine, and Robespierre rejected the religious dogmatism of the ancien régime. These political thinkers bestowed enormous philosophical importance upon reason, which became the sovereign standard of truth, the final court of intellectual appeal for the judgment of any individual, irrespective of country or social status. They recognized in deism its emancipatory character. They glorified it for its social values and for motivating the individual to transcend egotistic instinct according to the imperative guidelines of reason.

All three thinkers supported an internationalist agenda premised on private property and political equality. The 1789 *Declaration of the Rights of Man and Citizen* was a profound watershed. It granted voting rights to all individuals, the free exercise of their physical and intellectual powers, freedom of speech and press, equality before the law, equal rights to hold public offices regardless of birth, and, most importantly, the equal right to ownership. Regardless of the differences between Kant, Paine, and Robespierre regarding the best type of government to lead a revolutionary war, they ultimately agreed that a republican regime based on a system of checks and balances was the best type of government. It prevented the abuse of power, made war less likely, and guaranteed the application of the universal rights of man.

These thinkers envisioned the global system as an extrapolation of the republican state that would ensure peace through mutual interest, free trade, and worldwide citizenship. However, their vision of a brotherly community was soon consumed by strife within the Third Estate during the French Revolution. Kant argued that only propertied citizens were entitled to voting rights. By having property at stake, "active citizens," he maintained, would be the best custodians of peace. On the other hand, a few months after the Declaration, Robespierre and Paine opposed the Constituent Assembly's decision to deny voting rights to unpropertied citizens and thereby undermine their opportunity to make further social and economic demands in a parliamentary forum.

Despite their differences concerning voting rights, all three agreed on the inviolability of private property as a fundamental human right. What they did not perceive was that by making private property the core of their new republican state they were implicitly securing the future of inequality. On the one hand, inviolable property rights were revolutionary insofar as they disputed the basis of feudal property structures and released individuals from feudal bondage. On the other hand, the unrestricted accumulation of property would simultaneously benefit the economically advantaged bourgeoisie and generate discontent among its allies, the sans-culottes and the peasantry. The failure to establish equality in the political and economic spheres subverted the solidarity of the Third Estate and the universal aspect of internationalism. Indeed, the social conflict within the Third Estate intensified with the progress of the Revolution and ended with the Thermidorian victory of the bourgeoisie. The nature of internationalism was transformed: the popular appeal of unity succumbed to bourgeois control of the new social association.

Another obstacle to the full development of internationalism was these thinkers' inability to articulate a coherent political strategy for the universalization of republican ideals beyond the borders of France. Would France introduce the American model and inspire other nations to follow its example? Or was the use of bayonets necessary to spread republicanism and abolish old customs? Following the American example, Kant believed that the spirit of commerce was compatible with the proliferation of republican regimes; yet his position regarding the legitimacy of the French revolutionary wars remained ambiguous. Although he perceived the French Revolution as the "sign of the progress of civilization," he condemned all forms of rebellion and war as delegitimizing the nature of the original social contract. He rejected the view that revolution and war might be justifiable means toward his ethical end: perpetual peace.

Paine, aware that political transformations in France could not be reached in the same fashion as in America, regarded violence and war as essential to the spread of republican ideals abroad. Yet he was unable to show how these republican ideals could be exported without the concomitant centralized government required by the exigencies of domestic conflict and foreign wars (e.g., Robespierre's 1793 Committee of Public Safety). It remained unclear at which stage of the revolutionary war republicanism would blossom as a result of commerce.

Robespierre, on the other hand, accepted the revolutionary government as a necessary political means to transport the Revolution to foreign countries. He was oblivious, however, to the fundamental social differences within the Third Estate that were being intensified by the war and that ultimately led to the disintegration of internationalist solidarity.

Phase 3

Internationalism collapsed after the French Revolution into conflicting interests, mirroring the fate of Catholic universalism. An internationalist project seeking to reconcile political equality and economic interest at home and abroad seemed to threaten the political dominance

of the Thermidorian bourgeoisie and its allies, the repentant aristocracy. Thermidorians like Boissy d'Anglas[28] and Vergniaud strove to
recover domestic cohesion, regardless of social or economic criteria
of justice, and to pursue international trade.[29] Like the crusaders who
promoted the interests of their feudal monarchs under the banner of
universal charity, Napoleon, the so-called heir of the French Revolution, succeeded in advancing the interests of the bourgeoisie and the
aristocracy under the guise of internationalism. The emperor did not
emancipate his supporters politically; nor did he grant national
autonomy to his allies throughout his *imperium*. Instead, continuing
his politics of conquest, he fueled popular malaise, which was progressively translated into nationalist resentment.

The promotion of social equality associated with internationalism
during the French Revolution declined as a result of the Napoleonic
Wars, and internationalism thereby reached a third phase. A new
movement, romanticism, including individuals from opposite ends of
the political spectrum, emerged to challenge Napoleon's moral, political, and economic regime. In the philosophical realm, Romantics
like Herder and Goethe progressively replaced the rational postulates of the collectivity with emotional and subjectivist premises.[30]
Those who had first embraced the Jacobin ideas of the French Revolution ultimately repudiated the universal idea of reason—as a device that enabled French imperialism "rationally" to propagate its
particularist interests at the expense of its former allies. The new
Romantics appealed to faith and religion to stress the emotional
bonds between individuals and to invigorate the soul of the nation.
Those who, since the fall of the Bastille, had rebuked the rationalist
propositions of the revolutionaries as being divisive and conducive
to the ruling of the "canaille" invoked revealed knowledge to restore
their political privileges.

Internationalism was swept aside by its particularist tendencies;
nationalism emerged triumphant as the collective spirit of internationalism was also geographically circumscribed to the national
unit. Admittedly, although this new concept of national unity initially retained the organic definition of Rousseau's *Social Contract* as
espoused during the French Revolution, it was now morally justified
in particularistic rather than universalistic terms. The idea of national
interest was understood in its own terms. In other words, by arguing

that political and economic activities were morally right if they served the national interest, and by stating at the same time that the national interest was defined exclusively in terms of the moral aspect of political and economic enterprises, romantic thinkers provided a tautological definition of the concept of national interest. Such an obscure definition of national interest eclipsed the question of who were to be the primary beneficiaries of these political and economic rights.

In addition, the *Rechtsstaat* was reduced to the *Volksstaat*: the nation was no longer defined by universal criteria of reason and justice but by the cultural tradition of its own people. This cultural definition of the nation emerged in response to the imperialism of French policy. Throughout Europe, writers like Schelling, Manzoni, and Pushkin romanticized the medieval period and compared it favorably to their own. They began to work for the recovery of their national and cultural autonomy.[31] One could observe that the concept of the nation was reconceptualized in the same particularist fashion as during its initial phase of development. Nevertheless, the new nation differed in that the universalist base of solidarity changed; the bourgeoisie now acted in concert with the aristocracy.

On the worldwide scale, by focusing mainly on how social unity was an organic product of nationhood, Novalis and Schlegel in Germany, Sir Walter Scott and Wordsworth in Britain, and Chateaubriand in France all subverted internationalism in favor of experiential and nationalist ideologies.[32] The view of a peaceful world order regressed and began to resemble the particularist tendencies prevailing in the first phase of internationalism. Indeed, the idea of internationalism, which during the Revolution espoused political equality between individuals across countries, was superseded by instrumental and trade relationships, by the race for raw materials, and later by colonialist aspirations that exacerbated uneven economic development between countries and individuals.

The regression of internationalist ideals, allowing the development of nationalism on the political stage of the European theater, can be also be observed in the writings of Edmund Burke (1729–97), Joseph de Maistre (1753–1821), and Johann Gottlieb Fichte (1762–1814). The "elective affinity" of these three romantic political thinkers, drawn from diverse social backgrounds and countries, is evident in their displeasure with the French Revolution and its implications. Edmund Burke, son of an Irish solicitor, moved away from legal studies to become one of the most prominent British statesman at the end of the eighteenth century. Despite his middle-class origins, he was a champion of conservatism, developed in opposition to Jacobinism. In *Reflections on the Revolution in France,* he scorned the ideas of the French Revolution and became a source of inspiration for counter-revolutionary thought.

Joseph de Maistre was a French polemicist and a diplomat of aristocratic origin. After being uprooted by the French Revolution, he became a great exponent of the conservative tradition in exile. He called for the supremacy of Christianity and the return of the absolute rule of both the king and the pope. Johann Gottlieb Fichte, son of a ribbon weaver, became a philosopher, one of the greatest transcendental idealists of his time. Kant had a major influence on his ethical formation, as evidenced by *Versuch einer Kritik aller Offenbarung.* With his spiritual mentor, Fichte hailed the French Revolution, yet, frustrated by its unfulfilled promises of emancipation, he turned against Napoleon's regime and, in the *Reden an die Deutsche Nation,* developed a plan for national recovery and glory.

On the philosophical front, these thinkers transformed the universalist and rationalist premises of internationalism advocated during the French Revolution into the mystical and emotional experience of collective identity. Both Burke and de Maistre condemned the Revolution for dividing the nation, weakening moral stability, and encouraging belief in universal reason and political rights. They argued that reason — beyond the reach of the masses — and atheism were destructive forces and would lead France to chaos and social anarchy. Notwithstanding major differences, Burke and de Maistre agreed that reason was only accessible to political experts, who, inspired by wisdom and tradition, were better trained than the rest of the population to advance national interests.

Fichte, in constrast, had denounced the abuses and excesses of the Catholic clergy. Influenced, like Kant, by Protestant principles, he believed that the authority of the church should prevail in the spiritual and the "invisible world," and remain separate from the "visible world." He asserted that the penetration of religion into public affairs would restrain the free expression of the individual will.

Morality and justice could not be imposed by external agents, neither by the church nor, as he would later state, by Napoleon. Instead, they would emerge when individuals manifested their thought in action. His romanticized concept of the individual exalting himself through action laid the groundwork for the individualist free-enterprise spirit of the still-embryonic German bourgeoisie, and later served to inflame German nationalist spirit against Napoleon's domination. Taking a different route from Burke's constitutional monarchy or de Maistre's royalist position, Fichte began to move toward the same irrationalist interpretation of national unity.

Although Burke and de Maistre accepted the organic image of national unity that inspired Rousseau's revolutionary disciples, they rejected the idea that the "general will" should be articulated from "below." They argued that the nation should be controlled "from above," by a competent political elite found in the privileged classes. They excluded democratic or republican regimes as viable forms of government. Opposing the "anarchical ruling of the mob" during the French Revolution, Burke and de Maistre denounced the execution of Louis XVI, which, they believed, left France itself organically decapitated and culturally alienated. Burke considered that the British monarchy was the best type of regime for England, for it was shaped in harmony with its cultural history, whereas de Maistre yearned for the return of social order under the cultural splendor of the absolutist monarchy *à la française*.

In his early writings, Fichte stood in diametrical opposition to Burke and de Maistre. Influenced by the ideas of the French Revolution, he advocated the free expression of individuals' wills across boundaries, in a context where the state would only minimally intervene in private affairs. Frustrated by the vain promise of political and civil emancipation from revolutionary France, however, Fichte distanced himself from the original internationalist perspective by claiming that an individual is best substantiated if realized in a close unit: the nation. Indeed, in *The Closed Commercial State*, he suggested the construction of an autonomous and isolated nation, legitimized by the organic will of the people. Subsequent to Napoleon's defeat of Prussia in 1806 and anticipating Hegel, he explained that the organic will of the German *Volk* would be best represented by a bureaucratic elite. For the sake of the national interest, Fichte, like

Burke and de Maistre, translated internationalism into the love of
the nation, which now promoted the political and economic prerogatives of its self-appointed guardians: the ruling elite.

Despite their different motivations, vested in the realization of
the *Volksstaat*, Burke, de Maistre, and Fichte helped create the historical space for a global order predicated upon instrumental and
nationalist interests. Burke believed in the ineluctable process of industrialization and the spirit of laissez-faire on the foreign scene. He
asserted as well that, given the prevalent inequality of competence
among individuals and nations, the quest for political equality among
nations was erroneous. Only a worldwide system patrolled by the
balance of the major European powers would ensure stability in the
community of nations. Wars in certain instances, Burke commented,
were necessary to remedy situations in which a nation disrupted the
peaceful status quo. This proposition allowed him to justify wars
against countries that threatened English superiority (the French Revolution) and to deplore those wars that weakened it (the British-
American and British-Irish wars). Disguised by theoretical postulates
of "just war," Burke's views reflected strong nationalist sentiments.

De Maistre rebuffed the idea of laissez-faire capitalism as a framework that would promote political equality between states, as proposed by the radical Jacobins, or even Burke's economic cooperation
between individuals and nations. Nevertheless, he believed that a
certain harmony would be reached if nations followed the "enlightened" spirit of prerevolutionary France. In the wars of the French
Revolution, wrote de Maistre, one should observe the sign of God.
The Revolution purged France of its sin and prepared in the long run
for the flamboyant return of the monarchical regime. France had to
regain its supreme position in Europe and carry the torch of its intellectual force across the world.

On the global level, a nationalism of German flavor developed
in response to Napoleon's conquests. This jingoistic attitude, as expressed in Fichte's later work, differed substantially from his earlier
internationalist convictions. Indeed, at first he insisted that wars,
usually the product of barbarous and despotic regimes, should be
waged only to emancipate people and nations from their bondage. In
the spirit of Kant, he endorsed the idea of an equitable international
federation of states to protect peace between free commercial states.
Nonetheless, displeased by the political opportunism of the French

emperor, who had not kept his promises of political freedom and in-dependence for the states of his Continental System, Fichte directed his efforts toward the construction of a strong German national unity by praising German culture to the detriment of his universal prin-ciples of social justice, in the name of a world informed by particu-larist and nationalist aims. The nationalist lyricism of Fichte in the *Reden an die Deutsche Nation* contained the same frightening melody as that composed by Burke and de Maistre.

Burke, de Maistre, and Fichte reflected the involution of interna-tionalism. The inability to extend political and economic rights through-out Europe, the increasing political demands of the radical Jacobins, and the economic rivalries between European nations prepared a fer-tile soil for the development of nationalist and particularist interests. While de Maistre's and Burke's nationalism looked backward to a cherished past in the ancien régime, Fichte's nationalism laid the groundwork for the national unification program of 1848 that re-tained some form of progressive and republican elements.

Conclusion

The Congress of Vienna in 1815 had restored the power of the old absolutist dynasties. In Britain, France, and Spain—where national unity had already been achieved—nationalism was not so much a doctrine as a latent state of mind, easily aroused when "national in-terests" were questioned. Elsewhere—in Germany, Italy, Poland, and the Austrian and Turkish Empires—where people of the same nation-ality were politically divided or subjected to foreign rule, nationalism was becoming a deliberate and conscious program. It was undoubt-edly the example of the West, of Great Britain and France—success-ful and flourishing because they were unified nations—that stimu-lated the ambitions of other nations to become unified as well. The period after 1815 was, in Germany, a time of rising agitation over the national question, in Italy of the risorgimento, in Eastern Europe of a Slavic Revival.

Published after the collapse of the Napoleonic empire and the restoration of the Congress of Vienna (1815), Hegel's *Philosophy of Right* provides an interesting yet not unique sample of the progres-sive intellectual mood of that period. By fusing the particularist inter-pretation of internationalism, developed during the sixteenth century, with the Romantics' claim for national unity, Hegel's work illustrated the bourgeoisie's dual aspirations, and, more precisely, his own attempt to unify the Prussian nation and extend its economic interests worldwide. By introducing the civil code and religious liberty, by abolishing the tithe and feudal rights, Napoleon crushed many of the vestiges of feudalism in Germany; the country, nevertheless, remained fragmented. It was thus important, according to Hegel, to pursue the progress unleashed by revolutionary France and to further it under a unified constitutional monarchy. In *I Miei Ricordi,* Massimo d'Azeglio expressed a similar indebtedness to Napoleon's achievements, yet rejoiced with other Italian patriots "to see the French depart."[33]

Hegel's *Philosophy of Right* synthesized the political ambivalence of bourgeois consciousness, oscillating between internationalism and nationalism, or, in more abstract terms, between universalism and particularism. In the philosophical realm, Hegel's work incorporated both the prevailing ideas of the Enlightenment and the germinating conceptions of romantic nationalism. Indebted to the Enlightenment, he appealed to the universality of reason as the framework of his moral beliefs. Yet the universal and moral intentions of reason would remain abstract unless actualized through sensuous identification with the empirical world. It is interesting to observe how Hegel astutely integrated into his moral system the sensuous premises of romantic nationalism as a fundamental development of Enlightenment thinking. He thereby provided a comprehensive intellectual structure for understanding the changing character of history, reason, and bourgeois consciousness.

Furthermore, Hegel explained how the movement between the particularist and the universalist character of reason was transcended into higher forms of social unity: the civil society and the state. Civil society, Hegel argued, was the locus that enabled an individual to employ reason through the act of possessing. Due to the instrumental character of civil society, individuals were initially absolved both from the task of passing moral and ethical judgment on quality and quantity of property and from restricting the free accumulation of wealth. Individuals realize the need to enter into contracts, for contracts presuppose that individuals recognize each other as property owners. Once the ownership is established, Hegel argued in "The Law of Property," individuals can alienate their property by selling it or by exchanging it. Through these transactions, they entertain an external relation with other individuals, and therefore acquire a universal dimension of their beings; but this universality, characterized by necessity, stresses an instrumental identity of the social association.

Hegel realized that a civil state, embodying the instrumental and external interests of its citizens, was conducive to conflicts and disorders. Thus he dialectically juxtaposed the concept of civil society, reflecting the property interests of individuals, with the concept of the state, an institution standing above individuals and their competitive interests. According to Hegel, unity was the true content and moral end for the state. In short, with the Romantics, he interpreted the state as a locus that serves to unify individuals' cultural identification, and, with the classical liberal thinkers of the Enlightenment, he saw civil society as a milieu essential to individuals' freedom and self-fulfillment. Thus the major functions of the state should be twofold: to consolidate culturally and organically the *Volk,* while preserving the holdings and activities of property owners. Hegel elevated the Prussian state into an ideal form of national unity, into a philosophical existence. The Prussian state was designed as the *Aufhebung* (synthesis) of the instrumental principle of civil society and the cohesive and absolutist aspect of the state.

On the global level, Hegel dismissed the political feasibility of an international federation, for wars were the inevitable tests of national sovereignty and national cohesion. War prompted the unity of individuals' interest and the state that civil society could not establish by itself. War could prevent internal upheavals and strengthen the internal power of the state. While Hegel assigned an ethical end to the state, he maintained that such a goal was difficult to achieve in foreign affairs. Instrumental and economic relationship, as well as conflicts, will remain the only channel of interaction between states and individuals across borders. The only realm that, beyond the state level, was always moral and rational was the Absolute Spirit, or History, in which philosophy, art, and religion are its abstract moments, and in which the state remains its concrete manifestation.

Thus, following Hegel's view, one might conclude that internationalism in the global sphere is condemned to remain at the level of abstraction, while particularism, the state, and nationalism become its concrete embodiment. Therefore, by justifying universalism through particularism, or internationalism through the national unity of the state, Hegel implicitly assigned to world history the divine task of becoming the ultimate judge of aggressive nationalist behaviors. By precluding an institutional commitment to the internationalist ideal of human rights, Hegel's *Philosophy of Right* ultimately illustrates the contradiction of liberalism, which is still with us. Hegel's work also foreshadowed the development of international socialism and, though this theme is not developed in this book, its future contradictions.

This tension within internationalism can already be observed at its early stage of development. The next chapter depicts the historical and cultural context of the Reformation that encouraged the formation of internationalist views.

Part I

The Disintegration of the Universal Church and the Development of a New World Vision: Grotius, Vico, and Rousseau

One

The Wars of the Reformation and the Spread of Mercantilism

During the Middle Ages, Europe was dominated by a Christian commonwealth—the Respublica Christiania or Civitas Dei—the great medieval church, which the prudence of Constantine, the genius of Augustine, and the statesmanship of a long line of *imperii* had established upon the ruins of Caesarian Rome. The aim of the medieval commonwealth was to unite all individuals under the kingdom of God. Boniface VIII believed that the supreme power in Christian Europe should be the pope;[1] Dante thought that it should be the emperor;[2] others maintained that the two should share authority. Throughout the fourteenth century, the idea of a Christendom united through either a secular ruler or a general council representing the whole church remained the ideal for many individuals, like the Italian Marsiglio of Padua or the Englishmen Ockham and Wycliffe.[3] Throughout the next three centuries, the monarchs of Western Europe still regarded themselves as part of one Christian world polity. They legitimized their policies by referring to the universal goals of the church, the common fountain of all life and purpose. In their struggle for hegemony in Europe, the houses of Austria and France considered themselves the true protectors of the church and the most faithful adherents of Christian civilization. The Turks were still perceived as the principal threat to Christianity and a common enemy of Europe. Although the age of the Crusades had come to an end, its spirit had not yet entirely died.[4]

Yet the idea of a united Christian Europe never became a practical reality. It gradually gave way before the ambitions of national rulers and fiercely independent towns. The old central authority of the papacy and the empire were challenged and largely defeated by a burgeoning set of nation-states. The new masters rejected the claims of any universal pope or emperor to interfere in what they increasingly insisted was their own sphere of control. By the end of the sixteenth century, the universalist message of the church had been severely compromised by the territorial disintegration of the authority of the church and by the Reformation.

Indeed, while the separation of the Greek Orthodox churches from Rome had already provoked the first rupture in Christian unity, the Protestant Reformation of the sixteenth century contributed decisively to the decline of the universalism of the Catholic church. Protestantism contested the indisputable authority of the higher Catholic clergy, the spectacular and mundane ceremonies of the church, the infiltration of Catholicism into all spheres of human life, its claim to each person's body and soul, its control of the individual's destiny, and the promise of eternal felicity in Heaven provided that the faithful were obedient and loyal subjects of the "universal kingdom."

Protestantism proposed instead to view the Bible as the primary authority in issues of faith, to return to simple liturgies, to separate church and state, to assert the individual's responsibilities in matters of salvation and in seeking terrestrial happiness on earth, the realm of God's creation.[5] Such views, aiming at material felicity, encouraged the development of a bourgeois ethics, committed to God through the work of nature.[6] The proposed reforms of Protestantism had immediate political repercussions. They not only challenged the inherited Catholic dogma and authority, but, first and foremost, seriously undercut the hierarchy of privileges in the system of divine grace—the nervous system of the feudal regime. Not surprisingly, the progress of the Reformation alarmed the feudal guardians of the status quo and created a climate that incited animosity and engendered a period of extended conflicts between Catholics and Protestants.

The Religious Wars

Between 1546 and 1552 Charles V, with the help of foreign troops, tried to crush the Lutherans in the German states and the Low

Countries. In their turn, the Lutherans sought help from France against the emperor of the "universal monarchy."[7] Neither side won. In 1552, negotiations for peace began. With the Augsburg Peace in 1555, Lutheranism was officially recognized within the Holy Roman Empire. According to the maxim *cujus regio, ejus religio,* each prince was to decide for himself whether he or his state should be Catholic or Lutheran. Nonetheless, the parties involved soon showed their discontent regarding the peace agreement. Between 1555 and 1600 much ecclesiastical property was secularized and conveyed into Lutheran hands. In addition, Protestantism spread from Switzerland into Germany. However, it was no victory for toleration, for Lutherans disliked the idea of two religions within Germany as much as Catholics.[8]

The progress of Protestantism activated the emergence of the Counter-Reformation aimed at restoring the authority of Catholicism. Inspired by the Jesuits and encouraged by the papacy, the Counter-Reformation expelled Protestants from Catholic fiefs and made rapid progress in regaining property "wrongfully" secularized. A Catholic League was mobilized against the Calvinist Union. Hostilities began to cloud the horizon of the empire, and for forty years the rival alliances confronted each other. Civil violence erupted in Germany and soon escalated into a series of religious conflicts on an international scale: the French civil wars of 1562–94; the Dutch revolution against Philip II of Spain in 1581; the Spanish *armada católica* against England in 1588; the Scottish rebellion against Mary Stuart in 1637; the Thirty Years' War in Germany between 1618 and 1648; the Puritan revolution of 1640–60 in England; and the Glorious Revolution of 1688–99.[9]

Seventeenth-century religious wars were the final blow to hopes for the unity of the church. The Peace of Westphalia (October 1648) ended the wars of religion in central Europe but divided Europe in the following ways: in Germany, a balance of power between Catholics and Protestants was achieved, England asserted the Anglican colors, Calvinism maintained a strong foothold in the Netherlands, whereas France and the Italian states (despite intermittent occupations by the Austrian Empire) remained loyal to the papacy.

As the spread of religious wars eroded the universalist aspirations of Christendom, the international nature of the wars incited the development of a new vision of world unity based on rational and scientific premises rather than on revealed assumptions—principles that had shown their divisive nature during the wars of religion. Other historical events further undermined the Christian commonwealth: the scientific revolution, the growth of the nation-state, and the rise of the middle class.

The Scientific Revolution

It was during a period of religious crisis that scientific discoveries abounded. Why the seventeenth century was such a vital period in the history of science is a complex question. Undeniably, the long-term effect of both the Renaissance and the Reformation rekindled a questioning spirit among many scholars. In the search for intellectual independence, scientists were no longer strictly confined to the university, which was a bulwark of Catholic orthodoxy. Extra-academic and autonomous societies proliferated in the seventeenth century, as exemplified by the creation of the Royal Society in London, the Academy of Science of Paris, the Academia della Scienza of Naples, and the Collegium Curiosim Sive in Germany.

An additional factor that contributed decisively to scientific progress was the invention of the printing press. Rapid publication facilitated collaboration at a distance, so that the pace of scientific advance no longer depended upon the concentration of scholars in one place. Given the worldwide access to scientific information, technological discoveries spread rapidly. These included the development of precise instruments of measurement—such as the telescope, the microscope, the barometer, and the pendulum clock, which all made the scientific revolution possible.

These scientific inventions also had direct repercussions on the new social and internationalist outlook.[10] During the Middle Ages, mathematical inquiry had been limited to empirical observations and justifications. Any attempt to uncover the fundamental laws of the universe, or to compete with God's creation, was deemed sacrilegious, a challenge that led to the tragic fate of the Tower of Babel. "Beware of the Mathematicians," wrote Saint Augustine, "and all those who make empty prophecies. The danger already exists that Mathematicians have made a covenant with the devil to darken the spirit and to confine man in the bonds of Hell."[11]

The modern age, however, had no patience with Catholic quibbling, nor with the protoscience of the medieval period. Against the mystical vision of the medieval cosmos, Galileo and Descartes, whose influence remained unquestioned in the scientific and intellectual circles of the seventeenth century, stirred the imagination of their generation by painting a picture of the enrichment of human life through new discoveries, and by presenting a simple world open to human consciousness and built upon universal laws. Similarly, in *Principia mathematica*, Isaac Newton described the world as a giant machine, a huge clockwork device, from which universal and mechanical laws were discernible and could be used to predict further phenomena.[12] Newton's God, the great clockmaker, no matter how perfect his handiwork, was also more remote from human affairs than the Creator of the medieval scholars.[13]

In short, the spread of scientific reasoning not only worked toward the fragmentation of Catholic unity but also toward the development of a new spirit of international collective collaboration. Indeed, the scientific quest for simplicity and deductive thinking constituted a serious rebellion against feudal monarchs, who justified their privileges through revelation, standing behind tendentious interpretations of the Scriptures. In addition, the international spirit of scientific collaboration developed scholars' confidence in their search for the solution of social problems. Coeval with the international and scientific character of a new collective spirit was the emergence of an international solidarity between individuals predicated on commercial and trade interests. It is therefore important to analyze the development of the instrumental character of this internationalist vision in conjunction with the growth of the nation-state, mercantilism, and the rising bourgeoisie.

The Growth of the Nation-State, Mercantilism, and the Emergence of the Bourgeoisie

In concert with both the Reformation and scientific progress, the nation-state claimed its autonomy and emancipation from the jurisdiction of the Catholic commonwealth. The growth of the nation-state definitively reduced the imperial authority of the Roman church. Indeed, the Peace of Augsburg in 1555 allowed princes to escape papal control by determining the religion of their subjects. The nation became the cornerstone of their temporal power to further mercantile pursuits.[14] National sentiment was encouraged to solidify the nation-state.

Mercantilism was developed in Europe from the sixteenth to the eighteenth century. Coinciding with the decay of feudalism, it was an economic system to unify and increase the power, and especially the monetary wealth, of a nation by a strict governmental regulation of the entire national economy, usually through policies designed to secure an accumulation of bullion, a favorable balance of trade, the development of agriculture and manufacturing, and the expansion of foreign trade. Proponents of mercantilist theories maintained that global wealth was relatively fixed. The best way to conquer new resources and to keep as large a share as possible of this limited wealth was through a rationally and scientifically planned society. The scientific spirit of the time provided burghers and traders with incentives to develop a calculating and efficient spirit necessary for a future entrepreneurial society. Thus, along with the scientists, they applauded the concept of an organized secular sovereignty, including reasonable geographic size, military and economic strength as the principal components for its development.

However, in the sixteenth and seventeenth centuries, German and Italian cities—despite Niccolò Machiavelli's call in *Il Principe* for the unification of his country[15]—lacked the necessary political capacity to appropriate resources on a large scale. In Eastern Europe, states such as Austria, Poland, and Russia, although large in size, were overwhelmingly dominated by agrarian production and could not achieve the benefits of a mercantile economy. However, the conditions necessary for the progress of mercantilism were present in the Low Countries (especially from soon after the Westphalia peace treaty until the early 1700s), as well as in England and France.[16] By the first half of the eighteenth century, international trade, which had been centered in the north of Italy and the Low Countries, moved toward the two foremost expanding nation-states: France and England.

The growth of a mercantile economy was symbolic of the dynamic character of the emerging new Western world. The money market dissolved old social bonds. It transformed the guild character of the Middle Ages, enhanced the supremacy of the town economy, and made the surrounding countryside subservient to the interests of the town. The shift from the village to the town changed the landscape of social relationships that had prevailed in feudal societies, when individuals had been united by family bonds and by the land. The exchange involving individuals and nature, in which the latter was exchanged for the product of the former, constituted the feudal world, a world where the private and public spheres were closely connected.[17]

The collapse of Catholic unity coincided with the emergence of towns as the heartbeat of human life. Autonomous spheres of social activities—the private and the public, the political and the economic—proliferated on the ruins of the Catholic commonwealth. In addition, labor was divided according to specialization and segregated social realms. With the increased division of labor and the subsequent atomization of society, mercantilism reached new levels of speed and efficiency. Yet this fragmentation into various spheres of specialization undermined the self-sufficient character of the feudal society, and therefore exacerbated the need for a new form of social interdependence built around the exchange of commodities.

This parceling of sixteenth- and seventeenth-century political and economic life created the space for the development of a relatively autonomous class, the bourgeoisie, which was concentrated in urban sites.[18] The bourgeoisie stood economically between the nobility and the clergy on the one hand, and the peasantry on the other. Its members earned their living by manufacturing, shopkeeping, banking, trading, and in general by the various activities that had been stimulated by the expansion of commerce. In countries like England, France, or Flanders—where governments helped to create a national market and an industrious nationwide labor supply for their great merchants—the bourgeoisie became even more prominent, and succeeded in gaining economic strength outside the political and religious control of their provinces. Needless to say, a merchant backed by a national monarchy was in a much stronger position than one supported by a city, such as Augsburg or Venice. National governments could endorse local merchants, subsidize exports, pay bounties for goods whose production they wished to encourage, or erect tariff barriers against imports to protect their own producers from competition. Thus, a national tariff system was gradually superimposed on the old network of provincial and municipal tariffs.[19]

As long as kings supported mercantilist policies, a strong affinity was created between the monarchy and burghers. The interests of the rising bourgeoisie in the sixteenth century went hand in hand with the mercantile nobility, insofar as the former remained content with its social position. Only in the late eighteenth century, with the French Revolution, did the tension between the bourgeoisie and the aristocracy result in irreconcilable conflict. The bourgeoisie realized that the efficient progress of mercantilism was impossible without the abolition of local tariffs, as had already occurred in England, and a complete restructuring of the political realm, which remained in the hands of the aristocracy. In its attempt to conquer political power, the eighteenth-century bourgeoisie collided with the aristocratic system of privileges. This conflict of interest between the bourgeoisie and the aristocracy is discussed in Part II.

In brief, the growth of the mercantile nation-state, organized rationally and scientifically—in order to expand to new markets and acquire more resources—dismantled the territorial control of the Catholic commonwealth. Yet the extension of trade and the proliferation of human specialization on the global scale helped, in turn, to conceive a new form of international solidarity based on mutual interest, commodity exchange, and trade.

We have seen that while the religious wars, the scientific revolution, the development of mercantilism, and the rise of a class of traders dismembered Catholic universalism, the international nature of each of these events announced the development of an alternative form of social unity. The following chapters demonstrate how the disintegration of the Catholic commonwealth, prompting the elaboration of internationalism and a new realm of instrumental interaction, became manifest in the intellectual context of the seventeenth- and eighteenth-century works of Hugo Grotius, Giambattista Vico, and Jean-Jacques Rousseau. Their works encapsulated the movement from Catholic universalism to internationalism on three levels of analysis: as philosophy, political society, and the global order (discussed in chapters 2, 3, and 4, respectively).

Two

The Attack on Christendom

Throughout Europe, the disintegration of the Catholic commonwealth enlivened a new spirit of political and global cooperation. In search of new philosophical foundations, scientists and intellectuals shaped internationalism by gradually purging revelation from moral and scientific discourse, adopting instead more secular standards of reference, such as nature and reason. In Italy, Galileo, without rejecting faith, placed nature and reason at the center stage of scientific inquiry. Although his *Dialogues* were perceived by Rome as a work of heresy, they stirred debates throughout Europe about the need for freedom of scientific inquiry.[1] In England, Francis Bacon planned the *instauratio magna,* the mastery of humans over nature.[2] In Germany, Gottfried Wilhelm von Leibniz advocated Christian ecumenism in religion, codified Roman law, and introduced natural law in jurisprudence.[3] In France, Descartes disseminated a philosophical and scientific spirit of skepticism toward everything that was not certain or testable.[4]

It is in this lively intellectual climate that grew out of the Reformation that Hugo Grotius, Giambattista Vico, and Jean-Jacques Rousseau searched for new patterns of human cooperation. Their writings reflected the decay of Catholic universalism and a burgeoning spirit of internationalism.

Committed to a new vision of internationalist solidarity following the influence of the Protestant Reformation, Grotius rejected the

centralized authority of the universal church for practical and theoretical reasons. "For as a ship may be built too large to be conve-
niently managed," he wrote, "so an empire may be too expansive in
population and territory to be directed and governed by one head."[5]
He reminded those who asserted the dominion of the church over
unknown parts of the world that the apostle Paul himself had enjoined
Christians "not to judge those who were without the pale of their
own community."[6]

Although he accepted that the apostles held the seals of divine
grace on earth, Grotius maintained that their revealed judgment was
heavenly rather than earthly in character. Noting the complexity of
the Scriptures, he insisted that God's will was often perverted by
wicked monarchs and princes in their attempt to fulfill their personal
aims. Revelation was a device allowing them to promote their privileges and arbitrary version of the truth. Thus he deplored the dishon-
esty of the clergy and of the kings who masked their wars of conquest under the false pretext of propagating the universal message of
Catholicism and of avenging offenses committed against God. These
claims were self-contradictory, for they undermined God's omnipo-
tent aptitude to avenge himself.[7]

Observing the sanguinary battles launched under the flag of religious truth, Grotius urged avenging parties during the great religious
wars to maintain a spirit of tolerance. He insisted that no force should
be used to impose Christianity upon other nations and declared that

> it seems unjust to persecute with punishments those who receive
> the laws of Christ as true, but entertain doubts or errors on some
> external points taking them in an ambiguous meaning or different
> from the ancient Christian in their explanation of them.[8]

Thus, against the universalist pretensions of the church, Grotius introduced a new concept of solidarity committed to more than one
truth. The faces of truth, he explained, were multiple and difficult to
grasp by humans. Internationalism, unlike the universalism of the
Catholic church, was shaped by a new form of tolerance. The knowledge of truths has been "disfigured," he argued, "and almost entirely
obliterated among many nations by the lapse of time."[9] The words
of the prophets commanded by God, he stated, were aimed at satis-
fying popular needs during a particular time period.

Grotius's remarks were directed precisely against the means by which both the Catholic and the Dutch Calvinist churches maintained their intransigent power. Indeed, Grotius belonged to the sect of the Remonstrants or Armenians, who, influenced by Descartes, kept a certain level of skepticism regarding the existence of a unique Catholic truth. They advocated religious toleration, a decentralization of national power in favor of provincial sovereignty, and efforts to promote peace with the Spanish. However, once the Calvinists strengthened their power in the Low Countries, the Remonstrants were condemned as heretics. In 1618 they were outlawed, and Grotius was convicted of treason and given life imprisonment with forfeiture of all property. Three years later, he escaped to Paris, hidden in a trunk, with the help of his wife.

Nonetheless, one should not conclude too rapidly that Grotius's prospect for social harmony rested on secular ground. Like Galileo, Bacon, Descartes, Leibniz, and others, his rationalist foundation for a new collective identity was still linked by a sacred chain to God. Grotius postulated that reason was revealed to individuals in the process of working with nature "because of [God's] having willed that such traits existed in us."[10] He did not deny the existence of God.[11] Vesting his interest in individuals' ability to seek material felicity, however, Grotius emphasized the natural over the supernatural realm. Reason, he argued, guaranteed the ultimate progress of civilization.

Furthermore, the mathematical mind of the seventeenth century influenced the development of internationalism by providing a rational mode of investigating social and moral issues. Like the Cartesian formulation of mathematics, Grotius distinguished between scientific reason and uncontroversial axiomatic principles of morality, which could not allow any doubt. He then suggested checking the validity of the less evident postulates against the general principles of scientific reason:

> [We] should make an accurate distinction between general principles, such as living according to the dictates of reason, and those of a more particular though not less obvious meaning; as the duty of forbearing to take what belongs to another. To which many truths can be added though not quite so easy of apprehension: among which may be named the cruelty of that kind of punishment, which consists in revenge, delighting in the pain of another. This is the

method of proof similar to that which occurs in mathematics, the process of which rises from self-evident truths to demonstrations, the latter of which, though not intelligible to all alike, upon due examination obtain assent.[12]

By introducing mathematical modes of thinking to social science, Grotius contributed to the rational and theoretical proviso of the future bourgeois society—which would be based on a calculable and quantifiable monetary relationship between merchants, and hence would mold the early character of internationalism. In the words of Ernst Bloch:

> The universal rationalistic demand of [Grotius's] age was a genetic deduction from pure reason; here mathematics provided the model.... this is done in order to reconstruct the state out of its constitutive elements according to methodological purity, and, if necessary, in order to measure the empirical reality that is confused with this purity.[13]

Nature and reason were seen by Grotius as God's gift to individuals. His rationalist vision was nevertheless interpreted by Vico as a pure form of atheism and heresy. Grotius, explained Vico, avoided all but a few selective references to the Old Testament and was more inclined to confirm his assumptions by selecting evidence from the classical authors of Greece and Rome.[14] Although Vico openly proclaimed his fervent adherence to Catholic unity and his rejection of Protestantism, there was in fact no significant difference between his and Grotius's conception of morality.[15] Vico, despite himself, was influenced by the Protestant works of Grotius. Insisting that he was a genuine Catholic adept, he appeared unaware that the original conceptualization of his social vision had been tainted by the Reformation. This point is supported by Vico's own distinction between two realms of knowledge: God's domain, the *verum, ipsum factum,* in which God is the creator of all and thereby knows all,[16] and that of the human sphere, the *certum,* a narrower field of knowledge accessible to human minds, a confined world in which man is the creator and therefore is able to master the limited world of his creation.[17] Nations, institutions, laws, moral codes, and customs were all various aspects of civilization, and above all the product of human creation.

Thus, Vico's philosophical foundation of human solidarity, and indirectly of internationalism, was centered on the study of the palpable: the human territory. Engulfed in the study of men's creative work, Vico left God at the back stage of civilization, in the role of a hidden puppeteer. One can conclude that the *Scienza Nuova* was a de facto tribute to man's knowledge and labor. Vico inadvertently exacerbated the growing split between reason and revelation, as preached by Catholic dogma. In addition, by suggesting the possible development of various aspects of human morality, he was implicitly departing from the one-dimensional moral truth of Christendom. He sought, instead, a new collective spirit faithful to universal moral principles and founded on the diversity of competing cultural and religious values. His view reinforced the spirit of tolerance already associated with internationalism.

Vico shared Grotius's, Bacon's, Hobbes's and many other Enlightenment thinkers' interest in the terrestrial sphere. Like Grotius, the scientific revolution had influenced his rational and systematic understanding of human associations — as the title of his magnum opus, *The New Science,* suggests. Nonetheless, he rejected Grotius's and Descartes's optimism regarding the superiority of mathematical investigation, which emerges as an ex nihilo truth and represents the final progress of the "Age of Reason." Indeed, he asserted that natural reason was not the final phase of civilization. A new "barbarism of reflection" could turn civilized men into worse than beasts. The compromising and calculable spirit of scientific reasoning that linked individuals could also turn against itself and lead to social disintegration, to the emergence of particularism.

Although Vico viewed reason as a cohesive force in human association, he placed it within a sociohistorical perspective. In his section on natural reason, Vico evinced his point by referring to Roman history: "It came about that by abuse of eloquence like that of the tribunes of the plebs at Rome, when the citizens were no longer content with making wealth the basis of rank, they strove to make it an instrument of power."[18] These citizens would provoke civil wars and drive their commonwealth to total chaos. In such a situation, civil loyalties could be forgotten, the restraints of morality could turn into jests. Men would throng together in cities and jostle each other at public festivals, but they would live in deep solitude of spirit: under soft words and polite embraces they would plot against one another's lives. Their factions would grow into civil wars that decimated the lands and turned their cities into forests. Those who survived would be reduced to the barbarism of the senses, until they learned once more the necessary things of life.[19]

Vico's cyclical analysis of reason, unlike that of Grotius, contemplated the possible waning of social cohesion as well as its maturation. Reason was at different times "the daughter of ignorance, and the mother of knowledge,"[20] as it was also the product of human solidarity as well as the instrument of its own destruction. Whereas Grotius's belief in the coming of the final age of progress and reason was confirmed by the flourishing commerce and intellectual life of the Netherlands, Vico's cautious attitude regarding the advent of a long-lasting, peaceful, and rational harmony reflected his observation of the grandeur and decadence of the Roman and the Catholic empires, and of the Italian Rinascimento. In this respect, Vico implicitly announced the fluctuating nature of universal reason and internationalist aspirations.

Striking similarities can be found between Rousseau and Vico in terms of their analysis of reason. Among all characteristics of human faculties, Rousseau indicated that reason was the quality developed with the greatest difficulty. Rousseau, like his predecessor, recognized that reason could both consolidate individuals and isolate them from one another. Reason developed individual capacity for sociability; yet it is also "reason which turns man's mind back upon itself and divides him from everything that could disturb or afflict him."[21] Particular and instrumental interests, he knew, might supersede the collective spirit of compromise and lead to civil anarchy or the Hobbesian "war of all against all." Rousseau, like Vico, did not conceive reason as a fixed feature of human consciousness, but rather as a faculty that could be developed in the process of sociability. Inversely, in a corrupted environment, rationality could lead to the desire for luxury and depravation. In a selfish and greedy society, which, in Rousseau's opinion, was exemplified by the Parisian lifestyle, rationality lent itself to the interests of the few. It is therefore not surprising to see Rousseau ridiculing contemporary philosophers such as Voltaire, Condillac, Helvétius, and Condorcet for endorsing an instrumental rationality based on experience and that could lead to selfishness.[22] In such circumstances, reason fostered passions and rivalry. Reason, the new philosophical underpinning of internationalism, could only be understood in terms of the context of its emergence.

While exploring the two faces of reason, Rousseau emphasized the one fomenting mutual assistance, unmediated by the Catholic church. He explicitly rejected the revealed foundation of the universal ambitions of the Catholic church. In fact, the last part of his famous *Profession de foi du Vicaire Savoyard* attacks the very essence of revelation. The vicar warns Emile to attribute no authority to his words save that of reason, or, in the words of the vicar:

> The greatest ideas of Divinity came to us through reason only. Behold the spectacle of nature. Listen to the inner voice. Has not God told everything to our eyes, our conscience and our judgment? What can men [of the church] tell us more? Their revelation serves only to degrade God, by attributing to him the traits of human passions.[23]

Furthermore, Rousseau overtly condemned the Catholic commonwealth for cultivating division and inequality rather than human cooperation: "Religion commanded us to believe under the arbitrariness of revelation that the men God himself draws from the state of nature, immediately after the creation, are unequal because he wanted them to be."[24] "Christianity," continued Rousseau in the *Contrat Social,* "preached servitude and dependency," and favored tyranny by taking advantage of it. In such a world, the real Christians are made to be slaves.[25]

Rousseau recognized the universal message of the church as "embracing equally all men in a charity without limits," tearing down the fences separating nations, and convening all human races into one brotherly people.[26] Yet this message of charity stood in contradiction to its terrestrial application. Those who had politicized Christianity by mixing terrestrial interests with "celestial purity," wrote Rousseau, had to be condemned.[27] "How could a Christian Republic maintain a Christian army?"[28] Rousseau asked in reference to the crusaders. Such an idea was a contradiction in terms, for the crusaders could not have been both Christian and soldiers:

> I would be content to note that far from being Christians, they were soldiers of the priest; they were citizens of the church; they were fighting for their spiritual country. Frankly speaking, this enters into paganism.[29]

Rousseau relied less on the spirit of the church than on the Gospels, where the doctrine is simple and the morality sublime, where there is little practice and much charity.[30] He noticed that there should not be proscription or legitimation of one religion over another, but encouragement only of what reason and sentiment showed the individual to be just and moral. Defending the principles of the Reformation, he pleaded for tolerance of all forms of worship, the separation and peaceful coexistence between state and religion—in other words, for an internationalism based on pluralism and secular qualifications.

In short, despite their differences, Grotius, Vico, and Rousseau departed in their writings from the Catholic vision of universal human harmony. Their views nevertheless helped to develop the new philosophical foundation of internationalism, which would maintain separate spheres of human activities rather than the unified authority of the church, reason and natural law rather than revealed knowledge, and diversity of religious beliefs rather than uniformity. The next chapter will deal more specifically with these three thinkers' views of political society, a second dimension of internationalism.

Three

Natural Law and the Social Contract

The progressive reliance upon reason showed that revelation could not serve as a single criterion for establishing truth or for adjudicating grievances. It was thus plausible for Grotius, Vico, and Rousseau to concern themselves with the establishment of new rules for resolving conflict and developing cooperation. Natural laws would also become the legal foundation for tailoring new forms of social and political association. These laws were perceived as a system of rights, common to all humankind, derived from nature rather than from the rule of society or positive law. Natural law, though derived from divine law, assumed a life independent from divine laws. Yet the relationship between them constituted a source of tension.

The tension between divine and natural law can be traced through various historical periods. Aristotle had already held that natural law existed everywhere and should inform positive law. In the medieval period, Augustine elaborated the view of individuals living freely under natural law before their fall and subsequent bondage under sin and the positive law. Gratian in the eleventh century equated natural law with divine law. Inspired by Aristotle, Thomas Aquinas revived the classic distinction by suggesting that eternal and divine law, though inaccessible to individuals in its totality, was disclosed to them in part through revelation and in part through reason or natural law. Aquinas's distinction between divine and natural law was sharpened in later centuries. The supremacy of the human lawgiver was gradually posited by Machiavelli and in diverse ways during the Enlightenment by Bodin, Hobbes, Althusius, Pufendorf, and others.[1]

It is against this intellectual climate that Grotius delved into the pre-Christian past, remote from Catholic and Protestant religious rivalries, to examine through the eyes of Aristotle or Cicero natural law as the foundation for commonwealth. This journey into the past enabled him to discern two types of law: natural law and volitional law. The law of nature originated in the rational and social nature of man. "Natural right is the dictate of reason, showing the moral turpitude, or moral necessity, of any act from its agreement or disagreement with a rational nature."[2] Volitional law, which could be equated with divine law, was never in contradiction with natural law.[3] Volitional law did not play the same immanent role in Grotius's thinking as the law of nature. What Grotius hoped was that by privileging the laws of nature, inspired by Roman laws, he might offer a unified theory of natural law based on human rationality and social character, removed from the dispute about the "right" interpretation of the Bible. Ambiguity over God's real intention had already ignited too many wars:

> Since the divine words of permission are ambiguous in their meaning, it is better for us to interpret according to the established law of nature, what kind of permission it is, than from our conception of its expediency to conclude it conformable to the laws of nature.[4]

A universal theory of natural laws, Grotius commented, had to encompass a sacred, and if necessary, a profane morality.

The law of nature consisted, for Grotius, of strict and unchangeable principles of justice, necessary for the maintenance of a peaceful social order and consonant with human intelligence. It was also consistent with the will of God: "For since the law of nature is perpetual and unchangeable, nothing contradictory to it could be commanded by God, who is never unjust."[5] Eternal and timeless, Grotius's law of nature represented an ideal model that bordered on the perfection of geometric figures. Grotius presented his guiding model to rulers as a moral almanac to which they should refer in their act of governing. Different countries should keep a certain autonomy while drafting their laws. Yet these laws—he called them the "laws of nations"—ought to approximate the universal essence of natural law; for the

law of nature was the basis of *all* "laws of nations." Grotius introduced a normative and a human element into politics, a system of
values, such as justice, good faith, and fair contract, by which the
laws of nations could be critically evaluated. Grotius's departure
from the "invisible world" is shown by his focus on the "visible
world," where he distinguished between natural law and the laws of
nations, and by his concern to conform the laws of nations to a "terrestrial" ethic, to natural law.

Natural law preceded human conditions but was still applicable
once society was established. The rights enjoyed by the atomistic individuals in the state of nature permeated the moral world: the state
possessed no rights that individuals had not formerly acquired prior
to civil society. Grotius's optimism about the moral nature of individuals and the state of nature arouses a skepticism that underlined
the thought of Hobbes. Peace, argued Hobbes, is not achieved by individuals' altruistic motivation in the state of nature but is obtained
by their selfish interest in survival and security, when complying to
the state, *The Leviathan*. Internationalism was formulated in instrumental and economic terms.

Anticipating Locke, Grotius also regarded private property as one
of the most fundamental natural rights granted in the state of nature
that had to be secure in civil society. He justified the acquisition of
property through some sort of labor. In the *Iure Praedae,* he wrote
that

> common ownership could bring nothing but discontent and dissen-
> sion. Therefore, each one not only kept for him and his what he
> had made or labored, but unowned things also were possessed as
> well by whole peoples as by particular persons, and being pos-
> sessed came to be owned. For it is reasonable that what is open to
> all should go to the man who first takes it to keep it for himself.[6]

These lines showed how on the one hand Grotius legitimized the
possessions of the aristocracy, while on the other hand he created an
ideological space for the bourgeoisie to acquire property. He considered that these property rights should be protected in civil society
through fair contract. A fair contract was one that bound and oblig-
ated "free" covenantors to respect their agreement. Grotius insisted
upon the sacrosanct character of contracts in order to mitigate disputes and preserve civil order.

Individuals were the natural masters of their properties and they were free to strike bargains in all kinds of ways over their possessions. Whether men had the right to sell their freedom as part of their possession in a contract remained, however, ambiguous in Grotius's writings. In the *Inleidinghe*, he did not repudiate the idea of a contract by which an individual would renounce her or his liberty: "A man's honor belongs to him; first to protect it ... a man may renounce something that belongs to him as part of his honor."[7]

Grotius perceived the state as the aggregation of various independent associations, with responsibility for enforcing rules and compelling individuals to observe their agreements. Gierke identified Grotius as the advocate of the federalist trend within the natural school theory.[8] This tendency was developed against theorists such as Jean Bodin and Thomas Hobbes who argued for the absolute state. Grotius, like Pufendorf and later Kant, believed that the state existed to repair nature's weaknesses; the state should encompass the whole area of legal connection between persons, whether private or public, and should create the structure wherein various types of associations can enjoy an independent life. Such a theory had already been championed by Protestants in the Netherlands in their attempt to separate their religion from the state. This view paralleled the proliferation of independent spheres of activity. The atomization of society created a fertile soil for labor division and specialization, and thereby promoted a climate conducive to mutual exchange and contractual agreements. Internationalism was now divided into various spheres of specializations, which converged in the marketplace.

Furthermore, the political institutions of the state should enforce the dealings of fair contracts—to prevent possible misunderstandings and to palliate the use of force. It was through economic transactions, Grotius insisted, that the perfect form of reason and the highest level of a civilized state could be achieved. Conversely, it was only through rational thinking that private ownership and economic transaction could take place:

> Neither moral nor religious virtue, nor any intellectual excellence is requisite to form a good title to property. Only where a race of men is so destitute of reason as to be incapable of exercising any act of ownership, they can hold no property, nor will the law of charity require that they should have more than the necessaries of life. For the rules of the law of nations can only be applied to those

who are capable of political or commercial intercourse: but not to a people destitute of reason, though it is a matter of just doubt, whether any such is to be found.[9]

Grotius maintained that if not all people were ready for Christianity, they were undoubtedly all ready for commodity exchange, for the spirit of trade was based on reason and reason was available to all.

If each possessed the capacity to reason and the right to property, which form of government would prove most conducive for the conduct of trade? Inspired by Aristotle, Grotius seemed to argue at first that any government was acceptable insofar as it promoted commerce and trade. People could exercise political and legal authority through magistrates of their choice, he commented, or they could relinquish authority to some particular person:

> Just, in fact, as there are many ways of living, one being better than another, and every individual is free to choose from the many kinds what he likes the best, so a people may choose what form of government it pleases. Nor is his right to be measured by the excellence of this or that form, on which there is diversity of opinion, but by the people's will.[10]

In this passage, Grotius appears to be a "constitutional liberal." After all, "the sovereign power is vested in the people, so they have the power to restrain and punish the kings for an abuse of this power."[11] Nonetheless, he warned his reader of the "incalculable mischiefs" that could be occasioned by republican power.

Grotius even elaborated a justification for monarchy, based on a legal and contractual relationship: "There may be many reasons why a people may entirely relinquish their rights, and surrender them to another,"[12] without retaining any vestige of these rights for themselves. Grotius also thought that monarchical regimes were more in conformity with the law of nature and reason, and hence with internationalism. Such regimes would allow the progress of mercantilism while maintaining political order at home. A wise monarch, Grotius, and later the German political thinker Christian von Wolff, believed,[13] could advance the interests of the mercantile aristocracy while providing space for the rising bourgeoisie to join the aristocracy in its transatlantic economic venture.

The Wars of Spanish Succession in Italy influenced Vico's view in the same way as the wars of the Reformation shaped Grotius's political vision. Like his Dutch predecessor, Vico was interested in how to establish universal principles of social harmony in conformity with diverse cultural and legal systems. Vico observed three general principles. He maintained, first, that all nations, barbarous as well as civilized, although separated from each other in time and space, kept three human customs: all had some religion, all contracted solemn marriages, all buried their dead. Second, he maintained that all cultures passed through three stages: the age of God, the age of heroes, and the age of men. Finally, he believed that with these three stages went three kinds of laws, commonwealths, and religions. In this respect, Vico added a historical dimension to Grotius's work, and therefore to internationalism.

Unlike Grotius, Vico did not overtly condemn the Catholic church for perpetuating the belief in a universal dogma based on divine laws. Yet by devoting his study, *diritto delle genti,* to the development of natural law, he indirectly defied the supernatural foundations of the church. On this point, Benedetto Croce shrewdly observed that natural law during Vico's time meant "not supernatural."[14] Indeed, the study of the natural was considered sacrilegious and was often perceived as a form of heresy during the decay of Catholic unity. In addition, the title of Vico's masterpiece, *Scienza Nuova,* illustrated his attempt to investigate social questions in scientific terms, in the same way as Galileo and Descartes. Thus, with Grotius, Bodin, Wolff, and others, Vico reflected the social progress of Europe and of internationalism as it emerged from religious warfare and acquired a new scientific consciousness distinctively bourgeois and nonclerical in tenor.

As mentioned earlier, Vico, in spite of himself, was indebted to Grotius for the latter's distinction between the universal principles of natural law (*ius naturale*) and the laws of nations (*ius gentium*). No less than Grotius, Vico claimed that the universality of natural law (the *verum*) was to be differentiated from national laws (the *certum*). At the same time, however, he recognized the dialectical intimacy between the universal (*verum*) and the particular (*certum*) realm of natural law. In Vico's view, "natural law" embraced the aggregate of natural laws of an "eternal commonwealth," but this constantly varied in accordance with epochs and places.[15] He thus implicitly offered an understanding of internationalism that responded to cultural and historical changes.

Vico criticized Grotius, Selden,[16] and Pufendorf for misperceiving the historical importance of the development of natural law, whereby one custom of law grew into another. He condemned these seventeenth-century theorists for believing that a perfect legal system was attainable in their epoch:

> The three princes of this doctrine, Hugo Grotius, John Selden and Samuel Pufendorf, should have taken their start from the beginning of the *gentes,* which their subject matter begins. But all three of them err together in this respect by beginning in the middle; that is with the latest times of the civilized nations (and thus of men enlightened by fully developed natural reason) from which the philosophers emerged and rose to meditation of a perfect idea of justice.[17]

Natural law, Vico explained, was both a universal and a particular aspect of jurisprudence; it was also subject to change.[18] By omitting the process through which natural law evolved, Vico argued, these three theorists were unable to perceive the historical significance of a particular social association.[19] The various phases of jurisprudence, he claimed, were intertwined with the development of society.

Thus, in place of the usual speculation about the origins of social contracts, property, and so forth, Vico offered a framework in which the development of political society was studied in concert with laws and property relations between individuals. Internationalism would thus be informed by these social and political interactions, that would change their character mainly as a result of conflict over property relationships. Vico documented this position by first analyzing the development of society, *urbs,* as emerging from the cultivation of land. Ploughed lands were thus the first altars tended by nobles, who had descended from the gods. "To these altars, then, the impious-nomadic-weak, fleeing from the stronger, came seeking refuge, and the pious-strong killed the violent among them and took the weak under their protection."[20] Already, the granting of asylum to those weak nomads, called the *famuli,* was implicitly a sort of contract, one of submission, but the *famuli* achieved tenuous recognition status against which they mutinied and laid claims to the land they worked. The nobles, "to content the revolting bands of *famuli* and reduce them to obedience, granted them an agrarian law, which is found to be the first civil law born in the world" (par. 25).

Vico proceeded to explain how a new social arrangement was developed as a result of conflict of interests between the *famuli* and the nobility. A new commonwealth marked the beginning of fiefs and of a feudal system based on a mixture of domination and mutual benefit. "Since ownership determined power and since the lives of the *famuli* were dependent upon the heroes who had saved them by granting them asylum" (par. 597), the masters found it lawful to grant natural or "*bonitary*" ownership of the lands to their serfs, while retaining civil or "*quiritary*" ownership for themselves. In other words, the *famuli* were only granted "precarious ownership, which they might enjoy as long as it suited the heroes to maintain them in possession of the fields they had assigned them" (par. 597).

Gradually, the *famuli* merged to form the first plebs of the heroic cities, in which they were deprived of citizenship privileges. With the weakening of the heroes, the plebs succeeded in gaining *quiritary* ownership of their fields from the second agrarian law, which was conceded by the nobles in the Law of the Twelve Tables (par. 598). The struggle over the *connubium,* namely, the right of intermarriage between nobility and commoners, challenged hereditary rights, that is, the foundation of aristocratic privilege. In breaking through the privacy of "law," the plebeians in effect, though not with conscious intent, opened the way for the development of the universal nature of the law. The progress was implicit in the plebeian acquisition of civil ownership of land, since that could not depend on the goodwill of the nobles. This public determination of the laws removed them from the essentially arbitrary sphere of what was "certain" in the rigid noble code (pars. 110, 567, 587, 598, 612).

Vico, like Grotius, attached a great importance to the study of property relationships as the foundation of civil society. Yet, whereas Grotius viewed the universal accessibility of property as a satisfactory condition for peace, Vico claimed that civil harmony was not obtained once a republic of free men has replaced the aristocracy. Wealth and leisure would ultimately breed feebleness and greed, and will pervade the nature of fair contracts. Citizens would grow careless and lawlessness would prevail. Deliverance will come when a strong prince establishes order and takes authority into his hands. A single man must arise, as Augustus did in Rome, and take all public concern into his hands, leaving his subjects free to look after their private affairs. Thus, the people are saved when they would otherwise rush to their own destruction (sections 1102, 1104, pp. 865–66). The "history of Rome served to exemplify the irresponsibility of civilized men in the universal age of reason" that brought their civil society to destruction. Notwithstanding the differences between Vico and Grotius, internationalism was primarily conceived in instrumental and economic terms.

Which governmental institution, then, was capable of securing peace within civil society? Vico commented that "governments must conform to the nature of the men governed,"[21] with respect to their developmental stage. Despite the apparent relativism, he concluded with Grotius, Hobbes, and Bodin that aristocratic and republican regimes were unstable, and that states normally "come to rest under monarchies."[22] A strong monarchy might have both served to unify a dismembered, rivalrous Italy and reactivated its economic energy, following the English, the French, and the Dutch model.

Although Rousseau's concept of the laws of nature followed the principles of reason, his interpretation served to support the foundation of a political regime different from those advocated by his predecessors. Admittedly, Rousseau, like his two forerunners, believed that law, deriving from nature, was the pillar of a free society. However, wishing to assert the ethical content of the social bond, *le lien social*, Rousseau identified different rules deriving from nature, and therefore provided a new political perspective for internationalism. All bonds, or contracts, he claimed, must associate freely acting persons. Unlike Grotius and Bodin or Vico, Rousseau suggested that a civil association cannot be imposed by any external authority upon the will of the individual:

> The laws are only the conditions of the civil association. The people, subjected to laws, should, then, be the authors of these laws; for only those who associate can declare the conditions under which they want to associate.[23]

Subsequently, Rousseau declared that any theories of social contract that seek to derive a pact founded on subjection (*pactum subjectionis*) denied the universal and inalienable rights of individuals. Such basic rights included both the right to acquire private property and political equality. Thus he attacked Grotius for justifying the legal right of individuals to freely abnegate their freedom in a contract:

> To say that a man surrenders himself freely is to say something ab-
> surd and inconceivable; such an act is void, for it assumes that the
> one who performs it is senseless. To say the same thing for all people
> is to support a mad population: madness does not have accession
> to right.[24]

Grotius had arrived at this conclusion by deriving his concept of social union from factual assumptions.[25] Rousseau, on the other hand,
unlike his forerunners, proclaimed that legal standards should be exclusively inspired by moral and speculative criteria removed from empirical observations. Rousseau's social views contributed to strengthening the normative, speculative, and political aspect of a developing
internationalism.

The bourgeoisie during the time Rousseau wrote the *Social Contract* was no longer satisfied with short-term economic gain; the political state even more surely obstructed its long-term development.
Following the spirit of his time, Rousseau elaborated a theory of law
derived from speculative postulates in order to further ongoing political change. A new body of law should ensure the establishment of a
self-imposed social contract representing the will of the covenantors.
This definition of political society served to animate the spirit of "democratic" internationalism. He thus formulated a new theory of the
social contract, which was more than Locke's arithmetical sum of
the individual wills conceived as an organic entity. He described the
"general will" as a human body:

> The sovereign power represents the head, the laws and custom are
> the brain ... the commerce and agriculture are the mouth and
> stomach, the political finances the blood, which, thanks to a wise
> economy, fulfills the task of the heart and distributes the food and
> life throughout the body.[26]

His organic vision of the social contract provided the Third Estate
with a perspective by which it could transcend its particularist interests and restructure the state.

The concept of the *volonté générale* also anticipated many of the
substantive problems encountered by the French Revolution. Self-
defined concepts often lend themselves to relativism. Since the general will was always right once established, it was endowed with the

moral authority to legislate laws that were antagonistic to the welfare of minority groups by simply "forcing them to be free." Although Rousseau claimed that the exercise of the general will should remain within the framework of the "general convention," he did not clarify the moral nature of these conventions except — tautologically — in terms of the general will. A conceptualization of the collective good, unsupported by a priori standards of universal ethics, is condemned to be justified in its own terms, and thereby opens avenues for relativistic approaches. It is not surprising that this concept developed contradictory interpretations.[27] Despite the ambiguity of Rousseau's general will, his definition of the state was a revolutionary one for the eighteenth century since it condemned slavery and defied the crux of the feudal structure. For the first time, indeed, the nation was identified with the people, and internationalism with a democratic principle.

A major goal of Rousseau's view of the social contract was the preservation of property.[28] "It is certain," he wrote, "that the right of property is the most sacred of all human rights."[29] At the same time, however, he realized, with Vico, that discrepancies of wealth could engender inequality and social conflict between citizens. Thus he urged the taking of proper measures to attenuate social differences:

> Do you want to give the state some consistency? Bring together the extremes, as much as possible; do not accept opulent people and beggars. The two stages, naturally inseparable, are equally baleful to the common good; from one emerged those responsible for tyranny, and from the other the tyrants; it is always between them that the traffic of liberty operates: one buys and the other sells.

Thus, although inviolable and sacred, Rousseau asserted that the right of private property was subordinated to the general will, which was entitled to correct disparities of wealth.[30] He never stated clearly to what extent the state can regulate economic differences between citizens. However, he explicitly advised the Polish and Corsican governments to limit economic injustice without abolishing private property.[31] His ideal of a society consisting of owners of small property, each with a field or a workshop, greatly influenced radical Jacobins like Robespierre and Saint-Just, as well as Americans like Jefferson.

By favoring states with a self-sufficient agrarian economy, Rousseau sent an early signal of the flaws of an internationalist vision predicated mainly on instrumental and economic transactions. He favored agriculture over commerce because it was supposedly predisposed to freedom and independence. Those states whose economies were based on commerce were more inclined to abuses of power, corruption, and dependency. "Commerce produces wealth; but farming ensures liberty."[32] Thus Rousseau suggested to the Polish people not to make commerce their main source of national income. Instead, he argued that they should become self-sufficient through agricultural production: "Leave all that money to others ... [f]arm well your fields without worrying about the rest ... financial systems produce venal souls."[33] Rousseau's ideas were influenced by the Physiocrats, who looked upon commerce and industry as sterile and saw agriculture as the main source of wealth. The Physiocrats recommended that capitalism be applied to agriculture, rather than to commerce and industry, and that the tax burden be shifted to landowners — a process similar to what happened in England. In light of its agrarian bias, it is ironic that the physiocratic doctrine ultimately favored the middle class, which took the motto and the mentality of laissez-faire as its own. Adam Smith later reversed what the Physiocrats thought was profitable even while retaining the principle of laissez-faire.

It makes sense, then, that Rousseau should have believed that the nature of production, geography, and the size of the state determined the character of governmental administrations.[34] Rousseau observed that monarchy suited big and affluent states; aristocracy was adapted to states of middle wealth and size; and democracy conformed to relatively small and poor countries.[35] Like Vico, he believed that every regime had the potential to degenerate. When a government abused the confidence of its subjects, he argued, it would trigger a process of dissolution, from the larger number of people participating in the political realm to the smaller, that is, from democracy to aristocracy, and from aristocracy to monarchy.[36] The history of the Roman republic demonstrated this self-diminishing process.[37] Yet, unlike his two forerunners, Grotius and Vico, Rousseau vigorously rejected monarchy as an appropriate regime. Indeed, contrary to the English government, the eighteenth-century French monarchy was not inclined to reform the political system and therefore to decrease the frustration of the Third Estate. Rousseau might thus have favored the establishment of a small, self-sufficient government, like the communes of Switzerland, wherein all citizens would participate in the political affairs of the state and know one another, for in the large state, relations between citizens become impersonal and their interests, problems, and fortunes diversified. In small states, on the other hand, a clear national character could develop through civic education and personal bonds, knitted around public and moral concerns. Patriotic sentiments would represent the citizen's experience of moral and civic virtues.

Without disputing Rousseau's influence on nineteenth-century nationalism, it would be a mistake to understand him as a romantic nationalist.[38] Rousseau's eighteenth-century notion of patriotism should be clearly distinguished from nineteenth-century nationalism. The eighteenth-century view of patriotism served to exalt political and economic rights of all members of the Third Estate, from the French *patrie* to the rest of the world, in their fight against monarchical and absolutist regimes. Nationalism of the nineteenth century, on the other hand, fostered the cultural bond between individuals within the nation and at times the supremacy of one nation over another.

Furthermore, the distinction between patriotism, as a universal civic idea aroused by the state (or the *patrie*), and nationalism as an emotion aroused by a cultural identification with the nation was not known during the eighteenth century, for the Enlightenment did not make a distinction between nation and state. The French Encyclopedists provided a structural definition of the nation that could well have been used for the state: "a collective word used to designate a certain quantity of people, living in a certain size of territory, within certain limits, and who obey the same government."[39] The contrast between nation and state (and the corresponding distinction between nationalism and patriotism) would be made possible only when nineteenth-century nationalists chose to differentiate themselves from the universal aspirations of their Enlightenment precursors.

This should not suggest that the universal message of human rights was embraced in a similar fashion by Enlightenment thinkers. This chapter has shown the transformation of internationalism and natural law as understood, in the domestic sphere, by Grotius, Vico, and Rousseau. Central to Grotius's view of natural law was the individual's right to private property. This right, he claimed, derived from the state of nature and ought to be secured in political society. Grotius also argued that contractual arrangements, informed by the law of nature, would develop a spirit of domestic cooperation and peace.

Emphasizing a historical understanding of natural law, or internationalism, Vico showed a less optimistic picture than his predecessor and focused on how the precarious and changing character of natural and human law corresponded to the cyclical nature of political societies. Despite his apparently relativistic approach to governmental regimes, he agreed with his predecessor about the need for strong political institutions, in particular monarchical regimes, to unify individuals. Such regimes were in fact most compatible with mercantilist pursuits.

Rousseau's concept of natural law challenged Grotius's and Vico's by suggesting that private property rights were not the sole qualification of natural rights. With Rousseau, natural laws, or internationalism, would not just be determined by economic rights. These principles were to coexist with political rights as well. Rousseau shared with Vico a similar interest in relating natural law to its political context. Yet, unlike his forerunners' endorsement of monarchy, Rousseau maintained that the laws of nature were incompatible with the concept of strong monarchies. He thus proposed an innovative concept of political society identified with popular sovereignty, or the general will, and anticipated the aspiration of the Third Estate to seek a new political identity: the republican state. In the next chapter we shall see how Grotius's, Vico's, and Rousseau's respective principles, conceptualized in political society, manifested themselves in the global sphere, the third aspect of internationalism.

Four

Religious Wars and the Need for International Arrangements

Europe was still ensnared in incessant wars during the lifetimes of Grotius, Vico, and Rousseau. Their works were the product of minds revolted by the unparalleled atrocities of those wars: the assassination of leaders, the slaying of prisoners, the violation of women, the massacre of children, the pillaging of defenseless towns, the poisoning of wells, the wanton spoliation of peaceful populations. There appeared to be an urgent need for the formulation of a legal arrangement on the global level that could unify individuals, conflicting religious groups, and rival nations. What principles should be enunciated to condemn these barbarities? Under which standard could wars be justified? Upon what criteria could an authoritative body of rules be framed so that the public opinion of the civilized world would be compelled to observe them? On what foundation might a stable structure of global morality emerge?

These questions were already addressed in the fourteenth, fifteenth, and sixteenth centuries. Italian interstate conflicts prompted lawyers like Bartolo da Sassoferrato and Baldo degli Ubaldi during the fourteenth century to develop a doctrine of international law to tackle war issues.[1] Their doctrines became influential in Spain, Portugal, and Germany. In the fifteenth century, Machiavelli elaborated guidelines to temper conflicts and unify Italy. In the early sixteenth century, the Dominican friar Francisco de Vitoria condemned the conquests and colonial policies of the Spanish empire, defended the rights of the non-Christian population and American natives and founded the Spanish school of international law.[2] The spread of religious wars throughout Europe in the seventeenth century encouraged further debates in international law. The Italian scholar Alberico Gentili, the German publicist and jurist Samuel Pufendorf, the English scholar and jurist Richard Zouche, and the Swiss councillor of embassy Emmerich de Vattel were among the major participants in these discussions.[3]

The writings of the Dutch lawyer Grotius, however, remained the most influential. His diplomatic career undoubtedly helped him to shape a pragmatic theory of just war and to diffuse his ideas. Influenced by Alberico Gentili, Grotius developed a just-war theory, not only by classifying right or wrong motivations but also by advising head of states how to temper their conduct. Grotius's doctrine of *temperamenta* urged moderation for reasons of internationalism, humanity, religion, and farsighted policy. To the question of whether wars were justifiable or not, Grotius, keeping in mind that the revolt of the Protestant Reformation was conducted with canons and firearms, concluded that wars compatible with the spirit of natural law and free enterprise were justifiable. This position was aimed, as well, against the pacifism of many Christian thinkers who opposed bearing arms at all. He identified three justifiable causes of wars: defense,[4] recovery of property, and punishment.[5] Private wars could also be just when public laws were no longer effective: "For private war may be considered as an instantaneous exercise of natural right, which ceases the moment that legal redress can be obtained."[6]

Which types of wars were forbidden according to natural laws? Force, Grotius replied, cannot be used against individual property. Thus, unjust reasons to initiate wars included attacks launched out of fear of a neighbor's power, wars of expediency as opposed to necessity, wars "to subjugate any people by force on the ground that they deserve to be slaves," and wars prompted by religious differences. Furthermore, he emphasized the need for arbitration and negotiation when the just character of wars is unclear.[7] Grotius anticipated Kant by suggesting that certain acts during war could be irreversible and thereby obstruct all future efforts for peace:

In just war the right of dominion over a people, and the sovereign power, which that people possesses, may be acquired as well as any other right. But the claim to such a right ought by no means to be prosecuted beyond indemnity for aggression, and security against future evils.[8]

Grotius's plea for moderation and tolerance had a significant impact on our present international system of laws. He devised rules of conduct in the global sphere to ensure peace and the free flow of goods among individuals and nations. Christian von Wolff and Emmerich de Vattel became, in the late seventeenth and early eighteenth centuries, two early exponents of the Grotian views. Such ideas became increasingly important with the globalization of the world economy.

Grotius's rules derived from the law of nations, *ius gentium.* The primary purpose of the law of nations was to adapt the abstract principles of the law of nature, *ius naturale,* to concrete circumstances of time and space; thus, the law of nations derived from the law of nature. With Richard Zouche, Grotius distinguished the law of nations from municipal laws, or from laws within the state. The law of nations defined moral human conduct not only within single states but within the larger society of humankind, of which states were only parts. This law was characterized by its advisory nature. It informed nations of their mutual advantage and the range of "permissible" actions if they were to abide by the rules of nature and reason. The law of nations was the product of nations' consent:

> The law of nations ... deriv[es] its authority from the consent of all, or at least of many nations. It was proper to add MANY, because scarce any right can be found common to all nations, except the law of nature, which itself too is generally called the law of nations. Nay, frequently in one part of the world, that is held for the law of the nations, which is not so in another.[9]

From this perspective, international law was conceived as a customary law binding states in exactly the same way as associating individuals were bound in the prepolitical state. Grotius sought to show an affinity between customs among nations and the rational nature of man. Given these assumptions, states ought to be self-sufficient, entitled to the power of supreme sovereignty with no other human authority above it. He condemned the subjugation of states to another power, as was the case with the Roman provinces:

> For those nations are not sovereign states of themselves, in the present acceptation of the word; but are subordinate members of a great state, as slaves are members of a household.[10]

Yet Grotius's comparison between the rational individual, who had to submit himself to the legal authority of the state, and the nation-state acting in a legally noncoercive world was erroneous. His universal system of law applicable to all persons and nations overlooked the differences between the binding force of state law and the unauthoritative political structure of the global sphere. Grotius's rejection of any world government may have been the product of his aversion to the centralism of the Catholic commonwealth. Influenced by the Reformation, he was content to grant individuals the full capacity to shape domestic and international policies according to the rule of nature and reason. By assuming a dual legal standard, however, Grotius implicitly reflected the twin concerns of the emerging ruling classes, who were striving to create a contractual and legal spirit on the global level while simultaneously maintaining a strong authoritative nation-state capable of protecting their interests against foreign competition.

While Grotius's Low Countries asserted their independence and exemplified the progress of the Reformation, Italy was sinking into economic destitution. It was no longer the avant-garde country of the Rinascimento. Italy's rivals — France, England, and the Netherlands — had far outstripped it. Commerce was not widespread, industry and agriculture languished, and its princes had ceased to encourage even art and agriculture. Seventeenth- and eighteenth-century Italy was fragmented by the rivalry of petty city-states. The downfall of Italian prestige was precipitated by the mischievous careers of tyrants, statesmen, and conspirators animated chiefly by cupidity, envy, and revenge; the ambitions and intrigues in the court of Rome; the conspiratorial unity of the neighboring nations; and their consequent military superiority.

Living in Naples, Vico experienced the foreign rule of the Spanish, under Charles II of Spain, and of the Austrian viceroy as a result of the Spanish wars of succession. Observing the rapid changes occurring in his country, he argued, in contrast to Grotius, that any discussion of just or unjust wars according to any fixed criteria was a futile intellectual exercise. Wars and violent disruptions of the status quo were the manifestation of societies in transition from one historical phase to another: from birth to maturity, from maturity to decline, and from decline to rebirth. Thus Vico disputed Grotius's optimism regarding the final arrival of the "Age of Reason." Even when civil equality was fully attained, commented Vico, there could still be great inequality of wealth. This could engender grievous conflicts and wars, corruption among the rich, envy and aggression among the poor. In such a situation, a prince would arise to protect society from the worst effects of its own cupidity. He would become the substitute for the law that democratic license had rendered vain. In fact, the corruption of a nation may advance so far that no remedy can be found within itself, and hence must be sought from without. This could occur through defeat by a foreign enemy or simple internal decay. The conquest of one nation by another could take the conquered people back to the early stage of history.[11]

Vico's cyclical analysis of history did not paint the future with glowing colors, in contrast to the optimism of Italian predecessors Sassoferrato, Ubaldi, and Gentili, of Grotius, or of contemporary natural law theorists such as Wolff and Vattel. He was keenly aware of the gloomy and perplexing features of history and was convinced that all nations tended to decay. Despite Vico's pessimism, he was still a child of the Enlightenment. With the writers Lodovico Muratori, Apostolo Zeno, and Scipione Maffei, Vico reflected the awakening of historical consciousness in Italy.[12] One should remember that Vico was part of the Italian circle of lawyers who gradually became the progressive nucleus from which the progressive and liberalizing ideas of the seventeenth and eighteenth century would emanate. In the spirit of the Enlightenment, he wrote:

> Having entered upon civil life, [an individual] desires his own welfare along with that of his city; when his rule is extended over several peoples, he desires his own welfare along with that of a nation; when the nations are united by wars, treaties of peace, alliance and commerce, he desires his own welfare along with that of the entire human race.[13]

By recognizing that each nation did not pass through every stage in the same way, and that each nation had its own particularity, Vico exercised decisive influence over the nationalist thinkers of the risorgimento. It should be stressed, however, that he was not concerned with displaying the originality of the Italian character to the detriment of other nations. It was only in the nineteenth century that nationalists like the Carbonari updated Vico's theory and emphasized the superiority of Italian culture. Their position rested in a belief that Italy's natural development had been interrupted by foreign wars and occupation at a time when other states—France, Spain, and England—were able to consolidate their unification. Although he never saw the need to establish an international organization that could palliate the use of force between nations, Vico recognized the existence of universal principles that dictated the behavior of nations throughout history.

Vico's concept of recurrence (*ricorsi*) in the *Scienza Nuova* should be understood as an attempt to recapture over time both the organic universal message of the church and the particular essence of individual and national rights.[14] His implicit internationalism was founded on the linkage existing between universal principles, the *verum,* and particular circumstances, the *certum*. The religious wars of the sixteenth and seventeenth centuries fragmented the Respublica Catholica and created a space in which new boundaries had to be drawn in the "visible world." The establishment of autonomous confines of social activity and the sharpening division of labor would be propitious for the formation of capitalism, which required a separation between the public and private spheres, and between the national and global realms; in short, between the *verum* and the *certum*.

A quarter of a century after the first appearance of Vico's second *Scienza Nuova* (1725), Rousseau expressed his views on international conditions and wars. Although Rousseau was born in 1712, one year before the Treaty of Utrecht, which marked the end of the eleven years of the Wars of Spanish Succession (1702–13), peaceful relations between European states did not prevail during his lifetime. On the contrary, struggle between powers proliferated during the eighteenth century, which saw the wars of the succession of Poland (1734–38) and of Austria (1742–48), the Seven Years' Wars (1756–63), and the Polish partition crisis (1770–72). Consequently, it was not surprising to see Rousseau—along with Voltaire, Montesquieu, and others—using his pen to denounce the despotic nature of wars of conquests. These wars represented the interest of the princes, but never that of natural law, which Rousseau identified with the universal rights of the "general will":

> Finally, everyone can see sufficiently well that conquering princes wage wars as much against their enemies as against their subjects, and that the condition of the vanquishers is not much better than that of the vanquished.[15]

These observations plunged Rousseau into further meditations about the causes of war. Rousseau, like Grotius and Locke, believed that wars presupposed a constant set of relations that were formally established by states but that were not the product of relations between individuals in the state of nature:

> War is a permanent state, which presupposes constant relations, and these relations are a rare occurrence between men, for between individuals there is a continual flux that constantly changes relations and interests.[16]

The state of war, continued Rousseau, could not have existed before the institution of property and, therefore, not before the constitution of civil society. Unequal redistribution of property and resources by the state created covetousness, animosity, and wars of conquest: "Wars, money, and men, all the spoils one can possibly appropriate, become the main objects of mutual hostilities."[17]

Unlike Grotius and contemporaries like Voltaire and Hume, who believed in commodity exchange as an important way to promote peace, Rousseau was convinced that modern commerce was antithetical to the laws of nature, to global and universal harmony; instrumental exchange alone bred self-interest, competition, avarice, and ultimately war. "Ministers," he argued, referring to the political system, "need war to make themselves useful. . . . they need it to build in secret thousands of odious monopolies; they need it to satisfy their passions and to mutually exclude each other."[18] Rousseau expressed the Third Estate's growing disenchantment with the existing political apparatus and with its leadership, whose strength derived from war and privilege. Echoing Vico, he explained to the Polish people that wealthy countries always ended up being devoured by luxury and greed, and therefore were amenable to being conquered by other countries. In brief, wars were not just symptomatic of human nature or economic discrepancies but also of despotic governmental institutions, unresponsive to the "general will."

The sole justifiable ends of war, legitimized by natural laws, were those that defended the national rights of one community against another. In the light of this principle, Rousseau condemned all annexations of territory, or any form of war that amassed spoils and enslaved the population. On this point, Rousseau criticized Grotius for justifying the rights of the vanquished to barter their freedom for their lives during wartime. Rousseau shared Montesquieu's *L'esprit des lois,* and his condemnation of the fictitious rights of enslaved people. Peace promises, Rousseau argued, could not be actualized throughout coercion, human rights violations, or unfair contracts:

> I could question whether promises made to avoid death and extracted by force have an obligatory validity in the state of liberty; and whether any promises made by a prisoner to his master in this situation can mean something other than: I commit myself to obey you as long as you, being the strongest, do not threaten my life.[19]

Rousseau commented that, by allowing individuals to "freely" enslave themselves in wartime, Grotius ultimately showed his loyalty to monarchical regimes and absolutism. He did not hesitate to write that "Grotius, a refugee in France, ill content with his homeland, and desirous of paying his court to Louis XIII—to whom his book is dedicated—spares no pain to rob the people of all their rights and invest kings with them by every conceivable artifice."[20]

In addition, Rousseau argued that inequitable or unrepresentative political regimes were by nature the basis of global disorder. It is only in a just society, where individuals' autonomy and virtue can bloom, that wars will disappear. Governments, failing to represent the "general will," divert the resentment of their population to the external environment. Leaders of such repressive regimes point to the outside enemy as the cause of the population's discontent. World conflicts, Rousseau maintained, reflected internal political instability. He was the first thinker to suggest that the association of the sovereignty of the people with the nation-state was a major condition for world peace.

To underline, like Grotius, the formal significance and rationality of legal contracts without discussing the moral substance of pacts, or to grasp, in the spirit of Vico, the universal essence of the cyclical

nature of states were for Rousseau important but not sufficient efforts for sustaining a global peace proposal. Mutual exchange based
on economic opportunities was not a reliable criterion upon which to
found global solidarity. Only political equality between individuals,
within and between states, could secure the peace process and under-
pin the groundwork for internationalism.[21] Rousseau thus drafted
the future political agenda of the French revolutionaries[22] and highlighted a political, normative, and organic dimension to the internationalist yet instrumental vision of his forerunners.

Rousseau did not, however, conceive of a global system supervised by a world government. Given the status of the European powers,
he observed that peace was unlikely to be achieved. If the European
systems were undertaking just reforms, the need for a world government would become less and less pressing. Although he believed that
the idea of world federation launched by the Abbé de Saint-Pierre
was a laudable project, he was skeptical about its viability:

> One should not believe with the Abbé de Saint-Pierre, even with
> one's best will, which neither princes nor ministers would have,
> that it is too simple to find a favorable moment for the realization
> of such a system, for this would require that both the sum of the
> particular interests does not prevail over the common interests and
> that each sees in the well-being of all the aspiration of his own
> well-being. Yet this necessitates the fusion of so many interests that
> one should not expect from chance the congruence of the necessary
> circumstances. However, if this compatibility does not take place,
> there is only force that can supersede; and then there is no more
> question of convincing, but of constraining, and one should not
> write books, but should raise the troops.[23]

The bigger a state, Rousseau remarked, the heavier the administration, the greater its need for a strong executive with coercive power.
It would follow that, by stressing the administrative and formalistic
ties between states, an international confederation would inevitably
suffocate the needs and the voices of its citizens. Considering the decay
of the Catholic church, the failure of the confederation proposed by
Henry IV, and the monarchical aspect of the Abbé de Saint-Pierre's
peace project,[24] Rousseau concluded that the formation of such an
international society was impractical. Despite his call for universal
political equality, Rousseau rejected a supranational authority. Henceforth, he perpetuated with his predecessors the development of two

moral codes of behavior, the national and the global. Such a twofold moral structure enabled the rising bourgeoisie to promote, on the one hand, global legal arrangements between individuals within and between states, while striving, on the other hand, to keep a certain level of political control in order to contain the flow of commodities from abroad.

In short, Grotius's, Vico's, and Rousseau's internationalism defined natural laws as the guiding laws for nations and individuals. Each indicated that natural law should ensure universal cooperation while maintaining the independence of the nation-states. In the light of the flawed experience of the Catholic empire, they would have seen any endorsement of a centralized world government as obstructing the fundamental expression of individual rights and of free exchange. Each, however, viewed differently the ways to promote natural laws and internationalist solidarity. With Grotius, Vico indicated how trade relations would enhance cooperation; yet, with Rousseau, he also recognized how hostilities could emerge from unequal exchange. Grotius and Vico argued for the development of monarchies as the most stable and wise regimes to secure peace in the global order, whereas Rousseau contended that the institution of an organic and politically representative government (e.g., a republican state) would ensure domestic, and therefore global, peace.

None of these thinkers, however, could answer the question of how peace would triumph without delegating power to a world authority able to sanction recalcitrant nations. Thus, their understanding of natural law generated, or rather perpetuated, a nonidentical dual system of moral action: one for domestic policy, the other for foreign affairs. Their views epitomized the birth of internationalism rocking back and forth in its cradle, from an instrumental to an organic and normative view of global solidarity. With the development of the American and in particular the French Revolutions, discussed in chapter 5, the normative and organic school of solidarity would guide the infancy of internationalism.

Part II

Internationalism and the French Revolution: Kant, Paine, and Robespierre

Five

The Eighteenth-Century Democratic Revolutions and the Spirit of "Laissez-Faire"

By the mid-eighteenth century, a normative dimension had already been added to the earlier instrumentalist aspect of internationalism: political concerns now complemented its original economic character. Indeed, the eighteenth-century European imperial rivalries between major powers had proven that instrumental and economic links between individuals and nations could exacerbate hostilities rather than promote peace.

Unlike the sixteenth and seventeenth centuries, which were plagued by religious wars, the eighteenth century saw the struggle for wealth and empire take center stage. The treaty of Utrecht (1713) put an end to religious wars and proclaimed a new peace among the major European states: France, England, Spain, and Russia. Imperial rivalries, however, would soon rend it asunder. The next forty years were rife with flare-ups between opposing nations and coalitions, undercutting an already precarious balance of power.[1] Against that background of reciprocal mistrust, Frederick the Great's invasion of Saxony plunged the entire continent into war.

The Seven Years' War (1756–63) involved all the major European powers in a horrendous bloodletting, which ravaged each and every society. The key to the conflict lay in the strategic maneuvering between France and England to assert supremacy in the world economy, control over colonies, and command of the sea. The outcome of this struggle became one of the primary antecedents to both the French and American Revolutions.[2]

By the end of the war, the imperial ambitions of France had been sharply curtailed by British military might. While France retained important possessions in the Caribbean, the loss of territories in America exacerbated its dire financial condition and compelled the crown to search for new means of securing revenue. The heavy tax burden that the state extracted from the Third Estate accelerated resistance against the ancien régime and precipitated the fall of the Bastille in 1789.

The British victory would prove nearly as costly as the French defeat. Overburdened by the requirements of maintaining and supplying its new colonial possessions, England resorted to increasing the financial pressure on the American colonists through inequitable taxes. The British monarchy, moreover, stopped short of providing its colonies with the political autonomy they demanded to ameliorate these policies. The movement for economic and political independence, which culminated in the American Revolution, was hardly contemplated in the 1750s. It became, however, an irreversible force after the Seven Years' War, and thereby opened the door to new conceptions of political association.[3]

The American Revolution and Republicanism

The Declaration of Independence was more than an announcement of economic secession from the British Empire; it was an international justification of rebellion against any established political authority, organized around the republican idea. Although the American quarrel had been with Parliament, the Declaration arraigned no one but the king. "The history of the present King of Great Britain," wrote Thomas Jefferson in the Declaration of Independence, "is a history of repeated injuries and usurpations, all having in direct object the establishment of an absolute Tyranny over these States."[4] Boldly voicing the philosophy of the age, the Declaration held as self-evident, or, as evident to all reasonable men, that "all men are created equal, that they are endowed by their Creator with certain unalienable rights, that among these are Life, Liberty, and the pursuit of Happiness."[5]

These words electrified the world. The dissolution of old colonial governments threw open all political questions. The new republican state confiscated property from the counterrevolutionaries. People who before had no vote now voted for legislators and public officials. The principle, unknown to parliamentary bodies of Europe, was adopted that every member of a legislative assembly should represent about the same number of citizens. All states north of Maryland took steps toward eliminating slavery.[6] Many quasi-feudal institutions, similar to European ones, disappeared. Quitrent, which corresponded to some of the manorial fees paid by farmers in England and Europe, vanished in most of the new states. Primogeniture and entail, by which landed families aspiring to an aristocratic mode of life maintained themselves, went down before the demand of the democrats and small property owners.[7] The tithe was eliminated, while the established Anglican church in the south, and the Congregationalist church in New England, lost their privileged position in varying degrees.[8]

Universal principles stressing free access to commerce were embraced by a country that sought to provide an example. Property changed hands, but the law of property was modified only in detail. The inherited common law of England remained in effect everywhere. There was no such thing in British America as a native nobleman or even a bishop; clergy and aristocracy had been incomparably less ingrained in American than in European society, and the rebellion against them was less devastating in effect.

The major internationalist import of the American Revolution remained a justification of republicanism and even constitutionalism. The American cast of mind went back to the English Puritan revolution of the 1640s. At that time in England, the subparliamentary classes, the Levellers, and many radical sects, had insisted that every man ought to vote and that there should be some written constitution, some "agreement of the people," to protect man's natural or God-given rights from the encroachments of earthly powers.[9] Such ideas had died out in England, where they were replaced by the idea of parliamentary sovereignty. But older ideas remained alive in the English colonies, in which radicals of an earlier day had taken refuge. Five generations of life in America had sharpened the old insistence upon political liberty and equality. When the dispute with Britain came to a head, the Americans found themselves asserting the timeless and universal rights of man as barriers against the inroads of parliamentary sovereignty. With the triumph of Jefferson's ideals over Hamilton's, the Americans came to believe more than any other people that government should possess limited powers only, and should operate within the terms of a fixed and written constitutional document.[10]

All thirteen of the new states lost no time in providing themselves with written constitutions. All followed the thought stated in the Declaration that governments were instituted among men to protect their "unalienable" rights, and that, following the spirit of Locke, whenever government became destructive to this end the people had the right to "institute new government" for their safety and happiness. The constitutions undertook to limit the institution of even this republican government by instituting a separation of powers. A Bill of Rights was appended to the Constitution stating the natural rights of citizens and the things that no government might lawfully do. None of the state constitutions were as yet fully democratic, however; even the most liberal gave some advantage in public affairs to the owners of property.

The American Revolution inspired people throughout the world, people wishing to throw off their colonial status and replace it with independent republican institutions.[11] Constitutionalism, federalism, and limited republican government were not new ideas in Europe. John Adams would later report that the American Revolution was "Locke, Sidney, Rousseau, and de Mably reduced to practice."[12] Those who, like Lafayette, had helped the Americans against the British carried the republican and revolutionary message back to Europe. The American example made the realization of revolutionary ideas possible. It crystallized and made tangible the ideas that were spreading in Paris and throughout Europe. The American Revolution was now discussed in the press, in clubs, in Masonic lodges. It began to occupy the European mind.[13] In France, Chénier predicted that America "will soon change the world"; Alfieri saw in the American Revolution "a raging storm, which is bringing salvation and liberty to [Italians]"; Loosjes saw "the well being of [the Dutch countries] in the American liberty"; Anon perceived the America of 1776 as the "land to the singer dearer than the [German] fatherland"; and Radishchev acclaimed the Americans for revealing the new goal.[14] Undoubtedly the American republican views gave a new political energy to internationalism, and helped precipitate the events of the French Revolution. Parallel to political changes in North America, one can see the evolution of a similar trend in Europe, and more particularly in France.

The Development of the Bourgeoisie prior to the French Revolution

Republican ideas, an important aspect of internationalism, influenced writers and thinkers throughout Europe, and were embraced by the French bourgeoisie in its attempt to defeat the political control of the aristocracy. As a result of new conquests, there was a significant expansion of French overseas trade, which quadrupled in value between the Wars of Spanish Succession and the Revolution.[15] The position of merchants and businessmen was greatly strengthened and this rising class became of primary importance to the economic health of the ancien régimes. By some estimates, the ranks of the bourgeoisie nearly tripled between 1600 and 1789,[16] and, soon enough, the material survival of the absolutist regimes became tied to the fate of the bourgeoisie. Nevertheless, by the end of the eighteenth century the French bourgeoisie found itself trapped in a tale of two economies: between the prosperous international economy and the backward, traditionalist, and autarkic national market.

The financial institutions of the ancien régime were still rudimentary, and severely constrained the growth of merchants' wealth and influence. There were no state or private banks, no stock exchange, and virtually no joint-stock companies; the free flow of capital from one sector to another was continually impeded by the structural inefficiency of the ancien régime. An overhaul of absolutist economic institutions would necessarily require changes in the political realm, which continued to be relatively inaccessible to the bourgeoisie. As discussed earlier, the nobility dominated the government, the public administration, the church, and most social institutions. It resisted any change in the status quo that might undermine its privileges.

This oscillation between economic strength and political weakness was deeply resented by the bourgeoisie and underlined its irreconcilable differences with the aristocracy. These conflicts of interest were best exemplified by Molière's play *Le Bourgeois Gentilhomme*, which portrayed a ruined nobleman begging for more loans from an enriched bourgeois.[17] More than a mere theatrical event, this play captured the vital experience of a class.

The respective social positions of the aristocracy and the bourgeoisie also had strong ideological foundations: the ancien régime drew its political legitimacy and its ethos from Christianity. The bourgeoisie, often wealthier and more educated than the privileged order, drew its ideological strengths from reason and the sciences—fundamentally critical perspectives that inherently challenged the hitherto indisputable world of religious dogma. The French political philosophers Diderot, La Mettrie, and Helvétius; the German thinkers Lessing, Wieland, and Mendelssohn; the English Hume; and the Italians Alfieri and Beccaria were among the many contributors to an intellectual climate that strengthened the political confidence of the bourgeoisie.[18]

Despite its attempts to alleviate the earthly discontent of the people with promises of heavenly reward, the feudal order inevitably exacerbated the sharp antagonisms and tensions between the strengthened bourgeoisie and the established order. The Abbé de Sieyès ultimately called for the political representation of the Third Estate in the National Assembly. The growing hostilities between the Third Estate, on the one hand, and the aristocracy and the high clergy on the other hand, led to the outbreak of the French Revolution.

Numerous interpretations of its causes are possible. Mathiez and Lefebvre identified the outbreak of the Revolution as a series of class revolts; Soboul discussed the significance of the peasantry. These class-based analyses were challenged by a variety of explanations: Egret and Eisenstein contested the class demarcation of the revolutionary movement; Furet emphasized the struggle of the political elites; Skocpol focused on the structural weakness of the state and Goldstone on the growth of the population.[19] What is important here is not whether the bourgeoisie was significant in size or was behaving as a class, but to identify a trend: the expansion of capitalism and its relation to the evolving worldview of a class in formation.

Surely, the uncompromising position of the aristocracy in the face of reform was a critical explanation of why that revolution occurred in France and not in England. Indeed, after the Glorious Revolution, the English bourgeoisie had already been sharing economic power with the aristocracy for a century, in contrast with its French counterpart.

The English feudal orders, both lay and ecclesiastic, had been dispossessed. A "relative" modus vivendi prevailed between state and church. There was less social discrimination in the levying of taxes, less abusive regulation, and no restriction on commodity circulation within the country.

In the German and Italian states, however, social, political, and religious discrimination persisted. As a result of the fragmentation of these states, the faint beginnings of industrialization were confined to a few localities. The local burgeoning bourgeoisie had as yet no conception of its strength. It mainly resembled the sixteenth-century French, English, and Dutch rising bourgeoisie, content to reside in the shadow of the royal houses. The internal divisions of these states prevented the development of the middle class and the vitality of any concerted and conscious popular movement against the old establishment.

The Peasantry before the French Revolution

The bourgeoisie—the smallest, yet the most influential, sector of the Third Estate—was not the only social stratum seeking political changes and political rights. The republican ideas institutionalized in America were equally welcomed by the peasantry, who suffered under an overwhelming burden of taxes. It represented a force that was also interested in the overthrow of feudal institutions and the development of universal political rights, and comprised the immense majority of the population. Serfdom had almost disappeared from French territory by the end of the eighteenth century. The great mass of the peasantry, however, had barely enough land to eke out an existence. Its members were forced to seek extra wages as day laborers, take up an additional trade, or work in the rural industries run by merchants.[20] The long-leased peasant tenants paid their lords not only their rents (*cens*), but also a welter of dues for the estate owner's mill, oven, and winepress. They had to perform a stipulated amount of road maintenance on the estate.[21] Only a handful of farmers owned their lands. While other social groups had won exemption—the bourgeoisie escaped with few tax obligations, and the clergy offered only a contribution (*don gratuit*)—the peasantry had to pay almost entirely the taille, the state's tax on possessions and agricultural production. The peasantry bore a threefold burden to state, church, and landlord. All the subsequent peasant rebellions against tax collectors and land-lords, however, were suppressed by feudal authorities. For the peas-antry more than for any other social strata of the Third Estate, the source of affliction was rooted in the feudal structure.

As Albert Soboul observed, however, the peasantry (the largest segment of the population) and the urban popular sector — day laborers, salary workers, and *compagnons de métier* (journeymen and artisans) — were still incapable of imagining what rights they in fact possessed and what power they could exercise. It is only with the progress of the Revolution that the urban popular classes, the sans-culottes, developed a militant political consciousness. At the early stage of the Revolution, the middle class, the *possédants,* with its powerful economic base and its superior education, seemed to them quite naturally the only possible source of leadership.[22] Thus, in con-junction with the French middle class, the peasantry and the sans-culottes realized that the success of the French Revolution depended upon the alliance of *all* the sectors of the Third Estate against the ab-solutist institutions. Contesting the existing social order required a reorganization of society based on collective consciousness that would shape internationalism around democratic political principles.

The fall of the Bastille on July 14, 1789, marked the final transi-tion of internationalism from religious dogmatism to a new secular order, from absolutism to political freedom. The French Revolution signaled the progress of reason and opened the gateway to new polit-ical hopes. Revolutionary France embodied the aspiration of the people's will and inspired civic virtue through patriotic exaltation. It became the lighthouse of internationalism, spurring people oppressed by the old European dynasties to follow in its path. At the same time, however, it intensified the social differences within the Third Estate, which ultimately led to its decline.

The works of Robespierre, Paine, and Kant each demonstrated the republican aspect of internationalism. Their innovative social per-spectives also illustrated their attempts to seek an intermediate posi-tion between the exclusionary foundation of revelation and the athe-istic views of the French Enragés (chapter 6), between a society of republican politics and one of private investors, between war and commerce as means to extend republican principles beyond the bor-ders of the French *patrie* (chapter 7).

Six

Reason, Deism, and the
Internationalist Spirit of Solidarity

The normative and republican spirit of internationalism was invigo-
rated with the spread of deism after the fall of the Bastille in 1789.
Deism referred to a natural religion, to a religious and moral knowledge either inborn in every person or attainable by the use of reason,
as opposed to revelation. The democratic understanding of reason
preached in Europe and America by Bolingbroke, Voltaire, Lessing,
and Franklin stood in opposition to the orthodoxy of the church, the
last harbor of aristocratic privilege.[1] Deists gradually substituted a
philosophical commitment to the rule of reason for the revealed and
exclusionary knowledge of the clergy. Contrary to various sixteenth-
and seventeenth-century thinkers who highlighted the instrumental relation of the individual to the community (see chapters 1–4), Kant,
Paine, and Robespierre emphasized, by invoking deist ideals, the normative and altruistic relation of the individual to the collective body.

These three thinkers, like other deists, endorsed the French government's restriction of clerical privileges whereby church lands were
confiscated and placed at the disposal of the *patrie*. The nation was
still responsible for maintaining the clergy and for providing them with
an honorable annual stipend. Bishops and clergymen were elected like
any other public officials. After refractory priests rose in revolt on the
side of the aristocracy and allied with the royalists in the Vendéean
counterrevolution, however, the leadership of the young Jacobin

government was marked by attacks on priests, including the whole-
sale closure of churches and the enthronement of the Goddess of
Reason in Notre-Dame Cathedral. During the heyday of the French
philosophes, the boundary between deism and atheism was already
blurred, as evidenced by Voltaire, Diderot, d'Alembert, Holbach, and
La Mettrie.[2] The de-Christianization process, however, sharpened that
division and escalated into a virulent attack that threatened to sub-
vert the climate of solidarity within the Third Estate.

The "de-Christianization movement" greatly alarmed Robespierre,
who was then a major figure in the Committee of Public Safety. Believing in the immortality of the soul, he abhorred atheism and feared that
such extremism would cost the support of the religious peasantry.
According to Robespierre, the spread of atheism might actually engender support for the aristocracy: "To preach atheism is merely another way of absolving superstition and of putting philosophy itself
on trial, and all war declared on divinity is nothing but a diversion in
favor of monarchy."[3] In his address to the Jacobin Club in March
1792, Robespierre warned against antireligious excesses and encouraged moderation:

> Superstition is surely one of the props of despotism. But to pro-
> nounce the name of God does not mean to induce the citizens into
> superstition. I abhor superstition more than anyone else, all those
> impious sects that have expanded throughout the universe to favor
> ambition, fanaticism, and all passions and that protect themselves
> under the sacred power of the Eternal who created nature and hu-
> manity. But I am far from confusing it with those imbeciles armed
> with despotism.[4]

He despised the horrors that had been perpetrated under the guise
of revelation, but deplored as well the abuses of the atheist Enragés.[5]
As the de-Christianization process intensified, Robespierre asserted
that certain forms of religious incentives should be introduced in
order to moderate the outburst unleashed by the social upheavals.
He proposed a compromise alternative, a new civic religion based on
Rousseau's deism, which he called the cult of the Supreme Being, or
the cult of reason. At the 18 Floral II Convention (May 7, 1794), he
inaugurated the cult of reason, thereby enhancing the internationalist spirit and creating a sense of religious duty and patriotic unity

within the Third Estate. Robespierre maintained that deism predicated on reason was a revolutionary cult that could be shared by all men: "There exists for all men the same morality, the same consciousness."[6] The eternal laws of reason are "universal maxims of justice, inalterable, imprescriptible, formulated to be applied to all people."[7] Robespierre, following the footsteps of Bolingbroke, Voltaire, Rousseau, and others, believed in the ineluctable progression of history toward these moral ends. He supported his claim by referring to the scientific discoveries of the century. Since "all has changed in the physical order," he stated, "all must change in the moral and political order."[8] The worship of the Supreme Being symbolized these changes and was an attempt to place the new moral ideals on metaphysical foundations. Religious feasts were celebrated under the banner of reason and were organized in order to raise popular feelings of solidarity.

The cult of reason thus became an expedient tool for mobilizing patriotic fervor and for inculcating political virtue. Despite its religious character, the cult of the Supreme Being was inspired by historical necessity and social utility:

> In the eyes of the legislators, truth consists of all that is useful in the world and good in practice.... The idea of the Supreme Being is a constant reminder of justice; it is therefore something that is both socially valuable and republican.[9]

Albert Mathiez pointed out that, contrary to church dogma, religious elements were not only an elaborate system of domination, and an admirable machine for making slaves, they were also a rule of life, a morality.[10] "Let's leave the priests and return to divinity," Robespierre proclaimed, "let's attach morality to eternal and sacred foundations, and inspire in man this religious respect for his alter ego, these profound feelings for his duties which are the sole guarantee of social happiness."[11] Indeed, despite the controversies surrounding his deist beliefs, he always subordinated his religious to his social ideals, for he believed religion to be indispensable to the people.[12]

Like Robespierre, Paine struggled against both revelation and atheism, especially in the month of October 1793, and proposed deism to heighten the collective spirit of solidarity within the Third Estate. Although Paine believed in God and the immortality of the soul, he vehemently condemned revelation, miracles, and divine inspiration from the Bible as arbitrary systems aimed at protecting the privilege of the aristocracy and advancing the avarice of priests. He regarded religious beliefs inspired by revelation as implicitly denying the inherent ability of man to act morally and to respect the well-being of others. In *The Age of Reason,* he stated:

> I totally disbelieve that the Almighty ever did communicate any thing to man by any mode of speech, in any language, or by any kind of vision or appearance, or by any means which our senses are capable of receiving otherwise than by the universal display of himself in the works of creation, and by the repugnance we feel in ourselves to bad actions, and disposition to good ones.[13]

Everyone is endowed, according to Paine, with an inner light, and is able to act freely according to reason. In *The Rights of Man,* Paine, with the French philosophes, described reason as the beacon of Enlightenment: "The fear of slavery [perpetuated by monarchical systems] had made men afraid to think," for monarchs feared that reason encouraged rebellion, and hence "freedom was hunted around the globe." Paine believed that the march of reason and progress could not be obstructed; delaying its course, he argued, would only foment unrest:

> Reason and discussion will soon bring things right, however wrong they may begin. By such a process no tumult is to be apprehended. The poor in all countries are naturally both peaceable and grateful in all reforms in which their interest and their happiness are included. It is only by neglecting and rejecting them that they become tumultuous.[14]

The nobility and aristocracy had attempted in vain to ensure their survival by extinguishing the spark of freedom and reason. A "species" that distinguished itself by military conquests perpetuated itself both by the law of primogeniture and by "the base idea of man having property in man and governing him by personal right."[15] Degenerating through the common practice of intermarrying, this class was by its very makeup unfit to be the legislator of a nation. Monarchy and aristocracy were inevitably the product and employers of arbitrary power, and would always remain the enemies of reason.

During the French de-Christianization period of 1793, Paine commented, like Robespierre, that "religion has two principal enemies, fanaticism and infidelity, or that which is called atheism."[16] In addition, he shared Robespierre's deist creed. Deism stood at the crossroads between atheism (understood as leading to anarchy) and revealed religion (which fed tyrannical regimes). Deism retained from religion the sanctified value of moral duties and altruism. Yet Paine's universal principles of deism were not mediated by the church; his concept of Christian brotherhood was subordinated to the authority of nature and reason, both informed by God's wisdom. Furthermore, deism, in a view shared by Franklin, Mendelssohn, Paine, and others, instructed people to understand nature, and the mechanical laws of physics that governed it, as God's creation:

> The true deist has but one deity; and his religion consists in contemplating the power, wisdom, and benignity of the Deity in his work, and in his endeavoring to imitate Him in everything, moral, scientific, and mechanical.[17]

Contrary to Robespierre, Paine condemned any intrusion of the state into religious matters. In a letter to a friend, he wrote that "religion is a private affair between every man and his Maker, and no tribunal or third party has a right to interfere between them."[18] In another letter, Paine declared his preference for the simple worship of the Quakers—implicitly criticizing Robespierre's boisterous celebration of the cult of reason:

> The only people who, as a professional sect of Christians, provide for the poor of their society are people known by the name of Quakers. Those men have no priests, they assemble quietly in their place of meeting, and do not disturb their neighbors with show and noise.[19]

In addition, the doctrine of "common sense," that every man is capable of judging political institutions for himself, was a celebration of the private world and the right of the individual to enter the public one; it may well have been inspired by the Quaker notion of the inner light and the Protestant emphasis on the primacy of individual consciousness. Notwithstanding Paine's political activism, this view was rooted in Luther's stress upon the pure inwardness of religious experience, which in turn inculcated an attitude of quietism toward worldly power.

In this respect, a fair parallel between Paine and Kant can be drawn.[20] Kant's fervent belief in man's inner sense of morality was rooted in German Protestant pietism; it existed, as did the Quakers' religious life, independently of the state. Kant, like Paine and Robespierre, or like the enlightened German political thinkers Forster and Lessing, believed in the existence of God and the concept of immortality. Rather than deism, Kant preferred the concept of "moral theism," which he described as "consisting in believing not merely in God, but in a living God, who has produced the world through knowledge, and free volition."[21] Despite this semantic difference, Kant's moral view of religion showed striking similarities to those of Paine and Robespierre. Indeed, Kant generally viewed religion as a way to sanctify man's moral will while performing his altruistic and humanitarian responsibility. Religion encouraged the individual's best intention to attain the "summum bonum," or internationalism. In his preface to *Religion within the Limits of Reason*,[22] Kant, with Lessing and Mendelssohn, clearly showed how he departed from prevailing Christian ideology, placing the ideas of duty and reason at the center, and religion at the periphery. "Religion," he wrote, "is the knowledge of our duties as divine command."[23] His philosophy of religion comprised a corollary of his moral ethic.

Like Paine, Kant argued for the primacy of reason. "Was ist Aufklärung?" was the question he asked in his pamphlet on the "Enlightenment" published in 1784 by the *Berliner Monatsschrift*. He maintained that the time had come to cut the umbilical cord with the past. Men had remained too long in darkness, due to their "laziness and cowardice." "*Sapere Aude!*" This rebellious slogan of the Enlightenment was translated by Kant as "have the courage to avail yourself of your own reason." Kant believed that authoritarian voices inhibited people's full expression of reason. "Don't argue, do what you are told!" ordered the officer to his men; "Don't argue, pay!" shouted the official tax collector; "Don't argue, believe!" dictated the clergyman to his parishioners.[24] The time had come to silence these voices, and to reason for oneself.

The rising bourgeoisie did not remain insensitive to Kant's call: personal initiative had to be taken in order to shatter absolutism and create a democratic and entrepreneurial world. Kant assumed that the rules of reason were universal. These rules followed neither a providential course nor the laws of experience. In Kant's philosophical lexicon, these principles — based on reason, independent of experience, and capable of contradiction — were called "practical synthetic a priori judgment."[25] Here Kant's distinction between "hypothetical injunction" and "categorical imperative" became critical. The hypothetical injunction urged one to follow a course of action to attain a particular end or to fulfill one's own self-interest. A categorical imperative prompted one to observe one's moral duties. Kant believed that individuals were free to transcend their particular interests and to "act according to principles which can be adopted at the same time as universal law." It was, therefore, not surprising to see him acclaiming the French patriots who were acting disinterestedly in the name of universal principle. The French Revolution was the actualization of the principles of practical reason that derived from his categorical imperatives. However, as we shall see in chapter 7, it was by referring to these same categories that Kant disputed the legitimacy of resistance and rebellion.

The deist views of Kant, Paine, and Robespierre, joined by numerous other political philosophers of their age, helped to shape the organic spirit of global solidarity of the Third Estate in France and elsewhere. By invoking deism, Kant, Paine, and Robespierre stressed the altruistic duty of individuals and elevated the democratic vision of internationalist solidarity to the status of divine obligation. Their divergent opinions perhaps reflected the religious influence of their countries of origin. In prerevolutionary France, the Catholic church retained its wealth, privilege, and indisputable authority, and protected the inequities of the monarchical order. Such an unyielding religious climate incubated the most vehement attacks on privilege and the remnants of feudalism.

Consequently, during the French Revolution, a secular state religion — in the form of Robespierre's cult of the Supreme Being — was seen as the essential vehicle for transcending social inequality. In Protestant societies, such as England and most of Germany, a different climate prevailed. Church property had been partly secularized and monastic orders completely suppressed; in those countries, a multitude of free sects were tolerated, and individual and "quiet" religious worship proliferated beyond the reach of state interference. This might well have explained Kant's and Paine's inclinations toward a private vision of deism separated from state matters. Keeping in mind these differences, we will now examine these thinkers' formulation of deism and altruism, extended to both the political and global spheres, two realms closely linked by the revolutionary wars.

Seven

La Patrie: The Lighthouse of Internationalism

If deism emphasized the individual's moral duty, the *patrie* institutionalized the altruistic spirit of deism. With the French Revolution, internationalism, formerly built upon Grotius's enlightened monarchical power, was identified, thanks to Rousseau, with the people's nation, the *patrie*. Everywhere, progressive intellectuals endorsed the internationalism that emanated from the French Revolution. These thinkers included Forster and Kant in Germany; Radischev in Russia; Franklin, Jefferson, and Paine in North America; and the Italians Verri and Beccaria — whose work influenced directly Article 8 of the *Declaration of the Rights of Man and Citizen*.[1] The Declaration granted voting rights, freedom of speech and the press, equality before the law, rights to hold public office and to acquire private property.

Economic *and* political rights were now institutionalized in the French *patrie*, which was now perceived as the lighthouse from which civic ideas would spread throughout the world. Debating a cascade of questions regarding how to establish a democratic state internationally became fashionable: What were individuals' original relationships in political society? Which rights should be guaranteed by the state? What is the most felicitous type of government? How should democracy be spread to other lands? Robespierre, Paine, Kant, and many other liberal thinkers would address these issues.

At the National Convention, with other Jacobins such as Marat and Saint-Just, Robespierre echoed Rousseau's famous opening sentence of the *Contrat Social* in stating the relationship of individuals to society:

> Man was born for happiness and liberty, and everywhere he is enslaved and miserable! Society's aim is to conserve his rights and the perfection of his being, and everywhere society degrades and oppresses him. The time has come to remind him of his real destinies. The progress of human reason has prepared him for this great revolution.[2]

Following the ideas of Rousseau, Robespierre announced the fulfillment of individual freedom and happiness as he entered into the social contract. A contract representing the "general will" would not jeopardize the individual liberty that people possessed in the state of nature. On the contrary, such a bond would provide security and, most important, the possibility of cultivating civic virtue.

Robespierre maintained as well that the state had to guarantee the right to private property. Although in 1789 he regarded property rights as a "sacred and inviolable right," by 1793 he warned the Jacobins to limit the free accumulation of wealth. The right of property, he insisted, should not be permitted to infringe upon the rights of others — in particular those of the poorer citizens: the sans-culottes and the peasantry. Initially disadvantaged, the "Fourth Estate" — the peasantry and the sans-culottes — would remain a constant dependent force and would never be able to reduce the growing economic gap with the wealthier sector of the population. Robespierre rightly argued that once inequality developed beyond a certain point, democracy would become a sham.

Robespierre, along with Saint-Just, represented the Jacobin supporters of the popular classes. They believed in the possibility of social advancement through the extension of small-scale production and considered property regulation a fundamental element of social justice.[3] Robespierre thus opposed both the Gironde and Jacobin deputies such as Georges Danton, Pierre-Joseph Cambon, and François-Antoine Boissy, who favored a rapid expansion of commerce and the unrestricted accumulation of property. His 1793 property regulation proposal, however, was not adopted.

What type of governmental institutions should endorse the rights gained in civil society? In 1789 Robespierre supported a constitutional monarchy as long as the king remained an ambassador of the general will and maintained the separation of powers. However, after the flight of the king in 1791 to join the Austrian armies—which resulted in the bloody episode known as the "massacre du Champ-de-Mars"—Robespierre asked for the king's removal from office and denounced him as a "traitor to the French nation and a criminal against humanity."[4] From then on, he insisted that the republican executive had to function in a system of checks and balances. There would be no place for the king in this republic of elected officials in which no one held hereditary office. In the spirit of Rousseau and Montesquieu, he suggested that a republic was more convenient than direct democracy for the administration of the daily affairs of the sovereign will. Nonetheless, Robespierre was careful to distinguish between nominal republics—such as the Swiss cantons, or the United States, where suffrage was not universal and the government was in the hands of wealthy Virginian planters—and a republic that granted political rights to its propertyless citizens and abolished slavery in its colonies.

Robespierre's republican and obviously internationalist programs were defeated by the Constituent Assembly, in a decision that, a few months after the Declaration of Rights, denied the vote to "passive citizens"—domestic servants and all those who did not pay taxes equivalent to three days of labor. These groups were also excluded from the National Guard. At the same time, his attempts to emancipate slaves in the French colonial plantations were resisted by the French colonial landowners. It was only in Pluviôse II (1794), during the revolutionary government, that he succeeded in bringing about the decree for emancipation of slaves.[5] That success was preceded by the constitution of 1793, where Robespierre won a temporary victory for more political democracy: an elected legislative body with single-member districts, and an executive council elected by the legislative body from candidates designated by its own electorate.[6] Paradoxically, in the same constitution, women were excluded from universal suffrage, political activity, and clubs. From then on, women continued to lose what they had gained. In 1804, women's dependent status would be codified by Napoleon.[7]

The initial conflict within the Third Estate between maintaining property rights and extending democracy was exacerbated when the revolutionaries debated the way in which to spread republican ideals throughout Europe. Would the French offer a model capable of inspiring other nations, as the American Revolution had inspired them? Or was war the indispensable medium for propagating democratic principles? In January 1792, Robespierre believed that wars were unnecessary to extend the Revolution. He admonished Brissot to take a "longer look" at the internal situation in France before trying to take its liberty elsewhere.[8]

By 1793, however, the absolutist powers were advancing toward France and the counterrevolution was intensifying in the Vendée.[9] Robespierre was forced to change his position. He came to favor the idea of a war "for liberty." Armed patriots would compel the Prussian armies, through the war, to retreat and *par la force des choses* would propagate the ideas of the Revolution. Oppressed countries seeking to create a new brotherly community would welcome the wind of freedom blowing from the country of Marianne. A war for liberty, Robespierre claimed, would ensure the proliferation of republican states, where industry and commerce would provide the foundation for a happy future. At the February 5, 1794, Convention, he formulated the objectives of the Revolution:

> It is time to mark clearly the aim of the Revolution. We wish an order of things ... where distinctions arise only from equality itself;... where industry is an adornment to the liberty that ennobles it, and commerce the source of public wealth, not simply of monstrous riches for a few families.... we wish to substitute in our country morality for egotism, probity for a sense of honor, the empire of reason for the tyranny of custom.... May France stand for the glory of all free people, fight the terror of oppressors, console the oppressed, become the ornament of the universe; and in sealing our work with our blood may we see at last the dawn of universal felicity gleam before us. This is our ambition, this is our aim.[10]

With the spread of the Revolution, however, rising internal and external dangers induced Robespierre to reconsider the proper form of a political regime. With the counterrevolution on the rise, he called for instituting a strong centralized government. Robespierre legitimized the revolutionary government as an extreme and transitory measure, but nonetheless a necessary means of both surmounting wartime obstacles and laying down the foundation for constitutional democracy. "The object of constitutional government," he explained, "is to preserve the Republic; the object of revolutionary government is to establish it."[11]

For the next century, throughout the world, the Revolution became identified with the republican ideal. The revolutionary government, however, rested on contradictory social foundations, which
proved fatal to its chance of maintaining social cohesion within an
internationalist spirit. The war demanded unity, but the government
was split by the conflict between the nobility and the Third Estate,
which in turn was divided by the interests of the affluent bourgeoisie
on the one hand, and small consumers and small producers on the
other hand. In response to food shortages and price rises, Robespierre
passed the Laws of the Maximum, which imposed price controls on
all merchants whether rich or poor; discontent among producers
grew stronger.[12] Since the support of the merchants was essential to
the conduct of the war, Robespierre had to abandon the Maximum
law, which favored the small consumer. This time the consumers expressed their dissatisfaction with the new measures. Robespierre and
his friends on the Committee of Public Safety became prisoners of
these conflicts, which sharpened as a consequence of the war economy. In the words of Albert Soboul, Robespierre and Saint-Just
"were too preoccupied in defeating the interest of the bourgeoisie
to give their total support to the sans-culottes, and yet too attentive
to the needs of the sans-culottes to get support from the middle
class."[13]

Despite the economic tensions, which eroded the revolutionary
government, Robespierre could not unequivocally serve the interests
of the sans-culottes and the Fourth Estate. His ideal was a society of
small producers (an ideal shared by many internationalist bourgeois
thinkers) where men lived by their labor without being indebted to
anyone else. This vision, however, was neither consonant with the
emerging capitalist order nor a concrete alternative.[14] He was unaware that by setting private property and freedom of competition as
the linchpins of his republican ideal he would only make the future
safe for a large-scale concentration of capital, which might ultimately
undermine republican values. Robespierre failed to envision the development of a supranational executive body, which might have restricted economic exploitation of weak individuals and nations, and
prevented wars of conquest.

The internationalism of Thomas Paine was to some extent different
from that of Robespierre. His belief in a noninterventionist republican
government did not change significantly from his earliest writings,

such as *Common Sense*. In conceiving the relationship of the individual to the state, Paine, like Robespierre, was influenced by Grotius, Locke, and Rousseau. He described man as caught in an inner struggle between moral and selfish drives. He believed, however, that social association would ultimately foster people's altruistic and virtuous feelings. Political society was a blessing; government was "a necessary evil," or, in the words of Rousseau, a "denaturating agent." Paine affirmed that political society, not government (and even less a centralized government), was beneficial to man's personal improvement:

> Society is produced by our wants, and government by our wickedness; the former promotes our happiness positively by uniting our affection, the latter negatively by restraining our vices. The one encourages intercourse, the other creates distinction. The first is a patron, the latter a punisher.[15]

Paine maintained that social usage and custom were of far greater influence than any political institutions, however perfectly constructed or skillfully operated. Governmental institutions were necessary only in those cases where society could not appropriately act, such as in ensuring the free exercise of private property rights. The philosophical underpinning for these laissez-faire beliefs derived from Locke and Adam Smith.

From Locke, Paine concluded that individuals had the right to draw subsistence from whatever nature offered, provided that they had "mixed the labor of their bodies with nature." This right, claimed Locke, was inherent in the state of nature. Political society and government existed mostly to protect, rather than to limit, the right to private property. Like Adam Smith, Paine conceived of society as in a harmonious equilibrium. Governmental interference could only pervert the natural order.

This view stood in opposition to the ancien régime. It was characterized by self-interested individuals whose competitive activity produced, via the marketplace, public benefit. A free market, relieved of all factors of monopolistic restraint, would, through the work of the "invisible hand," serve the good of the greatest number.

Paine at first conceptualized internationalism mainly in instrumental and economic terms. In his early essays, he legitimized inequality of wealth within society. Some would inevitably surpass others thanks to their differences in "industry, superiority of talents, dexterity of management, extreme frugality, fortunate opportunities."[16] Loyal to Smith and Locke, he opposed any type of state interference and economic control, even in the critical economic crisis of 1793. When Robespierre imposed price and wage controls to protect people from inflation and from speculators, Paine wrote to Danton that in Philadelphia such regulation had not worked.[17] Although he condemned Babeuf's insurrection in 1796, this event stimulated Paine to reconsider his view that poverty and economic inequality were natural conditions.[18] In *The Agrarian Justice,* written after the "Conspiracy of the Equals," Paine became aware that "the great mass of the poor in all countries are becoming an hereditary race,"[19] and that instead of restricting the growth of monopolies, the free market stimulated the development of an economic abyss between rich and poor. A collective spirit could only prevail if a government were to intervene in civil society: internationalism was gradually defined in political terms.

He argued, therefore, that deprived individuals could not acquire property without the aid of the state: "All accumulation ... of personal property, beyond what a man's own hands produce, is derived to him by living in society from where all came."[20] Thus he proposed the creation of a national fund supplied voluntarily by landed property owners — a system where proprietors would donate to the state a "ground rent". The new national fund would allow all those who reached the age of twenty-one to receive fifteen pounds as a reparation for their loss of inheritance. In addition, the national fund would be used for pensions. "It is only in a system of justice," wrote Paine, "that the possessor can contemplate security." This appeal to the charity of rich people as a sufficient way to reduce the social gap was politically naive. Prisoner of the precapitalist age, Paine was unable to discern that such suggestions fundamentally contradicted the interests of the bourgeoisie. His political optimism also led him to believe that the disunity of the French revolutionaries was the mere result of "private malignancy and private ambition"[21] rather than a fundamental conflict of interests between two social groups.

With most of the enlightened thinkers of his age, Paine believed, perhaps too optimistically, that the ideal of political justice and property rights would coexist harmoniously in a republic. Direct democracy was an inconvenient system by which to conduct public affairs;

even before the king's flight, Paine insisted, unlike Robespierre, that republicanism and monarchy were incompatible.[22] If the independence of the United States established the internationalist climate for liberty, the French Revolution, by granting universal suffrage, raised the standard of freedom for *all* nations. As early as March 1780, Paine wanted to extend universal suffrage to black and mulatto slaves. These internationalist ideals clashed with those of the Virginian landowners, who had vested interests in keeping a cheap labor force in the Southern plantations.[23]

Unlike the American model, Paine thought that the democratic principles emanating from France — which differed in its geographical position and its social achievements — had to be extended via the bayonet in order to decimate once and for all the structure of the ancien régime. "O! ye Austrians, ye Prussians!" wrote Paine in his address to the people of France, "ye who turn your bayonets against us, it is for you, it is for all Europe, it is for all mankind, and not for France alone that she raises the standard of liberty and equality."[24]

Next, republican regimes would produce an international order, he believed, in which commercial competition would supplant wars of conquest. Both domestically and globally, Paine defined commerce as a system that would encourage republicanism by rendering individuals as well as nations useful to one another. Worldwide peace would thus emerge as the result of self-interest:

> If commerce were permitted to act to the universal extent it is capable, it would extirpate the system of war, and produce a revolution in the uncivilized state of Governments. The invention of commerce has arisen since those Governments began, and it is the greatest approach towards universal civilization that has yet been made by any means not immediately flowing from moral principles.[25]

Paine supported the wars of the French Revolution as necessary for conveying the republican message abroad, and believed that the proliferation of republican governments would be cemented by commerce and mutual interests. However, the same principles he entertained at the national level — that is, the establishment of a political authority that represented and protected the collective will and rights — were not carefully applied in the global sphere. That imprudent omission by Paine (and Robespierre) would ultimately help foster an internationalism premised on instrumental and economic competition, rather than secured by supranational political institutions.

Kant, like the two preceding theorists, grasped republicanism as the core of the new internationalism. In contrast to them, he also favored the vision of a supranational government. The idea of an international federation had been elaborated by Sully and Penn, but it owed its introduction to the Abbé de Saint-Pierre's *Projet pour rendre la paix perpétuelle*.[26] In the spirit of the latter, Kant envisaged the success of global peace as being predicated on democratic arrangements within existing states. He thus considered absolutist states predisposed to predatory behavior and republican ones to the promotion of peace. To ensure world harmony, then, would require combined efforts at the national and at the global level.

In civil society, Kant, with Grotius, pictured individuals as caught in a continuous struggle between selfish desires and moral imperatives. This inner conflict was not resolved by compliance to an enlightened monarchy as Grotius recommended, but by the state of law (*Rechtsstaat*). Inspired by Rousseau, Kant perceived the state as embodying a contract wherein individual gain reciprocated rights and duties in a commonwealth. The republican state was thus one in which individuals could preserve their freedom by remaining their own lawgivers and perpetuating the general will:[27]

> The equality of subjects may be phrased as follows: each member of the community has rights that entitle him to coerce every other member.... But this thorough equality of persons as subjects of the state is quite consistent with the great inequality in the quantity and degree of their possessions.... One man's welfare, therefore, is greatly dependent on another's will as the poor man's on the will of the rich; one must obey ... when the other commands.... And yet,... all of them are equal as subjects *before the law*.[28]

Nonetheless, Kant weakened his defense of political equality by asserting that "fitness to vote is the necessary qualification which every citizen must possess."[29] Individuals "fit" to vote were "active" and professionally independent citizens, as opposed to nonpropertied, "passive citizens," who were unqualified to vote because they were merely "auxiliary" individuals to the commonwealth.[30] By recognizing the importance of private property, Kant's primary intention was to reduce the restrictions that hampered the bourgeoisie's setting up of independent businesses. What he failed to consider was that, to sustain their economic superiority, "active citizens" would have to compete among each other for resources; however, this battle for wealth would distance them from the rest of the society. Such an outcome would inevitably challenge Kant's universal categories of rights.

Would the establishment of republican states and commerce be conducive to universal welfare? Or were violent means such as wars and rebellions necessary to reach peace on earth? Republicanism was, for Kant as for Robespierre, Paine, and Jacobin supporters throughout Europe, a necessary condition for perpetual peace. He explained that republican regimes, because of their checks-and-balances structure, rendered instigation of war a more difficult task for the head of the state.[31] To prevent the temptation of belligerence, he asserted that the legislative power should be vested in the hands of "active citizens." Kant believed that this class would be less inclined to promote war, since it would bear its costs. In any event, he considered property holders the best custodians of republicanism.

Kant pursued his discussion on the universalization of basic human rights by maintaining that, since individuals had relinquished their lawless freedom for their own good in entering the republican state, so now the state needed to surrender some of its "lawless freedom" for the global good. While Paine and Robespierre and most of their contemporaries refused to contemplate the idea of a world government, Kant argued that the family of nations needed a constitution and an executive body—for wars would continue so long as each state recognized no authority above itself. If it is true that a republic is the most favorable structure for developing morality and collective solidarity, then a world federation would be most inclined to temper aggression and cultivate a spirit of internationalism.

In concert with the establishment of a republican polity, Kant believed that a world federation of republics would ultimately emerge as commerce expanded:

> Civil freedom can no longer be easily infringed without disadvantage to all trades and industries, and especially to commerce.... the citizen is deterred from seeking his personal welfare in any way he chooses which is consistent with the freedom of others, the vitality of business in general and hence also the strength of the whole are held in check.[32]

The spirit of commerce, for Kant, was perfectly compatible with the progress of republicanism. The "circle of civilization" would be incomplete if republican institutions were jeopardized by wars. With the growth of republican states and trade, Kant argued, global harmony would prevail and the use of warfare would gradually disappear.

Would revolutionary wars produce a world federation? Kant's position remained ambiguous. On the one hand, he saluted the revolutionary patriotism of the French Revolution as the symbol of moral progress:[33]

> The revolution which we have seen taking place in our times in a nation of gifted people may succeed or it may fail. It may be so filled with misery and atrocities that no right-thinking man would ever decide to make the same experience again at such a price, even if he could hope to carry it successfully at the second attempt. But I maintain that this revolution has aroused in the hearts and desires of all spectators who are not themselves caught up in it a sympathy which borders almost on enthusiasm, although the very utterance of this sympathy was fraught with danger. It cannot therefore have been caused by anything other than a moral predisposition within the human race.[34]

At the same time, however, Kant could claim that revolutionary activity and wars violated moral law. In a footnote to "An Old Question," he thus wrote that the "realization of the republican state may not have to pass through revolutions which are always unjust."[35] He also reiterated his position in *On the Old Saw*, where he stated that

> any resistance to the supreme lawmaking power, any incitement of dissatisfied subjects to activity, any uprising that bursts into rebellion—that all is the worst punishable crime in a community.... And this ban is *absolute*, so unconditional that even though supreme power or its agent, the head of the state, may have broken the original contract,... even then the subject is allowed no resistance, no violent counteraction.[36]

How would France, the country of the Revolution, fight a war against despotism except through resistance to authority, rebellion, the breach of agreements, killings, or interference with the internal affairs of the enemy's country?[37] Kant's self-contradictory position results from his commitment to an epistemological ethic divorced from

"necessity." In *Perpetual Peace,* he thus praised the "moral politician," rather than the "political moralist" who justified the means by
the ends. Written in 1794, at the end of the reign of terror, this piece
offers an implicit attack on Robespierre's use of a revolutionary government to realize his internationalist aims. Kant should be praised
for having conceptualized the necessity for a world federation to mitigate wars. His project, however, did not provide a practical political
alternative to Robespierre's policy.

Nevertheless, like Paine and Robespierre, Kant's internationalist
agenda was premised on extending the *Declaration of the Rights of
Man and Citizen.* Their discordant views regarding voting rights of
"unpropertied citizens," their dissimilar opinions about the role of the
state in property regulations, their ambivalence concerning the way
to expand republicanism—all these reflected the tension within the
Third Estate. The idea of equal access to private property, stipulated
at the onset of the French Revolution, was a progressive and revolutionary principle insofar as it shattered the structure of feudal monopoly. By identifying the "inviolability" of property accumulation as
the crux of their social theory, however, Kant, Paine, and Robespierre—as well as the most progressive intellectuals and political
leaders of their epoch, including Saint-Just, Marat, Mendelssohn,
and Jefferson—implicitly privileged the position of the initially advantaged bourgeoisie. Internationalism reflected the interests of the
middle class. Indeed, after 1793, the bourgeoisie gradually imple-
mented policies restricting human rights, which it perceived as a threat
to its economic and social position. These policies engendered discontent among the sans-culottes and the peasantry. Social inequality
within the Third Estate, camouflaged before the downfall of the old
order, intensified with the progress of the French Revolution and
Thermidor. Henceforth, the universalist solidarity of the Third Estate
would give way before particularist tendencies.

The same particularist trend was exacerbated by the failure to
extend republican principles into the global sphere. Kant, in contrast
to Paine and Robespierre, may have conceptualized a supranational
democratic authority. He did not, however, foresee how to execute
his plan in the critical reality of 1789. Unable to realize internationalist principles, Kant, as well as Paine and Robespierre, continued to
perpetuate a dual standard of moral behavior. Their internationalist

theory ultimately favored particularism over universalism and the national interest over global principles of justice. With the establishment of the Directoire and the rise of Napoleon (examined in chapter 8), the commitment to universal rights gradually vanished and was superseded by beliefs in the superiority of one social group over others.

Part III

The Rise of Nationalism and the Counter-Enlightenment: Burke, de Maistre, and Fichte

Eight

Europe and the Napoleonic Wars

Internationalism did not long outlast Robespierre's revolutionary government. It declined after the Thermidorian reaction and provided a
fertile ground for the extension of particularist ideologies. The Thermidorians wanted to guarantee the social preeminence and the political authority of the bourgeoisie within the framework of a liberal
regime where civil and foreign war still held sway. In the Constitution of Year III, moderate republicans and constitutional monarchists,
such as Boissy d'Anglas and Lanjuinais, laid the foundations for the
regime of notables. The *Declaration of Rights of Year III* marked a
definite regression compared to the 1789 *Declaration of the Rights
of Man and Citizen*. For instance, the first article of the Constitution
abandoned the claim that "all men are born free and equal in rights,"
as a restrictive property franchise removed the masses from power and
influence.

The new Constitution reestablished the separation of powers and
prevented the executive from interfering in financial matters. The
newly established government, the Directoire (1795–99), maintained
a degree of centralization in seeking to assure the internal and external security of the state. The war situation, the economic crisis, and
the increasing militancy of the canaille brought the interests of the
property-owning bourgeoisie closer to those of the aristocratic émigrés.
The inclusion of the repentant aristocracy within the bourgeois nation
paved the way for a new ruling class. In 1799, with the expansion of

the war abroad and the growth of radical Jacobinism, the need for a still stronger executive was fulfilled by Napoleon after his coup d'état on 18 Brumaire. The 18 Brumaire of 1799 is best understood as an attempt to integrate the bourgeoisie and the aristocracy within one "nation." For a ruling elite eager to consolidate its power, foreign victories could help divert popular discontent.

Bonaparte, a military genius, was a seemingly perfect candidate. Gaining his support from the new republic of notables, he continued the work of the Directoire, improving institutions and strengthening the authority of the state.[1] In 1802, however, Bonaparte foiled the calculations of his supporters by taking away their freedoms—even their bourgeois freedoms—and establishing his own personal dictatorial power. From then on, Napoleon earned the hostility of his early supporters. Nevertheless, he still enjoyed the reputation of a potential liberator, a champion of the Constituent Assembly of 1792, and the heir of the revolutionary wars.

The French Revolutionary Wars of 1792–1815 and the Rise of Nationalism

By the Decree of November 19, 1792, the Constituent Assembly declared that "in the name of the French Nation it will bring fraternity to all people wishing to recover their liberty."[2] Revolutionary principles began to spread through all of Europe, not only via "wars of liberation" but also through well-organized local minority groups, influenced by French republican ideals. In the most despotically governed countries of Eastern Europe, such as Hungary, political unrest took the shape of conspiracies. In England and Prussia, Jacobin clubs, such as the London Corresponding Society and the "Wednesday Society," proliferated.

France, committed to the spread of revolutionary ideas, threw down the gauntlet to the Great Powers. The break with Great Britain came first. After the Austrian Netherlands had fallen to the French, and the Scheldt estuary was opened to French commerce, the British government under Pitt abandoned its policy of neutrality and passed a series of measures aimed at undermining the achievements of the French Revolution.[3] On February 1, 1793, the Convention declared war on both Britain and the Austrian Netherlands.

Gradually, all European countries, with the exception of the Scandinavian states and Switzerland, allied with England to protect monarchical privileges. This was called the First Coalition War; by the spring of 1795 the French armies had reached their "natural frontiers," the left bank of the Rhine, and had beaten their enemies on every front and occupied their lands.

The Directoire engaged in a politics of annexation.[4] Threatened by the new French conquests, the European powers launched two consecutive wars: the wars of the Second Coalition (1798–1800) and the Third Coalition (1805–07), which led to the consolidation of Napoleon's leadership, including the organization of a Continental System.[5]

The Continental System was a plan to unite Europe against the British export trade.[6] It attempted to develop the economy of continental Europe around France as its main center. It presupposed an internationalist ideology that sought common ground of consent between the Europeans. As mentioned earlier, European Jacobins still perceived Napoleon as their liberator. He spoke endlessly of the Enlightenment and urged all people to work with him against the medievalism, feudalism, ignorance, and obscurantism still prevailing in Europe. France was still vindicating the principles of liberty and equality, and Napoleon, whose victories spread these principles abroad, was the "man of destiny," or what Hegel called "the world spirit on a white horse." For the continental bourgeoisie, *The Declaration of the Rights of Man and Citizen* became the charter of a new world, the constitution of a universal society that Europe should exemplify.

The rhetoric of a French crusade to liberate enslaved people was soon belied by Napoleon's actual policies, as the deeds of the liberator began to resemble the play of old-fashioned power politics. The united European flag, which Napoleon brandished during the "wars of liberation" against the absolutist regimes, served mainly to increase France's economic and national prestige at the expense of its allies. Indeed, national emancipation was not really granted to Jacobins outside of France.

The unification of Italy, for instance, may have been implied by Napoleon's creation of the Italian Kingdom, but the new state was promptly truncated by France's annexation of one-third of the peninsula, including the territory extending from Rome to the French border.

Sections of Croatia, Carniola, and the Dalmatian coast, annexed as the Illyrian provinces, were given a strictly administrative unity: the name was borrowed from a Roman prefecture, yet the language favored there was not Croat, nor Italian, but French. The unfulfilled promises of national emancipation began to be ever more deeply resented by the subjects of the Napoleonic empire.

It should be stressed, however, that the rational reforms Napoleon introduced in Italy and in the German states helped to shatter the dikes of feudal particularism and cleared the way for the development of national institutions. As a champion of liberal reforms, Napoleon inadvertently taught the Italians and the Germans how to reorganize their national institutions—a lesson that would later help them to build their respective national states. Napoleon failed, however, to perceive that the national sentiments he aroused against absolutist regimes would soon turn upon him and his empire.

The first signs of Napoleon's decline coincided with what was ostensibly the period of his greatest power. As the expansion of French power became increasingly identified with blatant imperialism, the seeds of nationalist revolt began to bear fruit—first in Spain, then in Austria—and in the end broke Napoleon's power. The Continental System was so ambitious politically, administratively, and economically that it weakened the emperor as much as it strengthened him. The *imperium* eroded internally while the campaign of 1813–14 waged by the allies significantly weakened Napoleon's forces. After a brief escape from exile in Elba, he was defeated by allied forces at the famous Battle of Waterloo in 1815.

Romantic Nationalism and the Revolt against Reason

The Napoleonic dream of international unity was superseded throughout Europe by the belief that each nation in Europe had from its earliest formation developed a culture and a language of its own. Europe was now seen as a bouquet of diverse flowers rather than as a uniform civilization, stretching from Paris to Saint Petersburg, from London to Rome, and from Berlin to Lisbon, in which everyone spoke French and shared the same artistic ideals. The Continental System promoted the abolition of feudalism, the spread of the metric system, the extension of the prefectoral system, and the Napoleonic Code. However, the rational administration introduced by Napoleon Bonaparte did not emancipate the countries of his empire. Resistance began against the basic postulate of the Enlightenment and the French Revolution, namely, that only customs, beliefs, and institutions that could justify themselves before the bar of reason had a right to exist. Reason was now seen as veiling the particularistic "national interest" of France, disguised under the tricolor ensign: "liberté, égalité et fraternité."

Romanticism stressed the mystical quality of the nation (the *Volksstaat*), where individuals were organically attached to their native soil and shared an inborn understanding of all that has been created, rather than the rational character of the republican state (the *Rechtsstaat*), where citizens were bound by civic equality before the law. Romantics maintained an organic concept of the nation but idealized the subjective will; they elaborated racist views but entertained a taste for the exotic; they looked back to the tradition of the ancien régime but contemplated new avenues for cultural development. From the romantic perspective, national culture was not the conscious product fashioned by the ruling artists of the moment; it was the result of the slow development of centuries. It is therefore not surprising to observe the postrevolutionary passion for historical studies. Depending upon circumstances and needs, history was interpreted by conservative Romantics, such as Sir Walter Scott, Novalis, and others opposed to the brusque transformations of the French Revolution, as an evolutionary process orchestrated by the ruling elite. History was also perceived by politically frustrated liberal thinkers, such as Herder and d'Azeglio, striving to return their national patrimony to its "natural" historical path, as a cyclical mechanism in which wars and violence were romanticized.[7]

These cyclical and evolutionary ideas of history stemmed from biological studies that contemplated the slow growth and decay of the living organism. Versions of evolution, in the biological sense, were already adopted by Buffon's *Histoire naturelle* in 1750, and later developed by Lamarck at the turn of the eighteenth century, while Erasmus Darwin—the grandfather of Charles Darwin—had, by 1796, worked out for himself a compendious theory of similar thrust.[8] These biological inquiries undoubtedly reinforced the systemic and evolutionary definition of the nation, which was examined as an organism whose activities could not be understood merely as the sum of the activities of its parts. Yet functionalist examinations of organic political systems often obscured ethical considerations, such as the nature of individuals' solidarity, and at times even associated scientific assumptions with de facto moral postulates.[9]

Throughout the nineteenth century, romantic thinkers invoked the organic nature of the nation for different purposes: to unify their nation (e.g., Ranke and Mazzini in Germany and Italy) or, where national unity already existed (e.g., Bonald and Wordsworth in France and England), to reassert the status quo when the "national interest" was questioned. Generally speaking, by concentrating on the organic structure of the state to revive national pride, internationalism disintegrated in the thought of romantic political thinkers and writers.

In short, Romantics developed a distrust of reason (chapter 9), an emotional, cultural, and organic perspective of the state (chapter 10), and a skeptical view of a republican world order (chapter 11). The remaining chapters will focus on three writers who exemplify these views in various ways: Edmund Burke, Joseph de Maistre, and Johann Gottlieb Fichte.

Nine

The Revolt against Universal Reason

One main purport of the romantic movement was the philosophical rejection of rationalism, the precept of simplicity and harmony that typified the eighteenth century. The movement originated in England with the works of Blake, Wordsworth, and Coleridge; in Germany with Goethe's *Faust* and Herder; in Italy with the writings of Manzoni and Leopardi; in France with de Maistre and Bonald; in Russia with the poetic works of Pushkin; in Poland with the poet and novelist Mickiewicz; and in Spain with Rivas.[1] A number of eighteenth-century writers already anticipated a nineteenth-century conservative trend of romanticism. These thinkers included Edmund Burke and Joseph de Maistre, who called for the return of collective stability centered around faith, emotionalism, tradition, and discipline. Others, such as Herder and Fichte, initially championed reason and the universalist ideals of the Enlightenment. These views fell away, however, as Napoleon's troops betrayed the internationalist promises of revolutionary France. By the time of his death, Fichte's new vision of society built upon national duty, communal loyalty, tradition, and faith had come to resemble that of Burke and de Maistre.

As early as 1790, Burke began his attack on the secular premises of the Enlightenment. He denounced the National Assembly for having confiscated church lands and converted them into assignats, or paper guarantees issued to investors in the revolutionary loan, as well as for reducing clergymen to common employees of the state. The people of England, asserted Burke, would fight against "any project of turning their independent clergy into ecclesiastic pensioners of state."[2] Englishmen, Burke continued, had made their church, like their king and their nobility, independent.[3] The English people would never have permitted their ecclesiastic establishment to become dominated by the fluctuations of the "Euripus of funds and actions."[4] Admitting that the French clergy needed reform, he nonetheless maintained that the punishment inflicted by the revolutionaries was excessive.[5]

Burke's critique of the seizure of church lands underplayed the crisis that provoked it: the need to remedy the desperate state of French national finances. He continuously compared French policies unfavorably with those of the British (which he portrayed as an almost ideal example). In fact, the French use of national loans as inducements to invest in the future of the revolutionary regime had mimicked the role of the Bank of England after the Glorious Revolution. In Burke's eyes, however, the assignats were nothing but an act of confiscation, designed to destroy the established religion. He was oblivious to the fact that Whig families like his own gained their wealth from lands that were once monastic properties.

Burke deplored the destruction of religious institutions in France and the commitment to achieve a universal principle of reason, which he identified as the "appearance of the metaphysics of an undergraduate, the mathematics and the arithmetic of an exciseman" (p. 162).The Jacobins, declared Burke, were poor speculators on liberty. Their political zeal, unbounded confidence in their own enlightened rationality, and worship of mathematical reason entangled them in a labyrinth of metaphysical sophistry. Social union should be achieved by other means than those found in the temple of atheism: "It will be performed with other incense than the infectious stuff which is imported by the smuggler of adulterated metaphysics" (p. 67).The other incense was social restraint, tradition, political prudence, and sublime delight.

In contrast to the concept of beauty derived from reason and simplicity, Burke suggested in the *Philosophical Inquiry into the Origin of Our Ideas and the Sublime and Beautiful* an understanding of an aesthetic built on the sublime delight of the senses. The spectator's or reader's delight in the sublime, he explained, depended upon a sensation of pleasurable pain. In contrast to eighteenth-century metaphysicians, he added, reason required social restraint: it was not accessible to every individual. Burke's central doctrine was that the social order preceded the human intellect and set the moral and practical conditions under which theory and practice must be carried out. Thus, by striving to destroy the traditional fabric of culture, the French revolutionaries were destroying the lineage of their social patrimony: society itself. Echoed in 1798 by Wordsworth and Coleridge's *Lyrical Ballads,* Burke maintained that reason established *in abstractum* was a dangerous guide. Political action should be derived from different sources: tradition, faith, and prejudice. The English, contrary to the French, he proudly explained, treasured their prejudices:

> You see sir, in this enlightened age, I am bold enough to confess that we are men of untaught feelings, that instead of casting away all our old prejudices, we cherish them to a very considerable degree and to take more shame to ourselves, we cherish them because they are prejudices; and the longer they have lasted and the more generally they have prevailed, the more we cherish them. (P. 76)

Like Machiavelli, who advised his prince to use every possible means to remain in power, Burke recommended religion to preserve the peaceful edifice of society. He depicted society as too complex to be accessible to all through reason. Political affairs were a realm for experts—the only ones capable of connecting utility with intelligence, liberty with innovation, and power with discipline. "It is the business of the politician, who is the philosopher in action, to find out means towards ends, and to implement them with effect."[6] Burke rejected the speculative interpretation of reason; even instrumental rationality was useful only insofar as it served the ruling elite in consolidating the hierarchical order of society—which, in his opinion, was congruent with natural harmony. "The levelers," on the other hand, "only change and pervert the natural order of things; they load the edifice of society by setting up in the air what the solidity of the structure requires to be on the ground."[7]

De Maistre was often viewed as the "French Burke."[8] He was in complete agreement with the Irish thinker's contention that religion was a way to solidify the prerevolutionary status quo. He stressed, however, the importance of truth manifested only through revelation: "The first character of God's teaching is neither to reveal directly

God's existence, nor his attributes, but to suppose that the whole is anteriorly understood, without knowing how and why."[9] According to de Maistre, Catholicism was the only true revealed religion.[10] In *The Pope*, he attempted to reassert the spiritual authority of the papacy in the Christian world. He entrusted the pope with the power of releasing people from their duty of obedience to secular authority.[11] In this work, de Maistre explicitly described his desire to return to a unified Christendom under the supervision of the pope — a situation analogous to medieval times. He even criticized the Jansenists and the Gallican church for constituting a threat to the unity of Christianity. Only the goodwill of a Holy See had preserved the church from a more serious rupture.[12] Universalism could only be realized through the medium of the church.

What had to be condemned above all, he claimed, was the French attack on the clergy. In the same vein as Burke, he denounced the revolutionaries for confiscating church property and imposing secular sermons on priests: "The first blow at the church was the appropriation of its estate, the second was the constitutional oath; and these two tyrannical measures started the revision."[13] No less than Burke, de Maistre characterized the revolutionary government's expulsion of the priests as "against all justice and decency."[14] De Maistre neglected to mention that the banished refractory clergy had traitorously worked in concert with the aristocracy against the new state. He suggested nevertheless that

> the misery inflicted on the priests should be understood as part of providential design: the crime of the tyrants became the weapon of Providence. It was probably necessary for the French priests to be exposed to foreign nations; and they have lived among Protestant peoples, and this closeness has greatly diminished hatred and prejudices.[15]

He interpreted the migration of French priests, particularly of archbishops, to Protestant countries, as a providential sign that might invite the Catholic clergy to find a common ground with their Protestant counterparts. A Christian reunion, he believed, might facilitate the revival of the spirit of the lost Christendom. A formal solidarity should be reached through the medium of the church and papal authority, not via the cult of the Supreme Being inaugurated in 1793.

More harshly even than Burke, de Maistre denounced Robespierre's effort to subordinate religion to reason:

> One should remember the unique moments: Robespierre's speech against the priesthood, the solemn apostasy of the priests, the profanation of objects of worship, the inauguration of the Goddess of Reason, and the many ignominious events by which the provinces tried to surpass Paris. These all leave the ordinary realm of crimes and seem to belong to a different world.[16]

Like Burke, de Maistre rebuked the pretentiousness of the French revolutionaries, whose commitment to reason presupposed that everyone could take control over her or his life without previous experience or religious reverence. Such assumptions obviously undermined the monarchical order, whose authority was granted by the divine grace of God. Only the nobility, he insisted, was endowed with revealed knowledge and the intellectual ability to direct the people. Nor was scientific progress self-evidently justified. "Divine justice," declared de Maistre, "has no respect for geometers or physicists" who dared to question the knowledge of the Almighty.[17] The exaltation of reason during the French Revolution led, in his opinion, to scientific barbarism. Even Newton, he maintained, never would have ventured to say, like some of his malevolent disciples, that the law of gravity was a purely mechanical rather than a divine law.[18] Science cannot prevail without religious content. Religion, de Maistre concluded, was "the preservative that saves science from putrefaction."[19]

Echoing Hamilton and Madison in North America, Burke and Coleridge in England, Goethe and Gentz in Germany, de Maistre described the absurdity of reason left to itself:

> The more reason trusts itself, the more likely it attempts to draw strength from itself; and the more it is absurd, the more likely it shows its feebleness.... Philosophy is nothing but human reason working alone, and human reason reduced to its individual forces is nothing but a brute, which power is reduced to destroy.[20]

All questions regarding human association must be resolved through historical development and not through ad hoc postulates. In this respect, de Maistre anticipated major conservative historians such as Friedrich von Savigny and Leopold von Ranke.[21] Individuals, de

Maistre continued, are determined by the nature of their associations, which change according to circumstance. It would be useless, he argued against the philosophes, to study individuals in a void. Reason must thus give way before tradition and the sphere of prejudice in which it developed: "Let us not misunderstand the meaning of [prejudice]; it should not signify necessarily false ideas but, following the strength of the word, any opinions adopted prior to all examinations."[22]

Like Burke, de Maistre selected prejudice as the pillar of social unity. Prejudice privileged the experiences of the group that was hitherto in control of history and governmental affairs: the aristocracy. De Maistre insisted that opinions and prejudices were also essential for collective happiness; by happiness, however, he meant obedience to church and community. The point is thus to affirm the "general and absolute rule of national dogma" by an aristocratic elite.[23] His understanding of "national reason" is tantamount to Burke's explanation of "political reason." Whereas Burke called for the submission of individuals' reason to the authority of political experts, de Maistre depicted such compliance as a sublime and divine act of patriotism. Glorifying the submissive, mystical, emotional, and even sensual experience of the patriot, de Maistre was a more extreme and less thoughtful version of his British counterpart. "Faith and patriotism," he wrote,

> are the greatest thaumaturges of this world. The one and the other are divine: all their actions are prodigies. Do not talk to them about examination of choice, of discussion: they will tell you that you are blaspheming; they only know two words: *submission and faith*.[24]

This was not a position of which Fichte would have approved, at least until 1806. Fichte was a fervent advocate of the internationalist ideals that emanated from France. With the revolutionaries, he reprimanded the Catholic clergy for its excessive abuses of wealth. In the spirit of Luther, he argued that church activities should be limited to the "invisible world" as opposed to the "corporeal," or material, one.[25] Fichte thus justified the National Assembly, which both confiscated clerical property and declared the necessity for the priests to take an oath of allegiance to the state. Any infiltration of religious institutions into the public sphere, he maintained, restrained the expression of individuals' will and freedom. Morality and reason could be imposed by neither external agents nor institutions, whether church or feudal establishments, nor, as he argued later in his life, by the power of Napoleon's Continental System.

Fichte's ideas on religion, reason, and morality were strongly inspired by Kant's precepts. The similarity between Kant and the early Fichte was such that when Fichte's *Versuch einer Kritik aller Offenbarung* was published without his name appearing as the author, the literary world assumed that the book had been written by Kant. Kant then made it known that the book was from Fichte's pen, not his, and praised the work, thereby making Fichte a national figure. In this essay, Fichte stressed that the acceptance of moral principles deriving from theological postulates was not identical with the individual's strict compliance with the church. Insofar as reverence for moral law was the guiding rule of conduct, there was no room left for coercive laws pretending to promote morality. Following the spirit of Kant's *Critique of Practical Reason,* Fichte argued that divine will, once manifested in the material world, only coincided with the moral content of laws, or at most, gave additional strength to the latter. If there was revelation at all, he maintained, it should correspond only with the content of morality.[26]

Fichte, following Kant, also deplored morality derived from experience or tradition. Together the two philosophers criticized empiricists for placing experience rather than the universality of reason at the heart of their social theory.[27] "Experience," Fichte claimed, "is a box filled with attributes thrown helter-skelter; it is thus the mind that gives a meaning to this chaos,"and in this case the mind should aim toward universal reason and morality (pp. 77–78; my translation). The aristocracy, maintained Fichte, has constrained human reason and identified it with their experience (p. 123). Yet reason cannot be the exclusive prerogative of the few: "It is the commonwealth of humanity" (p. 197; my translation). Fichte addressed his remarks against the arbitrary evaluation of experience to Burke, through his German translator, Frederick Gentz, and blamed Burke for oscillating opportunistically between routine and reason:[28]

> Do you want me to tell you what is the debate between you and me? You probably do not want to get tangled up with reason, but neither do you care about routine. You want to split yourself into

two, and, by placing yourself between these two intractable mistresses, you put yourself in this unpleasant situation of contenting neither one of them. Rather, you should follow with resolution your grateful drive leading toward the latter; and we shall know what to expect from your side.[29]

Fichte explained reason as a process confirmed by the continuous actualization of individuals' will and freedom in the empirical world, rather than as an inherent and static feature of human intellect. By absolutizing the particularist source of reason instead of its universal aim, Fichte made a clear point of departure from Kant.[30] Fichte's ethical postulates presupposed that moral activity was a free and dutiful commitment of the will, triggered by ideal devotion. The dutiful will is the will of one's true self, pursuing in unremitting endeavor an expanding moral goal. In the course of action, explained Fichte, one is expressing the full recognition of oneself. One should never disavow the fulfillment of one's duty as being beyond one's ability. The true moral expression takes the form "If I ought, I can."

A person's true vocation is to achieve in ever fuller freedom an ever more loyal devotion to her/his spiritual ideals. The duty one assigns to oneself is the recognition of one's authentic being and the expression of true freedom. It is necessary for individuals to aim for their utmost potential for freedom, and reach their divine will. In the aspiration of the self, the divine itself is actively manifest and creates the spiritual bond between all finite beings:

> This Will pursues no solitary path withdrawn from the other parts
> of the world of reason. There is a spiritual bond between Him and
> all finite rational beings; and He himself is the spiritual bond of the
> rational universe.[31]

Fichte's evolution from the rational self to the spiritual one paralleled his growing dissatisfaction with the implications of the French Revolution. His exaltation of individuals' unlimited possibilities and their strong sense of duty contained elements of religious subjectivity and heroism that galvanized into nationalist action against Napoleon's pseudorationalist principles of morality. The long wait for freedom springing from the "objective" world had become, for Fichte, a futile hope. The German national soul, an empirical extension of the individual self in the sensuous and objective world, had to count only on itself to reconquer its lost spirituality, on its own sense of moral duty and discipline to reach an authentic freedom and national unity. Thus, departing from the Enlightenment's view of universal solidarity, Fichte began to envision social unity based on faith, sensuous and emotional experience, the consummation of moral piety, tradition, and self-discipline. His views assumed a form similar to the one developed at an earlier stage by Burke, de Maistre, Coleridge, Wordsworth, and Herder. Not only was the philosophical foundation of internationalism, as embraced during the French Revolution, transformed, but, as we shall see in chapter 10, so were its political aspirations.

Ten

Toward an Organic and Relativist Theory of the Nation

It is no wonder that Coleridge, Wordsworth, Novalis, Bonald, and others who challenged the philosophical foundation of the French Revolution should also have contested the liberal bourgeois view of the state. From Rousseau's organic definition of the nation, they retained the form rather than the universal content of the "general will." Yet, by privileging the organic notion of the nation, with no further qualification other than its formalist relevance, they ended up equating the structural or geographical parameters of the nation with its moral purpose, thereby promoting a relativist and arbitrary concept of the nation. For Burke and de Maistre, the ideal government was one that strengthened the national or monarchical interest; for Fichte, the aim of government was to unify the nation. Universal morality was now circumscribed by national boundaries. Internationalism was no longer premised on republican institutions but on any government representing the culture and the spirit of its people. Internationalism was being replaced by the national spirit, which became the sole arbiter of morality and liberty.

"What is liberty without wisdom and without virtue?" Burke inquired. "It is the greatest of all possible evils; for it is folly and vice, and madness, without tuition or restraint."[1] In England as opposed to France, he claimed, subjects had inherited their freedom; they asserted their franchise not only according to abstract principles but as patrimony derived from their forefathers. In keeping with these principles, Burke supported the cause of the Americans in 1776.[2] Contrary to the French, he later stated, the Americans had preserved the spirit of liberty developed and inherited by their English forerunners:

> The people of the colonies are descendants of Englishmen. England, Sir, is a nation which still, I hope, respects and formerly adored her freedom. The colonists emigrated from you when this part of your character was most predominant; and they took this bias and direction the moment they parted from your hands. They are therefore not only devoted to liberty, but to liberty according to English ideas and on English principles.[3]

What the French revolutionaries did not understand, Burke claimed, was that inequality was congruent and harmonious with the nature of civil society. The "characteristic essence of property, formed out of the combined principles of its acquisition and conservation, is to be *unequal.*"[4] With Madison and Hamilton, Burke justified the accumulation of property by the few.[5] He also defended the right to inheritance: "The power of perpetuating our property in our families is one of the most valuable and interesting circumstances belonging to it, and that which tends the most to the perpetuation of society itself."[6] The aristocracy was entrusted with the responsibility of regulating economic activities in conformity with organic social harmony, for "preference given birth was neither unnatural, nor unjust, nor impolitic."[7]

Nonetheless, Burke's friendship with Adam Smith also influenced his work. In the spirit of Smith, Burke condemned the heavy British taxation of the American colonies as an obstruction to laissez-faire theory.[8] Irish economic independence, he believed, would also further free competition.[9] Addressing himself to a merchant who was afraid of possible Irish competition, he said: "Indeed, Sir, England and Ireland may flourish together. The World is large enough for us both. Let it be our care not to make ourselves too little for it."[10] A month later, he pursued his point by suggesting to merchants in Bristol that "the greater [the Irish commerce], the greater must be your advantage. If you should lose in one way, you will gain in twenty."[11]

Burke's laissez-faire theory was not internationalist in its spirit:

it favored people of British and Irish origin. Despite Burke's indignation regarding British Governor General Hastings's exploitative rule in India, he never advocated Indian independence.[12] His belief was merely that the United Kingdom should not impede the development of any English-speaking societies, whether American or Irish, or attempt to subordinate them to its own.

By restricting property rights of nonaristocratic strata, while at the same time promoting a limited laissez-faire position, Burke reflected the oscillation between a bourgeois capitalist and an aristocratic order. In the spirit of Smith's *Theory of Moral Sentiments*, Kramnick provides an interesting psychological view of Burke as a member of the middle class, torn between love and hatred for the aristocracy.[13] Burke represented the affluent bourgeoisie that benefited after the Glorious Revolution from its alliance with the aristocracy. At the end of the eighteenth century, however, English Jacobins challenged this narrow alliance by requesting more political power. Throughout the 1770s, Burke usually could be counted on to support any parliamentary move to ease or lift civil obstacles that weighed down the Dissenters. He turned against his friends and allies in 1789, when he supported the effort of Charles Fox, a British parliamentarian, to allow Dissenters to hold government and municipal positions. With the spread of Jacobinism after 1789, however, he started to perceive the Dissenters as the domestic agents of "the worldwide Jacobin conspiracy."

Burke's organic concept of civil society included a threefold concern: to maintain the modus vivendi achieved by the aristocracy and the bourgeoisie after 1648, to prevent the challenge of Dissenters, and to modernize England. He thus defined the nation as a business contract, which, unlike other contracts, penetrated all spheres of human interaction in order to prevent the commoners from ascending freely each rung of the social ladder:

> Society is indeed a contract ... but the state ought not to be considered as nothing better than a partnership agreement in a trade of pepper and coffee, calico, or tobacco.... It is a partnership in all science; a partnership in all art; a partnership in every virtue and in all perfection.... Each contract of each particular state is ... linking the lower with the higher natures, connecting the visible and the invisible world, according to a fixed compact which holds all physical and moral natures, each in their appointed place.[14]

With Rousseau, Burke defined the organic concept of the nation as an indivisible and inalienable body superior to the sum of its parts. However, whereas Rousseau's general will displayed the interest of the population from "below upward," Burke's organic formulation of the nation was patterned from "above downward."[15] The political and universal prerequisite of internationalism was severely restrained.

There was no a priori governmental ideal for maintaining the cohesion of the nation. This concern, he asserted, was merely an abstract mental exercise, for a proper government was linked ineluctably to the historical development of its own culture, and could not vary "like mode of dress."[16] The function of political institutions was to preserve religions, laws, and liberties that had long been possessed. Instituting new liberties through democratic regimes was doomed to fail and would ultimately lead to the anarchic tyranny of the mob.[17] The only acceptable form of parliamentary representation was the one conducted under the leadership of a compact but public-spirited minority. Parliament should thus be mainly a place to assemble the leaders of this minority. Regardless of the type of government, contended Burke, a certain quantum of power should always exist in the community in some hands and in some appellation, preferably supervised by the crown.[18]

Comparing the English government to the French, Burke asserted that the English monarchy had been valuable because it fused the interests of the nation as a whole and secured it from the possible fragmentation of a "congress of ambassadors from different and hostile interests."[19] By degrading the king and his family, the National Assembly disempowered the only authority that could have consolidated the state. Burke claimed that the French had gained nothing by repudiating the proper exercise of the king's rule in the name of republicanism or internationalism. Under the monarchy, France was prosperous, whereas the National Assembly only succeeded in leading the country to economic bankruptcy and unemployment.[20]

De Maistre agreed with Burke and the statesman and philosophical writer Viscount Bonald that republican and internationalist ideas had worsened the economic situation of France. By deposing and decapitating their monarch, the French had destroyed the national unit.[21] In England, commented de Maistre, the king still exercised an honorable function and was able to preserve tradition and social cohesion.[22] Any comparison between the Glorious Revolution and the

French Revolution was thus ludicrous. "What a difference!" de Maistre exclaimed. "The monarchy was not overthrown in England. The monarch disappeared only to be substituted by another" (p. 135; my translation). Echoing Burke's view of tradition, he asserted that the Americans had not destroyed their English patrimony: "The Americans did not commit the extravagance of completely destroying their political system to create a new one; the operation was reduced to transporting, so to speak, the executive from England to America" (p. 212; my translation). Yet de Maistre pushed Burke's views to the extreme by arguing that no representative, mixed government *à l'anglaise,* no matter the configuration, should be adopted in France:

> I say more: when one would propose for France the mixed government of England, it was again an unforgivable imprudence to adopt it.... I know that many good minds, in the minority, had sympathy for this plan, but I think that I would not lack respect toward them by saying that the French, even the most educated ones, were not mature enough for the Revolution; that politics was too new in the realm, and that they were too hasty in assuming that the English government could be suited to their homeland. (P. 212; my translation)

De Maistre's concern with social unity was of a different sort from Burke's. Whereas the latter's antirevolutionary views sought to contain the spread of French propaganda within English society, de Maistre's attempted to give spiritual faith to the decimated French nobility in exile. Cultivating hope for a successful counterrevolution, which might reinstate the privileges and the wealth of the aristocracy, de Maistre urged his aristocratic audience not to despair; the cruelty of Robespierre's measures would bring about the death of the Revolution and would precipitate the return of the monarchy: "All the monsters, born during the Revolution have mainly worked,... for the royalty" (p. 19; my translation).

Like Rousseau, he conceived of the nation as an organism; and, like Burke, he criticized Rousseau for assuming that the people had the intellectual capacity to administer their public life. The people can, at most, be represented by delegates, but will never be in position to command. Accordingly, the idea of the *peuple souverain* was considered by de Maistre as an ironic proposition; for sovereignty is derived from God and the art of governing is revealed only to selected people. While rejecting the Rousseau of the *Social Contract,* which had such an influence on the French Revolution, he praised the Rousseau of romanticism and nationalism; the one who sought an emotional bond between citizens, rather than the one who celebrated civic solidarity; the one who depicted the nation as an extension of the inner light, rather than the one who claimed the rational and legal foundation of the state; and the one who asserted the unity between state and religion, rather than the one who advocated the total separation of these two spheres.

De Maistre's organic concept of the nation was stripped of its original universalist content and reinforced by the belief that monarchy alone could bind society with religion. Only the monarchy had the vigor and will necessary for strong government in great states. "The word of the king is a talisman, a magic power, which directs all its strength and talents in one single direction."[23] He claimed that impartiality was best secured when power was granted to one whose interest was that of the whole. Hereditary governments, he believed, were the best suited regimes for France and the European context: republicanism would produce only chaos.

Whereas Burke vacillated between a liberal laissez-faire economy and the maintenance of privileges by the aristocracy, de Maistre was an incontrovertible royalist in economic matters. Property should remain in the hands of the landed aristocracy and the crown. Burke's language was still indebted to Locke's teaching; de Maistre's was not. He despised the calculating bourgeoisie as carrying the "smell of the grocery shop." Only on rare occasions did he make reference to commerce or merchants, and then only in terms of their subordination to the king.[24] De Maistre reserved a profound disdain for the bourgeoisie, which, in contrast to England, was totally excluded from the political sphere.

As a champion of universal rights in the classical liberal tradition, Fichte argued that property should be accessible to everyone. He thereby dissociated himself from the conservative political economy of Burke as well as from de Maistre's feudal economic position. Following the Lockean tradition, he stipulated that our body belongs to us as property — "we are our property"[25] — and that the right to acquire property is justified by the labor invested in it.[26] He thus contended that limiting the right to property is legitimate only if that right infringes upon another individual's property right.[27]

The state provided the perfect condition for a society wherein citizens could acquire property while still performing their moral duty. Contractual arrangements regulated by the state thus had to be considered less an imposition of the outside world than an emancipation of inner morality. In his early writings, Fichte suggested that the state should have a minimal impact on the life of the individual: it should preserve what people had gained in the state of nature and civil society. Fichte's position reflected his hatred of absolutism; thus his first preoccupation was to weaken the power of the feudal state.

Fichte set the epistemological framework for individuals to act against feudalism and to shape their own destiny. "The original right [of man]," he argued, "is therefore the absolute right of the person only to be a cause in the sensible world and never to be an effect."[28] To express free will over the economic sphere, the role of the state had to be reduced to its minimal function; his ideas thus provided confidence to the burgeoning German bourgeoisie in its attempt to dominate the economic sphere. Fichte's concept of the state, however, also contained an element antagonistic to classical liberalism. He began gradually to ascribe to the state the positive task of ensuring all aspects of individual liberty in various spheres of human activity.

What kind of government would Fichte have sponsored to ensure such liberties? He did not specify any type. He made sure to note his opposition both to absolute monarchy and to pure democracy (which was not a viable regime).[29] Anything between these two poles was permissible. This position should not be surprising given that his attitude toward the state fluctuated throughout his lifetime. In his early writings, Fichte strongly supported the French Revolution and was a fervent adherent of natural law; he deeply distrusted absolutism.[30]

Under the influence of the French Convention, Fichte disputed the strict liberal split between the private and public spheres. Gradually, however, he began to subscribe to an organic image of the state. The organic character of the state had been depicted by Herder in *Ideen zur Philosophie der Geschichte der Menschheit.* Inspired by Herder, Fichte proceeded by depicting the state as a tree in which each single branch has a consciousness and a will but belongs to a living unit. Every part of a tree desires its own self-preservation, but nevertheless is compelled to will the survival of the entire tree, because its own survival is only possible on that condition.[31] In its internal life, the body politic is ruled, in Fichte's and Herder's view, by "common will," which Fichte derived in the same way as Rousseau and his revolutionary followers.[32] In the same fashion as Rousseau in the *Social Contract* and in Rousseau's position on property, Fichte argued that it was not sufficient for the state to endorse the right to private property and to presume that everyone would live by his or her work: "To say that everything will come about of its own accord, that everyone will always find work and bread and that this should be left to good luck, is unworthy of a constitution based upon justice."[33]

Fichte developed this view in *The Closed Commercial State.*[34] He conceptualized the state as being responsible for controlling the economic sphere. The influence of the radical revolutionaries in their attempt to reconcile political and equal economic rights was still blatant in this work. Fichte's main concern was the measures by which economic affairs could be rationally ordered. Every individual had to enter a trade and publicly declare his vocation. The state intervened to ensure a fair distribution of trades and a proper organization of the monetary system. Fichte envisaged four different classes: the producers of primary goods, the artisans engaged in the subsequent processing of these primary goods, the merchants who mediated between these two classes, and the officials who supervised the other three classes and allocated all resources so that every member of the state received an equal share of consumer goods. With this work, Fichte merged the radical Enlightenment tradition of universality of Babeuf and utopian socialists such as Saint-Simon, Fourier, and Owen with the autarkic tradition of German conservatives such as Adam Müller and Friedrich Schleimacher. In other words, he confined the internationalist spirit of the Enlightenment to the existence of a self-sufficient state.

The complete control of economic life was possible only if the state was self-contained. Trade with foreign countries must come to an end, for as long as there was any foreign trade, the state's economy would be dependent on the economic conditions of other countries. Like Vico and Rousseau, Fichte believed that conflict would result from the inequality of wealth between nations and hence frustrate rational economic and political arrangements on the domestic level. He might well have suggested gradually closing the commercial state, hoping to seclude the German people from French political and economic influence. One should remember that when *The Closed Commercial State* was published in 1806, during Napoleon's regime, Fichte still reluctantly believed that the French would provide assistance for the creation of a free and strong German economy. His work thus should be seen as a way to motivate the German quest for national and economic independence.

Infuriated by the humiliation that Napoleon inflicted on the Prussian troops in 1806, Fichte appealed to the German sense of patriotism to evict the foreign army from its soil. Inferring from Herder's *Ideen zur Philosophie der Geschichte der Menschheit,* Fichte stated that humanity had not one form but many and that the Germans were ready to initiate in this particular time and place their own cultural progress. The culturally relativist community (*Volksstaat*) was to take precedence over the state as a legal/formal entity (*Rechtsstaat*). The nation was now understood as the convergence of transcendental egos. In this collective and spiritual experience, Fichte assumed that individuals would achieve a higher level of morality, closer to infinity, closer to divinity:

> In a higher sense of the word, taken from the standpoint of the whole spiritual world, a folk is a people living together in a society and biologically and spiritually reproducing itself and subject to a particular law in accordance with which it reveals the divine.[35]

Frustrated by the lackadaisical nature of the German bourgeoisie and the empty promises of Napoleon, Fichte, Novalis, Schlegel, and others deviated from the rational premises of the Enlightenment. Thus, in 1806 Fichte abandoned internationalist principles and implored the German *Volk,* notwithstanding their social differences, to fulfill their moral duty as free individuals by uniting against the foreign aggressor. Fichte invoked Machiavelli's strategy to reach his ethical end. While condemning Machiavelli's goals, Fichte was convinced that everyone who wished to organize a republic—or any state, for that matter—must assume the maliciousness of man.[36] In other words, unlike Kant, Fichte justified unethical means to reach his national and moral goal. He thus perpetuated the uneasy marriage between universalism as developed during the Enlightenment and the particularist values of romanticism.

Despite important political differences between Fichte, Burke, and

de Maistre, their works illustrated the significant retreat of internationalism and republican ideas and the subsequent development of a
national spirit organized around sublime emotions and cultural
pride. Their concept of an "inalienable" and "indivisible" organic will
was confined to the control of the leading group of the nation, who
were believed to be the only effective advocates of social cohesion.
Their vision of the nation was reshaped in a relativistic way similar,
yet not identical, to the one conceptualized by theorists of the sixteenth century such as Grotius, Hobbes, Locke, and Vico (discussed
in chapters 1–4): the bourgeoisie had now become the major political ally of the aristocracy. The next chapter examines how Fichte,
Burke, de Maistre, and other thinkers viewed the role of the nation
during the revolutionary and/or Napoleonic Wars; in other words, it
traces the withering of internationalism not only in the philosophical
and the political societial realms, but also in the global arena.

Eleven

From Internationalism to Nationalism

Europe was shaken by the revolutionary wars, and later by the wars of the coalition against Napoleon. Although the Revolution itself had provoked a nationalist response among conservative thinkers such as Burke and de Maistre, it had initially inspired support among liberal thinkers like Fichte. Yet even among progressive thinkers the Revolution yielded over time to disillusionment and a growing embrace of nationalism. In Italy, the writers Cesare di Beccaria and Vittorio Alfieri acclaimed the French Revolution. Later, Massimo d'Azeglio deplored the internal division of Italy perpetuated under Napoleon's Continental System. The German political thinkers Kant and Forster hailed the French Revolution. In 1806, Novalis joined a chorus of German political thinkers in calling upon Saxony and Prussia to save Germany from destruction by the French emperor. The English poet Coleridge, though an early advocate of the Revolution, very soon turned against it. Later, in *Childe Harold's Pilgrimage,* the English romantic poet Lord Byron expressed the disillusion of the postrevolutionary and Napoleonic era and championed the cause of oppressed nationalities everywhere.

In light of the revolutionary and Napoleonic Wars, it was impossible for intellectuals throughout Europe to envision the nation without considering its role in war and in the community of nations. Burke regarded war as necessary to maintain order and the European balance of power. De Maistre declared war the result of divine intervention to purge humankind's sins. Fichte initially declared that the proliferation of free and rational governments would prevent war, but in his later works unconditionally justified war as a means to achieve German national unity.

Burke did not believe, as did Kant, that nations should possess equal rights to self-determination. A worldwide federation of nations was not likely to emerge in a world of hostile interests. No authoritative executive body could preside over independent states. "There is a Law of Neighborhood," he wrote in "The Regicide Peace," "which does not leave man perfectly master on his own ground; and as there is no judge recognized above independent states, the vicinage itself is the natural judge."[1] Peace and order would be realized through a stable balance of power.[2] The major powers in Europe should be the guardians and arbiters in the world arena. He considered the European states best suited for this international "peace force" function, since they might succeed in reaching a modus vivendi thanks to their common background:

> The nations of Europe have had the same Christian religion, agreeing in the same fundamental parts, varying a little in the ceremonies and the subordinate doctrines. The whole of the polity and the economy of every country in Europe has been derived from the same sources. It was drawn from the old Germanic or Gothic customary,... and the whole has been improved and digested into system and discipline by the Roman law.[3]

Acknowledging the tradition of natural law while transforming it, Burke differentiated just from unjust wars. Since wars were inevitable, he considered as just those wars waged to reach justice. Criteria of justice were, however, too often evaluated according to a posteriori judgments. He claimed, for instance, that the English wars were justified wars. "The revolution of 1688 was obtained by a just war, in the only case in which any war and much more a civil war, can be just. *Justa bella quibus necessaria.*"[4] This postulate, however, was tautological, for it assumed that wars were just when necessary, and therefore necessary when just. Burke believed that these natural law principles justified a nation's interference in the internal affairs of another state if the latter was internally divided. This allowed him to encourage a war against the divided French nation.[5] One can speculate that Burke would have proven less enthusiastic about prospective French interference on the side of the Dissenters in England.

Inspired by Grotius's and Kant's doctrine of *temperamenta*, however, he advised moderation in wartime. This theory called for the conqueror to refrain from abusing the conquered, because a state entered into war against another state and not against individuals. Victors should protect men who have surrendered and should avoid the confiscation of property. In this respect, the Commons's clerk reported:

> [Mr Burke] declared that the general confiscation of private property found upon the island [Saint Eustatius, a West Indies Dutch island] was contrary to the law of nations and to that system of war which civilized states ... by their consent and practice, thought proper to introduce.... Mr Burke said that a king conquered to gain dominion, not plunder; that a state does not take possession of private property.... Every monarch, however despotic, is bound to the very essence of his tenure to observe this obligation.... this is a principle inspired by the Divine author of all good; it is felt in the heart; it is recognized by reason; it is established by consent.[6]

Furthermore, Burke considered unjustifiable wars that pitted one English people against another. He admonished the members of the British Parliament not to pursue wars against the American colonists or the Irish separatists.[7] However, his theory of just war did not gravitate crudely around his interest in British culture; he supported the Polish and Corsican rebellions as well. Burke legitimized national rebellions aimed at defending a cultural heritage against foreign aggression, but he was especially supportive of those that did not threaten the English status quo and were consonant with the requirements of aristocratic order and discipline. Needless to say, the French Revolution was excluded from the just-war framework. So were the "rebellions" by "noncivilized" people that challenged Anglo-Saxon interests. No later than 1778, in a debate concerning the use of Indians and slaves in the American war, Burke hypothesized that "all Negroes and servants planning insurrection against their masters had as their principal objectives murders, rapes, and enormities of every kind."[8] Burke's Anglophilia is difficult to overlook when he distinguishes just from unjust wars or rebellions, since he often claimed the superiority and excellence of the English people over their "un-civilized" colonies and neighbors, and in particular over their French rivals.[9]

As with Coleridge and Wordsworth, Burke's anti-French senti-ments became more noticeable after the French Revolution. Relations between the French and the British were already strained by com-mercial rivalry, which predated the Revolution. The French Revolu-tion alarmed Burke, for it set a frightening example for the English Dissenters and could endanger the stability of the British system. Burke thus employed all his efforts to contain the effects of the French Rev-olution. It was important, in his opinion, for Britain to remain among the strong nations, if not to be the strongest, and to raise the national spirit. Burke was aware of the impact of nationalist propa-ganda on the people in times of crisis: "To do anything without raising a Spirit (I mean a National Spirit) with all the energy and much of the conduct of a Party Spirit, I hold to be a thing absolutely impos-sible."[10] He did not hesitate to use emotional, sublime, and religious appeal to advance what he considered the "national interest."[11]

De Maistre embodied an extreme version of Burke's nationalism. Like Burke, he depicted wars as a normal and an inevitable relation-ship between states: "History proves that war is a regular state and peace only a recess."[12] Looking backward, de Maistre showed that France had experienced eight hundred years of incessant wars with only short intervals of peace. Violence and violent death were laws of the whole universe. All animals were governed by the relationship of predator to prey, and man, to satisfy his needs and instincts, must kill or subdue the animal world. This same law mandated that men seized by "a divine fury" must seek to kill their fellows. The divine origins of war justified, even sanctified, the killing instinct. War was a noble experience. De Maistre demonstrated this claim by compar-ing the soldier with the executioner. Assessing the social utility of both occupations, he regarded the first as noble and the second as abject.[13] In contrast to the executioner, who was appreciated only for providing a necessary function, "military courage easily allies itself with virtue and even piety, and far from enfeebling the warrior, exalts him."[14]

"There is only one way of restraining the scourge of war," wrote de Maistre, "and that is by restraining internal political disorders, which lead to this terrible purification."[15] That assumption contra-dicted his providential view of war, whereby "every punishment is inflicted by [divine] love and justice."[16] By envisioning a providential perspective on war, de Maistre, even more so than Burke, distanced himself from the natural law tradition. Certainly there were "just and unjust wars," but only the Almighty could determine which was which.

Indeed, de Maistre argued that bloody wars were sacrifices needed to extinguish evil: "The whole earth, continually steeped in blood, is nothing but an immense altar on which every living thing must be sacrificed, without end, and without restraint, without respite, until the consummation of the world, the extinction of evil, the death of death."[17] Strangely enough, Christianity was never more sublime or compatible with God's justice than during war. In war, God punished and purified humanity. After the Lisbon earthquake of 1755, Voltaire cried out: "Can you say after seeing all these victims, that God is re-venged, that their death is the price of their crimes? These children crushed and bloody on their mothers' breasts, what crime or sin had they committed?" De Maistre shamelessly replied that these children, like all victims of natural disasters and scourges, were the object of divine wrath, that their deaths were the necessary means of expiating human weakness.[18] The innocent must expiate for the guilty. De Maistre's worldview was formed by the principle of original sin.

Given the purging effect of war and its inexorable recurrences in world affairs, de Maistre concluded with Burke that a world govern-ment, as the Abbé de Saint-Pierre conceived it, was an impractical vi-sion. In "Les Soirées de Saint-Pétersbourg," he elaborated his view by invoking three imaginary representatives of the old social order. Through one protagonist, the count, de Maistre asked a critical ques-tion: "How is it that God, the author of human society, allowed man, his cherished creation, endowed with divine attributes of per-fectibility, not to build a society of nations?"[19] His interlocutor, the senator, replied, without giving further explanation, that the project of civilizing nations was always attempted, but never successfully.

In keeping with his organic view of the nation, de Maistre, like Bonald, Novalis, and others, insisted that there could not be a world government, for there were no universal men in the world, only Italians, Frenchmen, Russians, and the like. A constitution made for all people would be satisfactory for no one, a mere scholastic endeavor.[20]

In the spirit of Vico, de Maistre argued that each nation was following a different evolutionary path, that each had a period of greatness and decadence, and therefore could not be considered as similar at a given point in time. France had achieved its moment of decadence after the French Revolution, and, after abolishing its negative elements, was preparing for a grand future.[21] "For nations," he stated, "the moment of their greatness is the one of corruption."[22] Such an apocalyptic vision of the world legitimized inherent hostilities between nations and the impossibility of world peace as part of God's design. Ironically, de Maistre ended up depicting God as a bellicose warrior vindicated each time blood was shed on earth.

Unlike Burke, de Maistre perceived France and not England as endowed with a mission: namely, to dominate Europe. In reaction to the French Revolution and Napoleon's regime, he developed the roots of French nationalism. De Maistre believed that France's geopolitical position gave it the opportunity to propagate its influence throughout the European continent: "Situated between seas, France attracts the commerce of all nations, and its warring fleet can reach and hit everywhere with an incommensurable facility and velocity."[23] Although the French had consistent problems throughout history in keeping conquered territories, they succeeded in extending their influence thanks to their superior culture and language. While Burke exalted English cultural superiority, de Maistre's pride in French cultural greatness over internationalist solidarity and equality made him the first French nationalist.[24]

In contrast to de Maistre and Burke, Fichte, endeavoring to retain the universal and rational aspirations of the Enlightenment, held that wars were not inevitable relationships between *true* and free states; wars were waged mostly by barbaric and enslaved countries and guided by masters insensible to the interests of their subjects.[25] Like Kant, Fichte argued that it was contrary to the interests of free states, or republics, to become bellicose. Wars could be justified only for self-defense or when treaties had been breached.[26] Preferably, ambassadors should be sent to mitigate potential conflicts. Fichte contended that, to avoid the outbreak of war, contracts between states should be clear and concise, and drafted in the spirit of equality and justice between neighboring states. Property rights of each state's citizens should also be mutually guaranteed; this would dissuade citizens from aspiring to acquire the property of their neighbors. States' rights within the global community should be similar to citizens' rights within states.

How would such treaties be guaranteed? Inspired by Kant, Fichte opted for a federation of states over an international state. A federation of states, after all, was not compulsory by its nature. Having outlined a treaty of federation, Fichte added:

> What I have described would be a *federation of nations*, and not an *international state*. The difference exists in the following: an individual can be compelled to enter a state, because outside a state no legal relationship with him is possible. But no state can be compelled in this association. It enters such a relationship with its neighboring states by recognizing them and by concluding with them the treaty which is described above.[27]

Although the federation must be armed, Fichte advised, a standing army would become unnecessary, since war would gradually disappear. He attempted to establish the theoretical legal framework to ensure principles of universal rights and cosmopolitanism for world citizens. "The right of the mere citizens of the world consists," he wrote, "in the right to walk freely about the world with the offer of forming a legal relationship."[28]

In contrast to Kant, however, Fichte did not stipulate that republican states were a major prerequisite for achieving international solidarity. He merely suggested, without specific qualification on the nature of government, that free states would first compel the transformation of neighbors into sisterly states. He therefore justified the wars against Napoleon, asserting that freedom would engender freedom, and once the involuted mechanism was triggered, it would expand progressively throughout the globe:

> Soon will the nations, civilized or enfranchised by them, find themselves placed in the same relation towards others still enthralled by barbarism over slavery, in which the earlier free nations previously stood towards them, and be compelled to do the same things for these which they were previously done for themselves; and thus, of necessity, by reason of the existence of some few really free states, will the empire of civilization, freedom and with it universal peace, gradually embrace the whole world.[29]

This internationalist idea of freedom, described as a self-propagating process, was abandoned as Fichte embraced the autarkic perspective of the closed state. As mentioned earlier, Fichte, echoing Rousseau, argued that by decreasing the interaction with other nations, a closed and self-sufficient state would evince its particular mode of life, institutions, and culture, and develop the citizens' love for their fatherland. Subsequently, a high degree of national honor and a clear national character would arise.[30] Like Herder, he began to discuss cosmopolitanism in terms of patriotism and vice versa: "In [the citizen's] mind, love of one country is his activity, cosmopolitanism is his thought; the former is the outer manifestation, the latter the inner spirit of the manifestation, the invisible in the visible."[31]

The spirit of internationalism vanished, and remained invisible, as Fichte became more suspicious of Napoleon's political intentions toward the German states. In *Beziehung auf den Namenlosen,* Fichte attacked Napoleon as a usurper who had betrayed the universal purpose of the state and its trust in the will of the people.[32] After the first Prussian defeat by Napoleon at Tilsit, Fichte's internationalism finally gave way to a German nationalist solution. France stood for everything Fichte opposed; the French conqueror had destroyed the internationalist aspirations of the French Revolution. It was the duty of the German people to take over the propagation of universal freedom:

> The German patriot wishes that this purpose [the acceptance of the new philosophy] be achieved first among the Germans and that the effects then be spread from them to the rest of humanity. The German can will this because the knowledge began with him and is written down in his speech. The greatest ability for understanding this knowledge lies with that nation which had the strength to create it. The German alone can will this; for he alone can, by means of the possession of this knowledge and of an understanding of the age through it, perceive that this is the next objective of humanity. The objective is the only possible patriotic one; the German can, therefore, be a patriot; for he alone can for the sake of his nation encompass entire humanity.[33]

Like Burke, de Maistre, and Novalis, Fichte believed that his nation must undertake a noble missionary role in Europe. He now boasted of the purity of German culture. Although for centuries nations had intermingled through wars with other nations, Fichte commented in the *Reden an die Deutsche Nation,* Germans had kept an authentic and unmixed cultural identity and a language that could be traced back to the Teutons. By sanctifying the nation, Fichte rekindled the spiritual energy required for German unification. This transition from Jacobin internationalism to nationalism turned Fichte from a rationalist into a romantic thinker.

Despite a political agenda that differed from the two previous thinkers, Fichte announced with de Maistre and Burke the regression of internationalist ideals, the capitulation of the universalization of human rights in the global and domestic sphere, and therefore the advance of nationalist values. Their writings reflected the prevailing political disillusionment with revolutionary ideas emanating from the French *patrie* and usurped by Napoleon Bonaparte. Yet Bonaparte's policy was not the only reason for the failure of internationalism. The tension within internationalism, which culminated in its demise, can be traced throughout the three historical phases discussed in this book.

Phase 1. The parallel development of both mercantilism and the nation-state informed the instrumental and divided character of internationalism during the Reformation. Grotius's writings illustrated the growing need for international law, stemming from burgeoning world trade, and later Vico warned of the prospective downfall of the growing nation-states. Their writings and those of other scholars of the same period also showed the initial ethical split between the global and the national order; their writings helped, on the one hand, to conceive a global peace premised on natural law, property rights, and economic exchange and, on the other hand, to orchestrate progress from a relatively strong national unit, the monarchy.

Rousseau's works echoed the growing political frustration of the eighteenth-century bourgeoisie seeking to develop the structure of the state and to achieve better political representation. A political and global society built on mutual and instrumental exchange, he believed, would yield inequality and conflicts of interest. Thus, unlike his precursors, he suggested a normative and organic link between individuals and identified the state with popular sovereignty. He also claimed that national self-sufficiency would prevent war. A world federation, he argued, was unfortunately not a viable system. It would involve governmental centralization, which would in turn repress democratic and individual expression. Despite his political and normative contribution to internationalism, his work ultimately perpetuated the initial fissure between global and political arrangements.

Phase 2. The advent of the American and, more importantly, the French Revolutions concretized Rousseau's republican aspirations. This achievement provided the French revolutionaries with the necessary confidence to reconcile political and economic rights not only in a representative domestic structure but also worldwide. Internationalism was now understood as advancing all of these issues. The writings of Kant, Paine, and Robespierre epitomized this new vision. Yet their aspirations were soon to be frustrated by domestic social cleavages (widened by the revolutionaries' inability to reconcile economic and political rights) and by the Jacobins', and later Napoleon's, failure to extend the republican spirit of liberty beyond the borders of France.

Phase 3. In this tumultuous climate, Burke, Fichte, and de Maistre, though starting from different approaches, ended up announcing the regression of internationalism. They replaced universal rights with cultural and nationalist claims. With other romantic thinkers, these intellectuals ultimately ossified the original gap between acceptable moral behavior in the domestic area and the global domain, and the breach between political equality and economic rights. Furthermore, by disregarding republicanism as a fundamental political institution for instituting universal human rights, they left political society and the global field open for the growth of particularist and relativist tendencies, for the development of nationalist and imperialist pursuits.

In brief, the first phase indicates the instrumental and economic character of internationalism, maintaining the split between the domestic and global spheres. The second phase adds a normative attribute to internationalism and strives to unify domestic and foreign affairs by developing universal political and economic rights, premised on equality. The third phase shows France's practical failure to reconcile this agenda in the domestic as well as the global sphere. It thus allows the unrestrained development of nationalism.

The liberal tension between universal human rights, developed during the Enlightenment, and nationalism, as conceived during the nineteenth century, is well exemplified by Hegel's *Philosophy of Right.* In short, Hegel's work illustrates the conflict between the particular-

ist and universalist trends, the global and political tension of internationalism; it also shows liberals' and general popular discontent with
the Napoleonic empire; and, finally, it serves as a springboard for the
understanding of internationalism as developed during the Industrial
Revolution by the emerging socialist movements. The exploration of
how international socialism followed the historical pattern of liberal
internationalism is, however, reserved for a future study.

Conclusion

The Great Fusion: A Commentary on Hegel's *Philosophy of Right*

Napoleon provided European poets and philosophers with the perfect hero. Hegel, Schelling, d'Azeglio, Byron, and Hölderin saw in Napoleon the historical hero fulfilling the destiny of the French Revolution: he was the man who expressed and actualized the need of his time, the one who linked individual freedom with universal reason, the one who fused internationalism with the claim for national unity. Napoleon introduced a degree of civil and religious freedom, abolished feudal taxes, developed economic and bureaucratic structures, and promised national emancipation throughout Europe. Hegel, however, recognized that the new states established by Napoleon were only a poor caricature of a modern sovereign state.

The reestablishment of the old dynasties during the Congress of Vienna in 1815 suppressed the "liberties" inaugurated by the French emperor. The major powers that defeated Napoleon were determined to produce an aristocratic balance of power throughout the European continent, to prevent its domination by a single power. The German states, thirty-nine in number, were joined in a loose confederation, in which each member remained virtually sovereign — a situation that precluded resolution of the Austro-Prussian states' rivalry. Further, the Congress ignored the yearning of German nationalists for a unified fatherland. For some Germans, Italians, Spaniards, and others the question was, then, how to maintain a commitment to the most progressive values of the French Revolution when the conditions for their realization had vanished; in short, how to secure Napoleon's reforms in a national order.

Hegel's *Philosophy of Right* illustrated this problem and attempted to provide an answer. It was concerned with the problem of how to unify, in a liberal state, the internationalist ideals unleashed during the French Revolution with the nationalist awareness that emerged in the wake of the Napoleonic episode. Hegel unfortunately did not succeed in reconciling internationalism and nationalism. His work instead illustrated the thesis developed in this book: internationalism, as advocated by early liberalism, incorporates particularist forces that would lead to its fragmentation and to the development of nationalist ideologies. Thus understood, internationalism remained a futile theoretical abstraction.

The *Philosophy of Right* has given rise to much controversy. For example, Karl Popper and Charles Taylor saw in Hegel's political study an open attack on universalism and liberal principles and an apology for romanticism, nationalism, and totalitarianism.[1] Herbert Marcuse and Shlomo Avineri defended Hegel's commitment to the universal principles of liberalism and the Enlightenment.[2] These opposed perspectives suggest the need to transcend both interpretations. Hegel asserted elsewhere that "philosophy is the epoch comprehended in thought," and his own work in fact reflected both the liberal and the romantic social forces of his time. It could also be suggested that Hegel's work sought to combine these apparently opposite movements with a dialectic discourse, that is, between liberalism and romanticism, internationalism and nationalism.

The revolutionaries, by denying the past, and the romantic thinkers, by rejecting the present, presupposed that history had been discontinued.[3] The French Revolution, Hegel asserted, was not a historical "accident," but it provided important momentum for historical evolution. Yet, in the *Philosophy of Right*, Hegel's dialectical method— which allowed him to unify the Enlightenment's desire for a better future with the Romantic's yearning for a glorious past—was frozen in the political aspirations of his time. The goal of philosophy was ultimately placed as a "rose in the cross of the present."[4] The "owl of

Minerva" could finally spread "its wings with the falling of the dusk" (section 270, p. 12).

Reason, Tradition, and Christianity

The movement of history would find its destination, argued Hegel, in the unified Prussian state. History had been propelled by the action of contradictory forces, by reason and the subjective will, reason and tradition, reason and religion, the Absolute Idea (universalism), and particularism. The Absolute Idea, or Reason, unfolds itself in the world and becomes real; and "the real becomes rational." Reason and the state, announced Hegel, would become one and the same in the speculative present. The liberal conflict between reason, on the one hand, and tradition and religion, on the other, would finally be reconciled.

With the French revolutionaries, Hegel condemned religion for offering an ideal life in another world, for suggesting "accidental and transitory life on earth" (section 270, p. 166). He thus disputed those who justified the state in terms of religion. "No doctrine," he maintained in this respect, "is fitted to produce so much confusion, more fitted indeed to exalt confusion itself to be the constitution of the state and the proper form of knowledge" (section 270, p. 164). On the contrary, the state was the institution where religion could flourish without impeding on the rule of law (section 270, p. 166).

Hegel, however, evoked the romantic spirit of Burke and de Maistre in his attempt to rehabilitate religion and the church as cohesive forces of social stability: "Since religion is an integrating factor of the state, implanting a sense of unity in the depths of men's mind, the state should even require all its citizens to belong to a church" (section 270, p. 168). Religion, he added, brings a sense of tradition and order to the state. Hegel sought in "true" and "just" religion the confirmation and justification of the rational state. Echoing, in different ways, Fichte, Rousseau, and de Maistre, he defined the state as the "divine will made present." Stating that "man must venerate the state as a secular deity" (addition to section 272, p. 285), Hegel, like those three predecessors, ended up deifying reason — in his case, in the form of the unifying German Prussian state.

He synthesized the abstract quest for universal reason, as espoused by Kant, Paine, Robespierre, and other enlightened writers, with the sensuous aspect of the subjective will, as advocated by Fichte, Schelling, and other thinkers of the counter-Enlightenment. The rational and universal postulates of the Prussian state were thus placed onto a subjective foundation. "The state," he argued, "must be treated as a great architectonic structure, as a hieroglyph of reason which reveals itself in reality" (addition to section 279, p. 288). Yet the organization of the state would also be the subjective application of the Absolute will, or History.

Following Kant, Paine, and Robespierre, Hegel also remarked that right, as achieved in the state, was nothing more than an extrapolation from the subjective will and individual impulses upon the moral realm. Right, he stated, is the product of individuals' subjective impulse toward "property and morality," toward the "impulse of love between the sexes," toward the "impulse of sociability" (section 19, p. 29). This impulse toward sociability led to the entire sphere of rights — namely, the right of the individual, the family, civil society, and the state. "Subjective will invested in the material world," he argued in the spirit of Kant, "purifies abstract universality from its crudity and barbarity" (section 20, p. 29). In the same breath, however, he added, against the Romantics, that subjective will, which does not aim its action toward a universal ethics, remains "self-enclosed and devoid of actuality" (section 149, p. 107).

The dialectic relationship between the Enlightenment and romantic worldviews, between the "abstract will" and the subjective will — or sensuous realm — led to a further development of bourgeois consciousness, exemplified by Hegel's discussion of property. In the act of possessing, individuals translated their subjective will as reason in the empirical world. Free will now becomes identified with acquired property. "I possess my life and my body, like other things, only insofar as my will is in them" (section 47, p. 43). It is in the process of acquisition, usage, and alienation of property that freedom becomes objectified and gains an external and sensuous quality.

This is not to imply that Hegel was oblivious to the tensions that arise between individuals as a result of conflict over property. He believed, as we shall see, in the importance of coordinating personal rights (the universal) with appropriated possessions (the particular). A lack of coordination, he insisted, can result in "wrong." By mutual agreement, individuals can decide how to commonly dispose of their property:

The sphere of contract is made up by this mediation whereby I hold property not merely by means of a thing and my subjective will; but by means of another person's will as well and so hold it in virtue of my participation in a common will. (Section 71, p. 57)

The development of just and moral contract elevated the individual's particularist claim for property rights to a universal dimension. This concern led Hegel to envision the fusion between universality and particularity in a different realm in terms of social and political institutions.

Between the Civil Society and the *Volksstaat*

The bourgeois conflict between reason and the subjective will ensured the successive progression and actualization of the Prussian state. Hegel's political inquiry began with the family (the sensuous and immediate universality), was developed in the civil society (the realm of self-interest and particularity), and culminated in the state (the fusion of the two preceding social stages). Society derived immediately from the union of natural opposites (male and female) through natural attraction (the immediate and sensuous sphere). The ethical institutions of the family — resulting inevitably from this natural attraction — can be considered as a groundwork for all ramifications of ethical life in society. Hegel conceived development of the private realm, the family, in three stages: love and marriage, property and capital, and dissolution.

The family is once again considered as the product of both the sensuous realm and reason. The romantic attribute of the existence of the in-itself, which implied an immediate sense of self-unity and a subjective will oriented toward particularism and individualism, is retained in the existence of the female. He further defined the existence of the male as the Enlightenment's perception of the existence for-itself, which implied a self-reflection of personality and an orientation toward universality.

The union of the existence in-itself of the female with the existence for-itself of the male corresponded to a fusion between the particular and the universal (or the Absolute Idea). It is through love that this union should be celebrated, commented Hegel, influenced by Romantics such as Schlegel and Goethe:

> Love means in general terms the consciousness of my unity with another, so that I am not in selfish isolation but win my self-confidence only as the renunciation of my independence and through knowing myself as the unity of myself with another and of the other with me. (Addition to section 158, p. 261)

Marriage becomes necessary to institutionalize love in an objective form. The new formal unity required property to maintain an aura of permanence and stability—property that might be designated as capital, or estate. Although administered by the husband, argued Hegel, the family capital has to be held in common:

> It is not merely property which a family possesses, as a universal and enduring person, it requires possession specifically determined as permanent and secure, i.e., it requires capital. (Section 170, p. 116)

By integrating romantic love and property concerns, the bourgeois family represented the preliminary stage of social union. It was also a natural place for the perpetuation of human relations through the process of child rearing. The family, claimed Hegel in the manner of Burke and de Maistre, established a stable relationship and tradition, thereby ensuring the continuity of tradition. Yet the family created its own antinomy. Children grow up and establish property-holding families of their own. The "natural" unity of the family thus breaks into a multitude of competing groups of proprietors, who essentially aim at their particular advantage:

> The family disintegrates ... into a plurality of families, each of which conducts itself as in principle a self-subsistent concrete person, and therefore as externally related to its neighbours. This is the stage of difference. This gives us, to use abstract language in the first place, the determination of particularity which is related to universality but in such a way that universality is its basic principles through still only an inward principle; for that reason, the universal merely shows in the particular as its form. (Section 87, p. 122)

From the perspective of the Absolute spirit, civil society is naturally prior to the emergence of the state, insofar as differentiation is naturally prior to unity-in-differentiation. Historically speaking, civil society may be temporarily posterior to some sort of state unity. The ancient monolithic states were based on religious or ethnic unity (e.g., the Babylonian empire), or on intellectual unity (e.g., the pre-Socratic Greek model). "In either case, they rested on primitive unsophisticated intuition" (section 185, p. 123). The emergence of self-reflection and civil society presents itself as a threat to social harmony. In Plato's *Republic,* individuals' aspirations and private property were to be subordinated to an extreme type of political unity. The idea of subjective freedom and property rights dawned in an inward form in Christianity and gradually gained an objective reality in the Roman world. From then on, individuals began to assert their rights and power over the early hierarchical, monolithic states. The development of personal freedom and subjective freedom in civil society shaped the instrumental character of internationalism:

> Individuals in their capacity as burghers in this state are private persons whose end is their own interest. This end is *mediated* through the universal which thus *appears* as *means....* In these circumstances, the interest of the Idea ... lies in the process whereby their singularity and their natural condition are raised, as a result of the necessities imposed by nature as well as of arbitrary needs, to formal freedom and formal universality of knowing and willing—the process whereby their particularity is educated to subjectivity. (Section 187, pp. 124–25)

The instrumental character of civil society was also emphasized by Hegel's discussion of the social system of needs. Hegel examined that aspect of human life in which the needs and therefore the interests of the individual govern her or his relationship with other individuals. He thus understood, in more concrete terms than Kant, Paine, and Robespierre, the inherent nature of civil society as "the battlefield where everyone's private needs and interests meet everyone else's" (section 289, p. 189). The burgher, he insisted, is a man related to other men strictly as a means to his own well-being. This is the sphere of economic life, whose regularities are expressed in the laws of the political, and whose content is the pursuit of selfish ends (cf. additions to section 182, p. 354).

In civil society, however, persons, unlike animals, have the ability to get beyond their restricted "natural" needs, by differentiating, universalizing, and categorizing their needs. The mediation and generation of needs through consciousness implies that, contrary to animal needs, human needs are infinite. Individuals have the ability to discern and to evaluate needs ad infinitum—a process leading inevitably to artificially induced want, deprivation, and depravity. The multiplicity of needs increases social interdependence, for each individual is free and at the same time dependent upon all others; the well-being or ill-being of each is defined by money and is secured only in its economic context. This position represented Hegel's instrumental aspect of universality.

Hegel's view of civil society, expressing the insatiable quality of individual need, stood in contrast to the romantic idealization of the state of nature—which was perceived as a model of unity and equilibrium between individuals and their needs:

> The idea has been advanced that in respect of his needs man lived in freedom with the so-called 'state of nature' when his needs were supposed to be confined to what are known as the simple necessities of nature.... The view takes no account of the moment of liberation intrinsic to work.... And apart from this, it is false because to confine to mere physical needs the existence as such and their direct satisfaction would simply be the condition in which the mental is plunged in the natural and so would be one of savagery and unfreedom, while freedom itself is to be found only in the reflection of the mind into itself, in mind's distinction from nature, and in the reflection of mind in nature. (Section 194, p. 128)

It was precisely the Enlightenment's quest for knowledge, Hegel insisted, and not the serene and satiated taste of romantic thought, that was conducive to the endless pursuit of commodities.

Hegel recognized the possible conflicts and injustice that might occur in civil society, for such a place was not the product of free, rational individuals but of chance, power, and arbitrariness. An observer of the conflicts over property that divided the Third Estate during the French Revolution, Hegel realized that an unequal distribution of wealth could undermine the principle of universal and equal rights:

> When the standard of living of a large mass of people falls below a certain subsistence level—a level regulated automatically as the one necessary for a member of the society—and when there is a consequent loss of the sense of right and wrong, of honesty and the self-respect which makes a man insist on maintaining himself by his work and effort, the result is the creation of a rabble of paupers. At the same time this brings with it, at the other end of the social

scale, conditions which greatly facilitate the concentration of dis-
proportionate wealth in a few hands. (Section 244, p. 150)

However, by equating, early on, freedom with the appropriation
of property, Hegel implicitly justified—no less than Kant, Paine, and
Robespierre—the accumulation of property as a never-ending expression of individual free will and needs. Like them, he failed to see
that the indiscriminate identification of property rights as political
freedom was a contributing factor to the tensions he deplored in civil
society. He reiterated Grotius's and Vico's prediction that political
societies are driven to seek solutions to domestic problems by expanding their foreign markets:

> This inner dialectic of society thus drives it—or at any rate drives a
> specific society—to push beyond its own limits and seek markets,
> and so its necessary means of subsistence, in other lands which are
> deficient in the goods it has overproduced, or else generally back-
> ward in industry, &c. (Section 246, p. 151)

Such an instrumental perspective was still incomplete from the
perspective of the historical development of internationalism.

Yet Hegel's analysis of poverty greatly influenced the socialist
thinkers of the mid-nineteenth century. Hegel, like Marx, explained
the origin of social differentiation in terms of the divisions of labor
and social production. Class divisions, he stated, determined not only
a people's economic life but its consciousness as well. A person's consciousness is molded in accordance with her or his membership in a
particular class. "When we say that a man must be a somebody," he
wrote, "we mean that he should belong to some specific social class,
since to be a somebody means to have a substantive being"; otherwise one's universality cannot be actualized (addition to section 207,
p. 271).

The three classes—the agricultural class, the business class, and
the bureaucracy—thus reflect three different modes of consciousness: conservatism, individualism, and universalism. Departing from
Rousseau's idealization of agrarian production, Hegel declared that
the social activity of the agricultural class, enclosed in immediate and
natural relations—the family and the soil—developed a stable and
conservative consciousness. Thus "the agricultural mode of subsistence remains one which owes comparatively little to reflection and

independence of will" (section 203, p. 131). In the business class, however, a higher level of consciousness was displayed:

> The business class has for its task the adaptation of raw materials, and for its means of livelihood, it is thrown back on its work, on reflection and intelligence, and essentially on the mediation of one man's needs and work with those of others. For what this class produces and enjoys, it has mainly itself, its own industry, to thank. (Section 204, p. 132)

Hegel considered the class of civil servants to be the universal class. It was a class that encapsulated the universal interest of the community:

> The individual functionaries and agents are attached to their offices not on the strength of their immediate personality, but only on the strength of their universal and objective qualities. (Section 277, p. 179)

Despite the socioeconomic awareness of class differences, Hegel, unlike Marx and his followers, bestowed enormous importance upon the middle class, businessmen, and civil servants.[5] He regarded them as the guardians of freedom, as the "pillar of the state, so far as honesty and intelligence are concerned" (additions to section 297, p. 291). The foundation of a just and stable state rested upon the middle class. Conversely, authoritarianism and instability in Russia resulted from the fact that the country had no countervailing middle class, but "a mass of slaves on the one hand and a mass of rulers on the other hand" (ibid.).

Hegel admitted that the bourgeois aspect of the state was still insufficient to resolve the tensions prevailing in civil society. He knew that once civil society develops, its main interest becomes concentrated in the expediency and satisfaction of individual needs. Various means of communication and standardized procedures are then developed. The division of labor, however, becomes so specialized that certain elements of society lose their human quality; the interests of producers and consumers come into conflict; families are uprooted, and individuals are thrown into an industrial milieu where the law is "everyone for oneself."

The classes, Hegel thought, thus had to be regulated by external mechanisms that were more powerful than the economic ones. His concerns prepared for the transition to the political ordering of society. In the section on the administration of justice, he maintained that laws have to be transformed in accordance with the organization of civil society. He insisted that once rights become law they assert their universal determinacy. He agreed with the Enlightenment legal scholars Grotius and Vico that laws should be guided by universalist drives that secure individual freedom and interests. Whereas in civil society the Absolute Idea has become particularized, in the administration of justice it has recovered its lost universality.

Hegel introduced as well the "police" (or public authority) as an external means for securing the interests of the universal. The aim of the police is to keep particularity under control; its justification is the ever-present possibility of wrong, that is, the transgression of particular rights. The police represent the interest of the whole against social forces that might threaten the proper functioning of the social and economic process of production. Policing is not, however, the only remedy. The uncompromising character of civil society has to be supervised by another institution: the "corporation."

The corporation is conceptualized along the lines of the old guild system. It consists of business corporations, labor, and professional organizations. Its purpose is to bring unity among the competing estates or to enforce bureaucratic decisions of the unifying state. As Marx rightly suggested, the corporation is the bureaucracy of the state; it is an "imaginary state alongside the real state."[6] Whereas the defense of particularity in terms of the universal is embodied in the police (or public authority), the corporation represents only a partial and restricted universality shaped in terms of the particular. The final reconciliation between particularity and universality is to be found in the state. Internationalism is now determined by the political institutions of the state.

Generally speaking, an individual in civil society counts as an individual by virtue of her or his individuality alone. It is only in the *Volksstaat* that she or he gains a national identity, becomes Jewish, Catholic, Protestant, German, Italian, and so on.[7] In the state, the individual is transformed into a *citoyen*. Individuals gradually transcended their particularity to join the organic and national will. Hegel congratulated Rousseau for having made the rational will the universal principle of the state:

The merit of Rousseau's contribution to the search for this is that, by adducing the will as the principle of the state, he is adducing a principle which has thought for both its form and its content, a principle indeed which is thinking itself, not a principle, like a gregarious instinct, for instance, or divine authority, which has thought as its form only.[8]

He believed, however, that Rousseau had failed to recognize the true relationship between the state and the civil society. Rousseau was unable to achieve a positive resolution of the contradiction between the *volonté générale* and the *volonté de tous*. Hegel argued that Rousseau understood the will of the all as the common will of the citizens, but not as something truly organic and general. Rousseau's *Social Contract*, commented Hegel, remains in the sphere of the capricious "indeterminate" will, and the results of forming a state with such a principle were manifested dramatically in the French "Reign of Terror." Hegel insisted that the state is a universal will, which ought to bind individuals into a popular spirit (*Volksgeist*). It must be differentiated from civil society, where the particular will is the only end and driving force.[9] Without judging the validity of Hegel's interpretation of Rousseau, it is interesting to note the German philosopher's concern for transcending the individualist character of civil society in the name of an organic unity of the people.

Hegel noted that an explicit unity and harmony was lacking in ancient states, in which insufficient respect was given to the particular, to the subjective, that is, to right and freedom. Universality should be explicitly linked with particularity in the state, insofar as the universal organism of the state is constructed on a twofold social foundation — the family (the universal) and the civil society (the particular).

The state, however, was not a static end in itself. The structural division of political institutions reproduced once again the tension between particularism and universalism. The power to determine and to establish the universal becomes embodied in the legislature; the power to subsume single cases and the spheres of particularity is encapsulated in the executive; the power of subjectivity, as the will with the power of the ultimate decision, is represented by the crown, that is, the monarchy. Hegel modified the traditional checks-and-balances trinity of powers: the judicial, the legislative, and the executive. The role of the executive power represented by the crown overlapped with the first two branches of power. Influenced by the unifying will of

Napoleon, he claimed that social alliance could be achieved only in the subjective persona of the king: the "absolute moment of the whole is not individuality in general but a single individual, the monarch."[10] Admitting the possible intellectual weakness of monarchs, he nonetheless endorsed their symbolic supervision over the rule of interested parties in the civil society.

By the same token, his insistence on setting the unity of the nation above any criticism led him to deify the nation in a romantic fashion. The constitution of the nation, he commented, "must be treated as something existent in and by itself, as divine therefore, and constant, and so exalted above the sphere of things that are made" (section 273, p. 178). Hegel's deified nation, however, did not parallel future fascist states. He strove to avoid social development that could lead to such an authoritarian nation. In this respect, his repudiation of Montesquieu's, Burke's, and de Maistre's (if not Fichte's) idea of the "monarchy of honor," a feudal monarchy based on privilege, should not be overlooked. The monarchy that Hegel endorsed was of a constitutional kind. He indeed claimed that "the development of the state to constitutional monarchy is the achievement of the modern world, a world in which the substantial Idea has won the infinite form" (section 273, p. 176). He postulated the unity of the state under the monarchy only to ensure the union of the universal with the freedom of the particular.

Hegel's exaltation of the state's political power has to be understood in the context of his time. The Congress of Vienna had left Germany fragmented and divided by aristocratic rivalries. In the same mercantilist spirit of the seventeenth century, Hegel, like Grotius and Vico, believed that a monarchy was conducive to the idea of national unification. Thus perceived, the monarch was entrusted to found the modern German state and to pursue the politics of freedom inspired by the French Revolution, which had been curtailed by the Restoration.

Hegel's commitment both to a strong state and to individual freedom is exemplified as well by his discussion of patriotism. Unlike Burke and de Maistre, Hegel did not regard patriotism as the devotion and sacrifice of individuals to an external being, to the state. The patriotic individual, he agreed with Fichte, thinks of the state as the full and necessary expression of his own individuality. Individuals do not view the state as something extrinsic to themselves, but rather as part of their own substance. This identification, and not the extraordinary fervor that induces individuals to make all kinds of dramatic sacrifices for their country, is the essence of patriotism:

> Patriotism is often understood to mean only a readiness for exceptional sacrifices and actions. Essentially, however, it is the sentiment which, in relationships of our daily life and under ordinary conditions, habitually recognizes that the community is one's substantive groundwork and end. (Section 268, p. 164)

The state constitution, Hegel maintained—in keeping with Kant, Paine, and Robespierre—generates and sustains patriotic sentiment. It is the true organism of the political sphere, insofar as it is the universal life substance.

His concept of patriotism fused and transcended the patriotic views of the Jacobins and the nationalist aspirations of the Romantics. For the Jacobins, patriotism was an exaltation of human rights throughout the globe; for the Romantics, nationalism was a celebration of the cultural superiority of one nation over another. Hegel derived his universal and legalistic enthusiasm from the Jacobins. From the Romantics, he retained the restriction of social concerns to the domain of the national.

One could still maintain that Hegel's support for a strong national state was opposed to the liberal concept of the state, envisioned as a means to satisfy the interest of individuals.[11] It is more plausible to argue, however, that his view of the state was developed in harmony with his view of bourgeois civil society. Thus, on the one hand, property owners seek to minimize the state's intervention in civil society, to ensure the free flow of commodities and to advance their own interests. On the other hand, the state is employed at times to unify society against military threats, for foreign aggression, or to protect domestic producers from foreign competition.

Internationalism and Its Betrayal

In the global realm, the struggle for recognition in civil society is rehearsed among sovereign states in the form of war. Hegel suggested that war was the ultimate test of sovereignty. War was neither an absolute evil nor some accident, but, from the standpoint of the Absolute Idea, a necessity that allowed the integration of interests that civil society could not achieve:

War is not to be regarded as an absolute evil and as a purely external accident, which itself therefore has some accidental cause, be it
injustices, the passions of nations or the holders of power, &c, or
something which ought not to be. It is what it is by nature accidental that accidents happen, and the fate whereby they happen is thus
a necessity. Here as elsewhere, the point of view from which things
seem pure accidents vanishes if we look at them in the light of the
concept and philosophy, because philosophy knows accident for a
show and sees in it essence, necessity.[12]

This should not suggest that Hegel denigrated the application of laws
that could temper wars; he supported the proviso of *ius gentium*,
which ensured the limited nature of war. Influenced by Grotius's *Law
of War and Peace*, he also argued that during wartime the safety of
envoys and agreements about the taking of prisoners should be re-
spected. Customary laws supervising trade relationship and movements of persons should prevail during peacetime.

Hegel maintained at the same time a skeptical attitude regarding
political solutions to the occurrence of war. Even if nations should
create such an international judicial power through a "league of nations," that power could never have absolute jurisdictional authority,
since the authority of the state is already absolute. Hegel therefore
was cynical concerning the prospect of a world confederation, as
prescribed by Kant, or of any possibility of political internationalism
in the global realm:

Kant had an idea for securing "perpetual peace" by a League of
Nations to adjust every dispute. It was to be a power recognized by
each individual state, and was to arbitrate in all cases of dissension
in order to make it impossible for disputes to resort to war in order
to settle them. The idea presupposes an accord between states; this
would rest on moral or religious or other grounds and considerations, but in any case would always be dependent ultimately on a
particular sovereign will and for that reason would remain infected
with contingency. (Section 337, pp. 213–14)

Grotius's, Vico's, and Rousseau's skepticism about the feasibility of a
supranational authority developed after the decay of the universal
Christendom. Hegel's pessimism regarding the application of such a
project coincided with the collapse of Napoleon's Continental System. Yet, by implicitly rejecting an authoritative jurisdiction superior
to the national sovereignty, Hegel perpetuated a double standard

developed by the seventeenth- and eighteenth-century thinkers: one rule for the state and another for the global arena. Such duality justified the development of national and instrumental foreign policies and, later on, led to Ranke's and Meinecke's formulation of a German *raison d'état* position.

Hegel saw the emergence of German national politics as the ultimate phase of the Absolute Idea. The national spirit developed in four stages. First, in the oriental world, the immediate state of existence, religion, philosophy, politics, and art are fused; except for static and ossified distinctions, such as castes, no real distinctions are tolerated. Second, the stage of the aesthetic union of immediacy and self-consciousness was developed in the Greek world and extended throughout the various city-states. Third, the Roman world before the time of Christ manifested the conflict between unity and abstract self-consciousness (in the rivalry between the aristocracy and the plebs); it dissolved into ineffectiveness after the advent of Christianity. Fourth, with Fichte and other Romantics, Hegel concluded that the Germanic world manifested the reconciliation of the divine and the human, universality and particularity, in the constitutional monarchy:

> This is the absolute turning point, mind rises out of this situation and grasps the infinite positivity of this its inward character, i.e., it grasps the principle of the unity of the divine nature and the human, the reconciliation of the objective truth and freedom as the truth and freedom appearing within self-consciousness and subjectivity, a reconciliation with the fulfillment of which the principle of the North, the principle of the Germanic peoples, has been entrusted. (Section 358, p. 222)

Hegel conferred on the German people the task of overcoming the universal and particularist drives of his period. The *Philosophy of Right* indeed articulated the development of bourgeois consciousness striving to surmount the progressive forces of the Enlightenment and the subjective will fueled by the romantic tradition. Yet, by viewing the *Volksstaat* as the panacea, Hegel ended up promoting the Prussian state over the claim of the internationalist project, the particular over the universal. He assigned the responsibility for assessing states' wrongdoing to "the history of the world which is the world's court of judgement" (section 340, p. 216). "For the only higher judge is the universal absolute mind" (section 192, p. 297). Beyond the national sphere, internationalism follows the route of the Absolute Idea, the route of an ephemeral utopia.

The late nineteenth- and early twentieth-century socialist thinkers attempted to provide a concrete definition of internationalism and, with the establishment of the First and Second Internationals, to create corresponding institutions. It seems, however, that socialists were to follow a pattern similar to the one adopted by their liberal forerunners. World War I rehearsed the socialists' abandonment of internationalism, dramatically staged by Stalin's "socialism in one country."[13] Internationalism remained an empty illusion, an idea condemned to the life of abstraction, a dream betrayed by even its staunchest defenders.

Notes

Preface

1. Immanuel Kant, "The Idea of Universal History with a Cosmopolitan Purpose", in *Kant's Political Writings*, ed. Hans Reiss, trans. H. B. Nisbet (Cambridge, Mass.: Cambridge University Press; repr. 1983), p. 51.

2. For an interesting account of the socialist perspective on internationalism, see Stephen E. Bronner, *Socialism Unbound* (New York: Routledge, 1990).

3. See Hans Kohn, *The Idea of Nationalism* (Toronto: Collier-Macmillan, 1969); Carlton Hayes, *Essays on Nationalism* (New York: Macmillan, 1933), chapter 1; Elie Kedourie, *Nationalism* (London: Hutchinson, 1960); Anthony Smith, *Theories of Nationalism* (New York: Holmes and Meier, 1983); E. J. Hobsbawm, *Nations and Nationalism since 1780: Programme, Myth, Reality* (Cambridge: Cambridge University Press, 1990); Benedict Anderson, *Imagined Communities* (London: Verso, 1986); Ernest Gellner, *Nation and Nationalism* (Ithaca, N.Y.: Cornell University Press, 1983); Julia Kristeva, *Nations without Nationalism* (New York: Columbia University Press, 1993); Liah Greenfeld, *Nationalism: Five Roads to Modernity* (Cambridge, Mass.: Cambridge University Press, 1992). For a comment on nationalism and patriotism by Hobsbawm, see note 39, chapter 3.

4. Despite the various meanings of liberalism in different countries, one might broadly divide liberals into those who see political freedom and property rights as something belonging to the individual that is to be defended against the encroachments of the state, and those who see political freedom and property rights as something belonging to society that the state, as the central instrument of social betterment, can be made to enlarge and improve. While some fit clearly into one of these categories, the greatest names in the history of liberal thought, including John Stuart Mill, are poised between these two positions. Despite differences within the liberal tradition, one could argue that these ideas often served to defend the interests of the middle class.

5. For a communitarian understanding of liberalism, see Charles Taylor, *Multiculturalism and the Politics of Recognition*, ed. Amy Gutman (Princeton, N.J.: Princeton University Press, 1993), and Michael Walzer, *Just and Unjust War* (New York: Basic Books, 1977). Alan Gilbert, *Democratic Individuality* (Cambridge: Cambridge University Press, 1990) provides an interesting criticism of Walzer on communitarian relativism. In "Must Global Politics Constrain Democracy?" in (*Political Theory* [February 1992], pp. 8–37), he criticizes liberal realists' lack of commitment for democratic value in their assessment of states' behavior in the international community.

6. See, in this respect, Micheline Ishay, "European Integration: The Enlightenment Legacy," in *History of European Ideas*, no. 208 (1994).

Introduction

1. E. J. Hobsbawm, *Nations and Nationalism since 1780: Programme, Myth, Reality* (Cambridge: Cambridge University Press, 1990).

2. Ernest Gellner, *Nation and Nationalism* (Ithaca, N.Y.: Cornell University Press, 1983), pp. 1–2.

3. Liah Greenfeld, *Nationalism: Five Roads to Modernity* (Cambridge, Mass.: Cambridge University Press, 1992), pp. 9–12.

4. See Benedict Anderson, *Imagined Communities* (London: Verso, 1986), pp. 17–40; Hobsbawm, *Nations and Nationalism*, p. 87. For a more extensive discussion of patriotism, see Hobsbawm's chapter 3.

5. See Karl Deutsch, *Nationalism and Social Communication: An Inquiry into the Foundation of Nationality* (Cambridge, Mass.: Cambridge University Press, 1966); Robert Keohane and Joseph Nye, *Power and Interdependence* (Boston: Little, Brown, 1977); Immanuel Wallerstein, *The Modern World System* (New York: Academic Press, 1980); and Andre Gunder Frank, *Dependent Accumulation and Underdevelopment* (New York: Monthly Review Press, 1979). In "Must Global Politics Constrain Democracy?" (*Political Theory* [February 1992], pp. 8–37), Alan Gilbert also provides an interesting critique on realism and dependency theories.

6. Cf. Thomas J. Schlereth, *The Cosmopolitan Ideal in the Enlightenment* (London: University of Notre Dame Press, 1977), p. xix.

7. For an insightful account of the collapse of the Roman Empire, see Perry Anderson, *Passages from Antiquity to Feudalism* (London: Verso, 1974).

8. Antony Black, *Political Thought in Europe 1250–1450* (Cambridge: Cambridge University Press, 1992), p. 162.

9. My use of the term "political society" corresponds to Gramsci's. By political society (or the state), he meant the political institutions of the state, which "is the instrument for conforming civil society to the economic structure, but it is necessary for the state to 'be willing' to do this; i.e., for the representatives of the change that has taken place in the economic structure to be in control of the state" (Antonio Gramsci, *Selections from the Prison Notebooks*, ed. and trans. Quintin Hoare and Geoffrey Nowell Smith [New York: International Publishers, 1971], p. 208; see also pp. 12–13, 206–9).

10. It will suffice to mention the works of Paul Hazard, *La Pensée Européenne au XVIIIème Siècle* (Paris: Fayard, 1963), pp. 13–50; Ernst Cassirer, *The Myth of the State* (New Haven: Yale University Press, 1946), pp. 176–86, and *The Philosophy of the Enlightenment* (Princeton, N.J.: Princeton University Press, 1951); Peter Gay, *The Enlightenment* (New York: Alfred A. Knopf, 1967), pp. 75–126; and Thomas J. Schlereth, *The Cosmopolitan Ideal in the Enlightenment*.

11. Lucien Goldmann, *The Human Sciences and Philosophy* (London: Chaucer Press, 1969), p. 35.

12. Martin Luther, *Ausgewählte Deutsche Schriften,* ed. Hans Volz (Tübingen: Niemeyer, 1966); Jean Calvin, *Institutes of the Christian Religion,* trans. John Allen, 6th American ed. (Philadelphia: Presbyterian Board of Publication and Sabbath-School Work, 1911).

13. See René Descartes, *Discourse on Method,* trans. Lawrence J. Lafleur (New York: Liberal Arts Press, 1956); Samuel Pufendorf, *De officio hominus et civis juxta legem naturalem* (Cantalorigiae: Ex Officiana Joan Hayes ... Impensis Joan Creed, 1682); and Francis Bacon, *Novum Organum,* trans. M. D. (London: University Micro-films International), printed for Thomas Lee, 1876.

14. See Thomas Hobbes, *The Leviathan,* intro. A. D. Lindsay (New York: Dutton, 1950); and John Locke, *The Second Treatise of Government* (New York: Macmillan, 1956).

15. See Alberico Gentili, *De jure belli tres,* translation of the edition of 1612 by John C. Rolfe, introduction by Coleman Phillipson (New York: Oceana, 1964); Emmerich de Vattel, *The Law of Nations* (London: W. Clark and Sons, 1811); and Christian von Wolff, *Gesammelte kleine philosophische Schriften* (Hildesheim, N.Y.: Olms, 1981).

16. Although the use of this concept may seem anachronistic in a precapitalist age, it accurately describes the sector of the Third Estate that belonged neither to the peasantry nor to the affluent bourgeoisie.

17. Giambattista Vico, *Opere,* ed. Fausto Nicolini (Milan and Naples: Riccardo Riccardi, 1953).

18. See Rousseau's *Écrits sur l'Abbé de St.-Pierre,* in *Œuvres complètes,* ed. Bernard Gagnebin and Marcel Raymond (Paris: Gallimard, 1964).

19. Emmanuel Joseph Sieyès, *Qu'est-ce que le Tiers État?* ed. Roberto Zapperi (Geneva: Droz, 1976).

20. François-Marie Arouet de Voltaire, *Œuvres complètes* (Paris: chez Th. Desoer, 1817); Denis Diderot and Jean le Rond d'Alembert, *Encyclopedia* (New York: Pergamon Press, 1985).

21. J. G. Forster, *Ansichten vom Niederrhein, von Brabant, Flandern, Holland, England und Frankreich in April, Mai und Juni 1790,* 2 vols. Leipzig: n.p., 1790; and Gotthold Ephraim Lessing, *Nathan der Weise* (Berlin: Wagenbach, 1977).

22. See William Wollaston, *Religion of Nature Delineated* (Delmar, N.Y.: Scholars' Facsimiles and Reprints, 1974).

23. See Louis-Antoine-Leon de Saint-Just, *Œuvres complètes de Saint-Just,* intro. and ed. Charles Vellay (Paris: Charpentier et Fasquelle, 1908). See also Jean-Paul Marat, *Textes choisis,* ed. Lucien Scheler (Paris: Éditions de Minuit, 1945).

24. See Marie Joseph Paul Yves Lafayette, *Memoirs of General Lafayette* (Hartford, Conn.: Barber and Robinson, 1825); and Pierre Victurnien Vergniaud, *Œuvres de Vergniaud,* ed. A. Vermorel (Paris: A. Faure, 1867).

25. See Jean-Denis Lanjuinais, *French Revolution and Napoleonic Era Pamphlets on Nationalized Property, 1790–1814* (Ithaca, N.Y.: Cornell University, Department of Rare Books); Honoré-Gabriel Riqueti Mirabeau, *Discours,* ed. François Furet (Paris: n.p., 1973); Georges Jacques Danton, *Œuvres de Danton,* comp. and ed. A. Vermorel (Paris: Cournel, 1866); and Camille Desmoulins, *Œuvres de Camille Desmoulins,* published by Jules Claretie (Paris: Charpentier, 1874).

26. Adam Smith, *The Wealth of Nations,* ed. and intro. Edwin Cannan (New York: Modern Library, 1937).

27. J. G. A. Pocock, *Virtue, Commerce, and History* (New York: Cambridge University Press, 1985), p. 69. See also Albert O. Hirschman, *Passions and Interests* (Princeton, N.J.: Princeton University Press, 1977).

28. François Antoine Boissy d'Anglas, *Loi qui rapporte celle du 27 Mars*; microfilm (Woodbridge, Conn.: Research Publication, 1976).

29. Albert Soboul, *The French Revolution* (Bristol: Western Printing Services, 1974), pp. 453–54.

30. Johann Gottfried von Herder, *Reflection on the Philosophy of the History of Mankind* (Chicago: Chicago University Press, 1968); Johann Wolfgang von Goethe, *On Art and Literature*, ed. John Geary (New York: Suhrkamp, 1986).

31. Friedrich Wilhem von Schelling, *Introduction à la philosophie de la mythologie*, trans. S. Jankelevitch (Paris: Aubier, Éditions Montaigne, 1945); Alessandro Manzoni, *I Promessi Sposi*, trans. Danile J. Connor (New York: Macmillan, 1924); Aleksandr Sergeevich Pushkin, *Eugene Onegin*, trans. V. Nabokov (New York: Pantheon Books, 1964).

32. See Novalis (Friedrich von Hardenberg), *Weltanschauung der Frühromantik*, ed. Paul Kluckhohm (Leipzig: P. Redam, 1932); August Wilhelm von Schlegel, *Neue philosophische Schriften*, ed. Joseph Körner (Frankfurt am Main: Schulte-Bulmke, 1935); Sir Walter Scott, *The Political Writings of Walter Scott*, ed. B. J. Legie Robertson (London: Oxford University Press, 1964); William Wordsworth, *A Wordsworth Selection*, ed. Edith C. Batho (London: University of London, Athlone Press, 1962); and François-René de Chateaubriand, *Grands écrits politiques*, ed. Jean-Paul Clément (Paris: Imprimerie Nationale, 1993).

33. Massimo d'Azeglio, *I miei ricordi* (Milan: Rizzolini, 1956).

1. The Wars of the Reformation and the Spread of Mercantilism

1. Donald W. Treadgold, *A History of Christianity* (Belmont, Mass.: Nordland Publishing Company, 1979), p. 118.

2. Cf. Dante Alighieri, "L'inferno," *The Divine Comedy*, Italian text and translation (Princeton, N.J.: Princeton University Press, 1970), canto 19, line 53; see Hans Lietzmann, *The Founding of the Universal Church*, trans. Bertrand Lee Woolf (New York: Scribner's, 1938); also Edward M. Pickman, *The Mind of Christendom* (London, New York, and Toronto: Oxford University Press, 1937).

3. For further references, see Robert Roswell Palmer and Joel Colton, *History of the Modern World* (New York: Alfred A. Knopf, 1965), pp. 73, 82–85.

4. Treadgold, *A History of Christianity*, chapter 7, pp. 89–100.

5. For valuable accounts of the Reformation, see Alistair McGrath, *Reformation Thought: An Introduction* (Oxford and New York: Basil Blackwell, 1988); Heinrich Boehmer, *Luther and the Reformation in the Light of Modern Research*, trans. E. S. G. Potter (New York: Dial Press, 1930); Charles Hardwick, *A History of the Christian Church during the Reformation* (London: Macmillan, 1877); and Jean Delumeau, *Naissance et Affirmation de la Réforme* (Paris: Presses Universitaires de France, 1965).

6. See Max Weber, *The Protestant Ethic and the Spirit of Capitalism*, trans. Talcott Parsons, with a foreword by R. T. Tawney (London: George Allen and Unwin, 1930).

7. Charles V ruled not only in Germany but also in the Netherlands, Spain, and much of Italy, thus encircling France. The spread of Lutheranism in Germany and the Netherlands was a threat to his Catholic empire; see Palmer and Colton, *History of the Modern World*, pp. 73, 82–85.

8. Ibid., p. 74; see also Treadgold, *A History of Christianity*, pp. 134, 140.
9. See Palmer and Colton, *History of the Modern World*, pp. 122–26, and Treadgold, *A History of Christianity*, pp. 141–47.
10. See Peter Gay, *The Enlightenment* (New York: Alfred A. Knopf, 1967), pp. 156–80; see also Alistair C. Crombie, *Medieval and Early Modern Science* (New York: Doubleday Anchor Books, 1959), 2 vols.
11. Arthur T. Winfree, *The Geometry of Biological Time* (New York: Springer Verlag, 1980), Series Biomathematics, vol. 8, p. 1. See also Alistair C. Crombie, *Augustine to Galileo* (Cambridge, Mass.: Harvard University Press, 1953).
12. Isaac Newton, *The Mathematical Principles of Natural Philosophy* (London: Sherwood, Neely and Jones, 1819).
13. See Eduard J. Diksterhuis, *The Mechanization of the World Picture* (London, Oxford, and New York: Oxford University Press, 1961).
14. For an interesting argument on the unifying concept of the nation-state, see Eli F. Hecksher, *Mercantilism*, trans. Mendel Shapiro (London: George Allen and Unwin, 1935), vol. 1, pp. 19–32.
15. Niccolò Machiavelli, *Il principe,* intro. and notes by Luigi Rosso (Florence: Sansoni, 1958).
16. For a discussion of the conditions of the development of mercantilism, see Hecksher, *Mercantilism,* vol. 7, pp. 326–456; see also Laurence B. Packard, *The Commercial Revolution* (New York: Henry Holt and Company, 1927), pp. 7–20.
17. Cf. Karl Marx, *The German Ideology* (New York: International Publishers, 1939), p. 63.
18. The very name of the bourgeoisie (dweller in a burg or town, hence burgher or bourgeois) reveals its origin.
19. Cf. Palmer and Colton, *History of the Modern World,* pp. 102–3.

2. The Attack on Christendom

1. See Galileo Galilei, *Dialogo sopra i due massimi sistemi del mondo,* ed. F. Flora (Milan: Rizzoli, 1959).
2. See Francis Bacon, *Great Instauration Proomemium Preface, Plan of the Work, and Novum Organum* (Garden City, N.Y.: Doubleday, 1937).
3. See Gottfried Wilhelm von Leibniz, *Philosophische Schriften und Briefe,* ed. Ursula Goldenbaum (Berlin: Akademie Verlag, 1922).
4. See René Descartes, *Discourse on Method,* trans. Lawrence J. Lafleur (New York: Liberal Arts Press, 1956).
5. Hugo Grotius, *The Rights of War and Peace,* ed. A. C. Campbell, intro. David J. Hill and M. Walster (New York: M. W. Dunne Publisher, 1901), book 2, chapter 22, section 14, p. 271.
6. Ibid.
7. Ibid., chapter 20, section 44, p. 249.
8. Ibid., p. 254.
9. Ibid., p. 252.
10. Hugo Grotius, *The Law of War and Peace,* trans. F. W. Keisley, intro. J. B. Scott (New York: Bobbs-Merrill, 1925), Prolegomena 12, p. 141.
11. Grotius's view paralleled Descartes's. In the Fifth Meditation, Descartes wrote: "I see that in some way I have in me the notion of God before that of myself. For how would it be possible that I should know what I doubt and desire, that is to say, that something is lacking to me, and that I am not quite perfect, unless I had within me

some idea of a Being more perfect than myself, in comparison with which I should recognize the deficiencies of my nature?" (*Œuvres complètes* [Paris: Librairie Joseph Gibert, n.d.], vol. 2, p. 149).

12. Grotius, *The Rights of War and Peace,* book 2, chapter 20, p. 248.

13. Ernst Bloch, *Natural Law and Human Dignity,* trans. Dennis J. Schmidt (Cambridge, Mass., and London: MIT Press, 1986), p. 55.

14. Dario Fauci has noted that Vico constantly portrayed himself in his writing as the Catholic anti-Grotius ("Vico and Grotius: Jurisconsult of Mankind," in *Giambattista Vico: An International Symposium,* ed. Giorgio Tagliacozzo and Hayden V. White [Baltimore: Johns Hopkins University Press, 1969], p. 73). For a similar argument, see Benedetto Croce, *La Filosofia di Giambattista Vico* (Bari: Laterza, 1962), pp. 89, 92–93; and Isaiah Berlin, *Vico and Herder: Two Studies in the History of Ideas* (New York: Viking Press, 1976), p. 77.

15. Fausto Nicolini, *La Religiosità di Giambattista Vico* (Bari: Laterza, 1949), Introduction and chapter 2.

16. See Giambattista Vico, *Scienza Nuova,* in *Opere,* ed. Fausto Nicolini (Milan and Naples: Riccardo Riccardi, 1953), sections 331, 335, pp. 479–81; Robert Flint, *Vico* (Edinburgh: William Blackwood & Sons, 1884), pp. 146–47.

17. Vico, *Opere,* sections 137, 138, pp. 438–39.

18. Ibid., section 1102, p. 865.

19. Ibid., section 1100, p. 865, and section 1106, pp. 866–67.

20. Ibid., section 189, p. 449.

21. *Discours sur l'inégalité des hommes,* in *The Political Writings of Jean-Jacques Rousseau,* ed. from the original MSS and authentic edition with introduction and notes by C. E. Vaughan (Oxford: Basil Blackwell, 1962), vol. 1, p. 162 (my translation).

22. See Voltaire, *Œuvres complètes* (Paris: chez Th. Desoer, 1817); Etienne Bonnot Condillac, *Essai sur l'origine des connaissances humaines* (Paris: Galilée, 1973); Claude Adrien Helvétius, *De l'Esprit* (Paris: Durand, 1758); and Marquis de Condorcet, *Œuvres de Condorcet* (Paris: Frimin-Didot, 1847–48).

23. *La Profession de foi du Vicaire Savoyard,* in *Rousseau's Religious Writings,* ed. Ronald Grimsley (Oxford: Clarendon Press, 1970), p. 168 (my translation).

24. Jean-Jacques Rousseau, *Discours sur l'inégalité des hommes,* in *Œuvres complètes,* ed. Bernard Gagnebin and Marcel Raymond (Paris: Gallimard, 1964), p. 133 (my translation).

25. *Du Contrat social* (first version), in Vaughan, ed., *The Political Writings of Jean-Jacques Rousseau,* vol. 1, p. 504 (my translation).

26. Rousseau, "Lettres à La Montagne," in *Rousseau's Religious Writings,* p. 324 (my translation).

27. Ibid. (my translation).

28. Ibid., pp. 504–5 (my translation).

29. Ibid. (my translation).

30. See Rousseau, "*La Profession de foi du Vicaire Savoyard,*" p. 188.

3. Natural Law and the Social Contract

1. See Jean Bodin, *Les œuvres philosophiques* (Paris: Presses Universitaires de France, 1951–52); Thomas Hobbes, *The Leviathan,* intro. A. D. Lindsay (New York: Dutton, 1950); Otto Gierke, *Johannes Althusius und die Entwicklung der naturrechtlichen Staatstheorien* (New York: H. Fertig, 1966); Johannes Althusius, *Politica*

methodice digesta of Johannes Althusius (Cambridge, Mass.: Harvard University Press, 1932); and Samuel Pufendorf, *De officio hominus et civis juxta legem naturalem* (Cantalorigiae: Ex Officiana Joan Hayes ... Impensis Joan Creed, 1682).

2. Hugo Grotius, *The Rights of War and Peace,* ed. A. C. Campbell, intro. David J. Hill and M. Walster (New York: M. W. Dunne Publisher, 1901), book 1, chapters 1, 10, p. 21.

3. Ibid., p. 25. For a discussion on natural and volitional law, see Peter R. Remec, *The Position of the Individual in International Law according to Grotius and Vattel* (The Hague: Martinus Nijhoff, 1960), pp. 63–70; Richard Tuck, *Natural Right Theories: Their Origin and Development* (Cambridge: Cambridge University Press, 1979), p. 68.

4. Grotius, *The Rights of War and Peace,* book 1, chapter 1, section 17, p. 29.

5. Ibid., p. 28.

6. Hugo Grotius, *Grotius's Jurisprudence of Holland,* ed. and trans. R. W. Lee (Oxford: Clarendon Press, 1936), vol. 1, p. 81.

7. Cited in Tuck, *Natural Right Theories,* p. 71 .

8. Otto Gierke, *Natural Law and the Theory of Society* (London: Cambridge University Press, 1934), p. 70.

9. Grotius, *The Rights of War and Peace,* book 2, p. 269.

10. Hugo Grotius, *The Law of War and Peace,* ed. Walter J. Black, trans. Louise R. Loomis, with an introduction by P. E. Corbett (New York: Published by W. J. Black for the Classics Club, 1949), book 1, chapter 3, section 8, p. 44.

11. Cf. Grotius, *The Rights of War and Peace,* book 1, chapter 3, section 8, p. 63.

12. Ibid.

13. See Christian von Wolff, *Gesammelte kleine philosophische Schriften* (Hildesheim, N.Y.: Olms, 1981).

14. Benedetto Croce, *La Filosofia di Giambattista Vico* (Bari: Laterza, 1962), pp. 77–78.

15. Cf. Dario Fauci, "Vico and Grotius: Jurisconsult of Mankind," in *Giambattista Vico: An International Symposium,* ed. Giorgio Tagliacozzo and Hayden V. White (Baltimore: Johns Hopkins University Press, 1969), p. 69.

16. See John Selden, *Two Treatises* (London: Printed for Thomas Basset and Richard Chismell, 1683), and John Selden, *Mare Clausum of the Dominium or Ownership of the Sea* (London: Printed by William Dugard, 1652).

17. Giambattista Vico, *Opere,* ed. Fausto Nicolini (Milan and Naples: Riccardo Riccardi, 1953), section 394, p. 513.

18. See A. Robert Caponigri, *Time and Idea: The Theory of History of Giambattista Vico* (Chicago: Henry Regnery Company, 1953), p. 51; and E. Gianturco, "Vico's Significance in the History of Legal Thought," in Tagliacozzo and White, eds., *Giambattista Vico,* p. 329. Both argued for Vico's superiority over Grotius by showing how Vico transcended the duality of universal and positive law. I would tend, however, to espouse the argument of G. Fasso (*Vico e Grozio* [Naples: Guida Editori, 1971]) and A. Agnelli ("Motivi e sviluppi della costanza del diritto di Giambattista Vico," *Rivista internazionale di filosofia del diritto* 30, [1956], p. 632) for stressing Vico's indebtedness to Grotius's theory of law. By showing the intimate interaction between *ius naturale* and positive law, Grotius prepared the theoretical platform for Vico's historical approach to natural law.

19. Isaiah Berlin, *Vico and Herder: Two Studies in the History of Ideas* (New York: Viking Press, 1976), pp. 34, 37, 85.

20. Vico, *Opere*, par. 18.

21. "I governi debbon essere conformi alla natura degli uomini governati" (ibid., section 246, p. 460). See also Croce, *La Filosofia di Giambattista Vico*, p. 107.

22. Vico, *Opere*, section 1025, p. 823; or Croce, *La Filosofia di Giambattista Vico*, p. 106.

23. *Du Contrat social* (first version), in *The Political Writings of Jean-Jacques Rousseau*, ed. from the original MSS and authentic edition with introduction and notes by C. E. Vaughn (Oxford: Basil Blackwell, 1962), vol. 1, book 1, chapter 7, p. 476 (my translation).

24. *Du Contrat social* (final version), in ibid., vol. 2 (my translation).

25. "His most consistent way of reasoning is to establish the right by the fact" (ibid., book 1, p. 25 [my translation]); or see Robert Derathé, *Jean-Jacques Rousseau et la science politique de son temps* (Geneva: Slatkine reprints, 1979), pp. 69, 73.

26. *Économie politique*, in *The Political Writings of Jean-Jacques Rousseau*, p. 241 (my translation).

27. Among the various interpretations of Rousseau's "general will," it will suffice to mention three. J. L. Talmon (*The Origins of Totalitarian Democracy* [New York: Praeger, 1960]) asserted that by identifying the "general will" with the principle of popular sovereignty, Rousseau gave rise to totalitarian democracy. Likewise, Jean Lemaître's *Jean-Jacques Rousseau* (New York: Macluse Company, 1907) denounced Rousseau's *Social Contract* for the worst excesses of the French Revolution. Yet, unlike Lemaître and Talmon, Albert Meynier's *Jean-Jacques Rousseau, révolutionnaire* (Paris: Schleicher Frères, 1911) perceived Rousseau as an advocate of liberal parliamentarism by drawing a comparison between the *Social Contract* and the Constituent Assembly. For a discussion of the historical interpretations of Rousseau, see also Joan McDonald, *Rousseau and the French Revolution, 1762–1791* (London: Athlone Press, 1965).

28. Cf. Jean-Jacques Rousseau, *Discours sur l'inégalité des hommes*, in *Œuvres complètes*, ed. Bernard Gagnebin and Marcel Raymond (Paris: Gallimard, 1964), pp. 169, 176; *Économie politique*, p. 259.

29. Rousseau, *Économie politique*, p. 259.

30. See also Ernst Cassirer, *The Question of Jean-Jacques Rousseau*, ed. and trans. Peter Gay (New York: Columbia University Press, 1954).

31. Cf. *Considération sur le gouvernement de Pologne et sur sa réformation projetée* and *Projet pour la Corse*, in *The Political Writings of Jean-Jacques Rousseau*, vol. 2, p. 474, and pp. 303, 320, 327, respectively.

32. Rousseau, *Projet pour la Corse*, p. 312 (my translation).

33. Rousseau, *Considération sur le gouvernement de Pologne et sur sa réformation projetée*, vol. 2, p. 477.

34. *Du Contrat social* (first version), book 1, chapters 3, 4, in *The Political Writings of Jean-Jacques Rousseau*, vol. 1, p. 461.

35. Rousseau, *Du Contrat social*, book 2, chapter 6, in *Œuvres complètes*, p. 403, and chapter 7, p. 415.

36. Ibid., book 3, chapter 6, p. 403; chapter 7, p. 415.

37. Cf. Rousseau, "De l'abus du gouvernement, et de sa pente à dégénérer," *Du Contrat social*, book 3, chapter 10, in *Œuvres complètes*, pp. 421–22.

38. Critics such as Alfred Cobban (*Rousseau and the Modern State* [n.p.: George Allen and Unwin, reprint 1964], pp. 104, 108, 114), George Sabine (*History of Political Theory* [New York: Holt, Rinehart and Winston, 1966], pp. 543–93), and Anne M. Cohler (*Rousseau and Nationalism* [New York: Basic Books, 1970) might have

exaggerated Rousseau's nationalist and romantic position. In *Rousseau, Kant and Goethe* (New York and London: Harper & Row, 1963), Ernst Cassirer suggests that "critics of Rousseau who see in him nothing but the Romantic enthusiast have never done justice to [his ideas on law and the state]" (p. 25). These critics, according to Cassirer, have forgotten how Rousseau helped "the Rights of Man to attain victory" (p. 27). For the latter interpretation, see also Ernst Bloch, *Natural Law and Human Dignity*, trans. Dennis J. Schmidt (Cambridge, Mass., and London: MIT Press, 1986), pp. 61–65.

39. *L'Encyclopédie*, art. "Nation" (my translation). In French: "Mot collectif dont on fait l'usage pour exprimer une quantité considérable de peuple, qui habite une certaine étendue de pays, renfermé dans certaines limites, et qui obéit au même gouvernement." In the words of Eric Hobsbawm, "The original, revolutionary-popular idea of patriotism was state based rather than nationalist, since it related to the sovereign people itself, i.e. to the state exercising power in its name. Ethnicity or other elements of historic continuity were irrelevant to the 'nation' in this sense, and language relevant only or chiefly on pragmatic grounds" (*Nations and Nationalism since 1780: Programme, Myth, Reality* [Cambridge: Cambridge University Press, 1990], p. 87).

4. Religious Wars and the Need for International Arrangements

1. See Bartolo da Sassoferrato, *La Tiberiade* (Rome: G. Gigliotto, 1587); Microopaque (New York: Readex Microprint, 1972); Cecil Nathan Sidney Woolf, *Bartolus of Sassoferrato: His Position in the History of Medieval Political Thought* (Cambridge: Cambridge University Press, 1913); and Joseph Canning, *The Political Thought of Baldus de Ubaldi* (Cambridge, England, and New York: Cambridge University Press, 1987).

2. See Francisco de Vitoria, *Relecciones sobre los indios y el derecho de guerra* (Buenos Aires: Espasa-Calpe Argentina, 1946); Francisco de Vitoria, *Political Writings*, ed. Anthony Pagden and Jeremy Lawrance (New York: Cambridge University Press, 1991); and Berenice Hamilton, *Political Thought in Sixteenth-Century Spain* (Oxford: Clarendon Press, 1963).

3. See Alberico Gentili, *De jure belli tres*, translation of the edition of 1612 by John C. Rolfe, introduction by Coleman Phillipson (New York: Oceana, 1964); Samuel Pufendorf, *De officio hominis et civis juxta legem naturalem* (Cantalorigiae: Ex Officiana Joan Hayes ... Impensis Joan Creed, 1682); Richard Zouche, *Juris et Judicii Fecialis*, ed. Thomas E. Holland (Washington, D.C.: Carnegie Institution of Washington, 1911); Emmerich de Vattel, *The Law of Nations* (London: W. Clark and Sons, 1811).

4. See Hugo Grotius, *The Rights of War and Peace*, ed. A. C. Campbell, intro. David J. Hill (New York: M. W. Dunne Publisher, 1901), p. 76; Peter R. Remec, *The Position of the Individual in International Law according to Grotius and Vattel* (The Hague: Martinus Nijhoff, 1960), pp. 88–89.

5. See Grotius, *The Rights of War and Peace*, book 2, chapter 1, pp. 73–84; book 2, chapter 20, pp. 220–55; Remec, *The Position of the Individual*, pp. 88–89.

6. Grotius, *The Rights of War and Peace*, book 2, chapter 1, p. 83.

7. Ibid., p. 398.

8. Hugo Grotius, *The Law of War and Peace*, ed. Walter J. Black trans. Louise R. Loomis, with an introduction by P. E. Corbett (New York: Published by W. J. Black for the Classics Club, 1949), book 2, chapter 23, pp. 250–54.

9. Ibid., book 1, chapter 1, section 14, p. 25.

10. Ibid., p. 62.

11. Giambattista Vico, *Opere,* ed. Fausto Nicolini (Milan and Naples: Riccardo Riccardi, 1953), par. 1105. For a historical application of these principles, see also pars. 1106, 1048, 1049, and "Ricorsi dei Feudi," pars. 1086, 1087.

12. Lodovico Muratori, *Opere* (Milan: Riccardo Riccardi, 1964); Apostolo Zeno, *Euristeo* (London: Printed by G. Wood Fall, 1757); and Scipione Maffei, *Merope* (London: Sold by J. Chrichley et al., 1740).

13. Vico, *Opere,* par. 341, p. 101.

14. For a similar discussion, see A. Robert Caponigri, *Time and Idea: The Theory of History of Giambattista Vico* (Chicago: Henry Regnery Company, 1953), pp. 127, 131–32.

15. *Jugement sur la paix perpétuelle,* in *The Political Writings of Jean-Jacques Rousseau,* ed. from the original MSS and authentic edition with introduction and notes by C. E. Vaughn (Oxford: Basil Blackwell, 1962), vol. 1, p. 390 (my translation).

16. Jean-Jacques Rousseau, *L'État de guerre,* in ibid., p. 294 (my translation).

17. Ibid., p. 300 (my translation). See also Robert Derathé, *Jean-Jacques Rousseau et al science politique de son temps* (Geneva: Sklatine reprints, 1979), p. 134.

18. Rousseau, *Jugement sur la paix perpétuelle,* p. 391 (my translation). See also Stanley Hoffmann, *The State of War: Essays on the Theory and Practice of International Politics* (New York: Praeger, 1965), p. 69; and Rousseau, *Du Contrat Social* (first version), in *The Political Writings of Jean-Jacques Rousseau,* vol. 1, p. 510.

19. *Fragments,* in *The Political Writings of Jean-Jacques Rousseau,* vol. 1, p. 310 (my translation).

20. Jean-Jacques Rousseau, *Du Contrat Social* in *Œuvres complètes,* ed. Bernard Gagnebin and Marcel Raymond (Paris: Gallimard, 1964), book 2, chapter 2, p. 370; quote from *The Social Contract and Discourses,* trans. and intro. G. D. H. Cole (London: Everyman's Library, 1973), p. 184.

21. *Jugement sur la paix perpétuelle,* in *The Political Writings of Jean-Jacques Rousseau,* p. 391.

22. See Carol Blum, *Rousseau and the Republic of Virtue* (Ithaca, N.Y.: Cornell University Press, 1986), chapter 8.

23. Rousseau, *Jugement sur la paix perpétuelle,* p. 392 (my translation).

24. Ibid., pp. 393–96.

5. The Eighteenth-Century Democratic Revolutions and the Spirit of "Laissez-Faire"

1. See David Ogg, *Europe of the Ancien Régime, 1715–1783* (New York: Harper & Row, 1965).

2. In reference to this period, see the fine volumes of W. L. Dorn, *Competition for Empire, 1740–1763* (New York: Harper & Brothers, 1940); M. S. Anderson, *Europe in the Eighteenth Century* (New York: Holt, Rinehart and Winston, 1961), vol. 8; and C. E. Carrington, *The British Overseas: Exploits of a Nation of Shopkeepers* (London: Cambridge University Press, 1950).

3. L. H. Gipson, *The British Empire before the American Revolution* (New York: Alfred A. Knopf, 1936), 4 vols.; and *The Cambridge History of the British Empire,* ed. Holland Rose, A. P. Newton, and E. A. Benians (Cambridge: Cambridge University Press, 1929–59), vol. 8.

4. Cited in Herbert G. Gutman, ed., *Who Built America?* (New York: Pantheon Books, 1989), p. 156.

5. Ibid. See also Carl L. Becker, *The Declaration of Independence: A Study of the History of Political Ideas* (New York: Vintage Books, 1942).

6. Allan Nevins and Henry Steele Commager, *A Pocket History of the United States* (New York: Simon & Schuster, 1976), p. 96.

7. Ibid., pp. 92–93.

8. Ibid., p. 94.

9. Ibid., pp. 13–15.

10. See Gutman, ed., *Who Built America?* pp. 160–75.

11. For an analysis of the effect of the American Revolution in Europe, see Robert Roswell Palmer, *The Age of the Democratic Revolution: A Political History of Europe and America* (Princeton, N.J.: Princeton University Press, 1959), pp. 239–82.

12. John Adams, *The Works of John Adams*, 10 vols. (Boston: Little, Brown, 1850–56).

13. Palmer, *The Age of the Democratic Revolution*, pp. 242–43. Palmer offers a very good account of the influence of the American Revolution throughout Europe.

14. For full quotes and references, see Palmer, ibid., Appendix II, pp. 238 and 506.

15. F. Crouzet, "England and France in the Eighteenth Century: A Comparative Analysis of Two Economic Growths," in Donald Maxwell Hartwell, ed., *The Causes of the Industrial Revolution in England* (London: Methuen, 1967).

16. W. Doyle, *The Old European Order 1600–1800* (New York: Oxford University Press, 1978), p. 144.

17. Molière, Jean-Baptiste Poquelin, *Le bourgeois gentilhomme* (Paris: Librairie Générale Française, 1985).

18. Denis Diderot and Jean le Rond d'Alembert, *Encyclopedia* (New York: Pergamon Press, 1985); Julien Offray de La Mettrie, *L'Homme machine* (Paris: Frereric Henry, 1865); Claude Adrien Helvétius, *De l'Esprit* (Paris: Durand, 1758); Gotthold Ephraim Lessing, *Education of the Human Race*, ed. John D. Haney (New York: Teacher's College, Columbia University, 1908), and *Nathan der Weise*, ed. Gustav Steiner (Basel: Birkhauser, n.d.); Christoph Martin Wieland, *Geschichte des Agathon* (Munich: Goldman, 1965); Moses Mendelssohn, *Selections: Moses Mendelssohn: Eine Auswahl aus seine Schriften und Briefen* (Frankfurt am Main: Kauffman, 1929); David Hume, *Essays: Moral, Political and Literary* (London: Oxford University Press, 1963); Franco Betti, *Vittorio Alfieri* (Boston: Twayne Publishers, 1984); and Cesare di Beccaria, *On Crimes and Punishments*, trans. Henry Paolucci (Indianapolis: Bobbs-Merrill, 1963).

19. Albert Mathiez, *The French Revolution* (New York: Russell & Russell, 1962); Georges Lefebvre, *La Révolution Française* (Paris: Presses Universitaires de France, 1968); Albert Soboul, *Histoire de la Révolution Française* (Paris: Gallimard, 1962); Jean Egret, *The French Pre-Revolution* (Chicago: University of Chicago Press, 1977); Elizabeth Eisenstein, "Who Intervened in 1788? A Commentary on the Coming of the French Revolution," *American Historical Review* 71 (October 1965), pp. 77–103; François Furet, *Penser la Révolution Française* (Paris: Gallimard, 1978); see also Simon Schama, *Citizens* (New York: Alfred A. Knopf, 1989); Theda Skocpol, *States and Social Revolutions: A Comparative Analysis of France, Russia and China* (Cambridge, England, and New York: Cambridge University Press, 1979); and Jack Goldstone, *Revolution and Rebellion in the Early Modern World* (Berkeley: University of California Press, 1991).

20. Georges Lefebvre, *The French Revolution*, trans. Elizabeth Moss Evanson (London: Routledge and Kegan Paul/Columbia University Press, 1962–64), vol. 1, p. 48.

21. Alfred Manfred, *La grande Révolution Française* (Moscow: Foreign Language Edition, 1961), p. 24; see also Raymond Birn, *Crisis and Absolutism, Revolution: Europe, 1648, 1789/91* (Lasalle, Ill.: Dryden Press, 1977), p. 159.

22. Soboul, *Histoire de la Révolution Française*, vol. 1, p. 16.

6. Reason, Deism, and the Internationalist Spirit of Solidarity

1. Henry St. John, Viscount Bolingbroke, *Letters on the Spirit of Patriotism* (London: Printed for A. M. Millar, 1752); François-Marie Arouet de Voltaire, *Œuvres complètes* (Paris: chez Th. Desoer, 1817); Gotthold Ephraim Lessing, *Education of the Human Race*, ed. John D. Haney (New York: Teacher's College, Columbia University, 1908); and Benjamin Franklin, *The Works of Dr. Benjamin Franklin in Philosophy, Politics and Morals* (Philadelphia: W. Duane, 1808–18).

2. Voltaire, *Œuvres complètes*; Denis Diderot, *Le Rêve de d'Alembert* (Paris: L'avant-scène, 1987); and Jean le Rond d'Alembert, *Essai sur les éléments de philosophie*, ed. Richard N. Schwab (Hildesheim, N.Y.: Olms, 1965); Baron von Holbach, *The System of Nature or Laws of the Moral and Physical World*, trans. H. D. Robinson (Boston: J. P. Mendum, 1868); and Julien Offray de La Mettrie, *L'Homme machine* (Paris: Frereric Henry, 1865).

3. Maximilien Robespierre: *Œuvres*, ed. Laponneraye (New York: Burt Franklin, 1970), National Convention, February 5, 1794, vol. 3, 557 (my translation).

4. Ibid., p. 305 (my translation).

5. The Enragés were the extreme revolutionary party, led by Jacques Roux, Jean Varlet, and Théophile Leclerc, who were strongly suspected by Robespierre and the Jacobins of instigating popular uprisings, that is, grocery riots, and de-Christianization in 1793 (George Rudé, *Robespierre: Portrait of a Revolutionary Democrat* [New York: Viking Press, 1975], pp. 148–49, 226).

6. Maximilien Robespierre, *Discours et rapports de Robespierre*, ed. Charles Vellay (Paris: Fasquelles, 1908), Constituante, May 31, 1790, p. 45 (my translation).

7. Ibid., Constituante, February 5, 1790, pp. 10–11 (my translation).

8. Robespierre, *Œuvres*, National Convention, May 7, 1794, vol. 3., p. 609 (my translation).

9. Albert Soboul, *Histoire de la Révolution Française* (Paris: Gallimard, 1962), vol. 2, p. 110; or, in English, *The French Revolution 1787–1789: From the Jacobin Dictatorship to Napoleon* (Bristol: Western Printing Services, 1974), vol. 2, p. 398.

10. Albert Mathiez, *The Fall of Robespierre and Other Essays* (London: Hazell, 1927), p. 103.

11. Robespierre, *Œuvres*, vol. 3, p. 633, Jacobin Club, April 15, 1794 (my translation).

12. Robespierre's deist views have provoked considerable debate. I agree with Mathiez's position in his *Fall of Robespierre* that Robespierre tolerated religion for social, practical purposes, but not as a system for class domination: "Si Dieu n'existait pas, il faudrait l'inventer" (If God did not exist it would be necessary to invent him), wrote Robespierre, with a wink to Voltaire. Cobban and Aulard, on the other hand, maintained that what Robespierre truly wanted in the anticlerical raid was to be the "défenseur des catholiques" (Alfred Cobban, *Aspects of the French Revolution* [New York: George Braziller, 1968], p. 177).

13. *The Writings of Thomas Paine*, ed. Moncure D. Conway (New York: AMS Press, 1967), vol. 4, p. 184. See also W. Carey McWilliams, "Civil Religion, in the

Age of Reason: Thomas Paine on Liberalism, Redemption, and Revolution," *Social Research* 54, no. 3 (autumn 1987), p. 475.

14. *The Rights of Man*, in *The Essential Thomas Paine*, ed. Sidney Hook (New York and Toronto: Mentor Books, 1969), p. 281.

15. *Common Sense*, ibid., p. 164.

16. *The Writings of Thomas Paine* (A Discourse at the Society of Theophilanthropists in Paris, January 16, 1797), p. 229.

17. *The Age of Reason*, in *The Writings of Thomas Paine*, p. 67.

18. Ibid. (A letter to Mr. Erskine, January 16, 1797), p. 229.

19. Ibid. (A letter to Camille Jordan, summer 1797), p. 250.

20. In his editorial note, Moncure D. Conway informs us that Paine did not understand German, but Kant was well acquainted with the literature of revolution in America, England, and France (ibid., p. 184).

21. Immanuel Kant, *Vorlesungen über die philosophische Religionslehre*, ed. Karl Heinrich Ludwig Politz (Leipzig: Verlag der Taubertschen Buchhandlung, 1830), p. 15; also cited in Allen W. Wood, *Kant's Moral Religion* (Ithaca, N.Y., and London: Cornell University Press, 1970), p. 161. Contrary to Wood, who distinguished sharply between deism and Kant's theism, I argue that Kant's moral theism was fundamentally similar to the deism of Paine and Robespierre.

22. Immanuel Kant, *Religion within the Limits of Reason*, Preface to the first edition (Chicago: Open Court Publishing Company, 1934), p. 141.

23. Ernst Cassirer, *Kant's Life and Thought* (New Haven: Yale University Press, 1981), p. 385.

24. Cf. Kant's *An Answer to the Question: What Is Enlightenment?* in *Kant's Political Writings*, ed. Hans Reiss, trans. H. B. Nisbet (Cambridge, Mass.: Cambridge University Press, repr. 1983), p. 50.

25. Immanuel Kant, *Critique of Practical Reason*, trans. Lewis White Beck (Indianapolis: Bobbs-Merrill, 1956; repr. 1982), p. 4.

7. *La Patrie*: The Lighthouse of Internationalism

1. See Benjamin Franklin, *The Works of Dr. Benjamin Franklin in Philosophy, Politics and Morals* (Philadelphia: W. Duane, 1808–18); Thomas Jefferson, *The Writings of Thomas Jefferson*, selected and edited by Saul K. Padover (New York: Heritage Press, 1967); and *The Declaration of Independence and the Constitution of the United States of America*, intro. Richard G. Stevens (Washington, D.C.: Georgetown University Press, 1984); Pietro Verri, *Basta con la tortura* (Rome: Organizzazione editoriale tipografica, 1944); Pietro Verri, *Reflections on Political Economy*, trans. B. McGilvray and P. Groenewegen (Fairfield, N.J.: A. M. Kelley, 1993); and Cesare di Beccaria, *On Crimes and Punishments*, trans. Henry Paolucci (Indianapolis: Bobbs-Merrill, 1963).

2. Maximilien Robespierre, *Œuvres complètes de Maximilien de Robespierre*, ed. Marc Bouloiseau and Albert Soboul, Société des Études Robespierristes, National Convention, May 10, 1793, vol. 9, p. 495 (my translation).

3. Georges Lefebvre, "Sur la pensée de Robespierre," in *Études sur la Révolution Française* (Paris: Presses Universitaires de France, 1963), p. 147.

4. *Robespierre*, ed. George Rudé (Englewood Cliffs, N.J.: Prentice Hall, 1967), p. 31. See also George Rudé, *Robespierre: Portrait of a Revolutionary Democrat* (New York: Viking Press, 1975), p. 24; and Lefebvre, "Sur la pensée de Robespierre," p. 210.

5. See Robin Blackburn, "The French Revolution and New World Slavery," in *Socialism and the Limits of Liberalism,* ed. Peter Osborne (London and New York: Verso, 1991), pp. 73–90.

6. Georges Lefebvre, *The French Revolution,* trans. Elizabeth Moss Evanson (London: Routledge and Kegan Paul/New York: Columbia University Press), vol. 2, p. 117.

7. See Darline Levy and Harriet Applewhite, "Women and Political Revolution in Paris," in *Becoming Visible: Women in European History,* ed. Renate Bridenthal and Claudia Konz (Boston: Houghton Mifflin, 1987); and Anne Sa'adah, "Toward the Politics of Exclusion," in *The Shaping of Liberal Politics in Revolutionary France* (Princeton, N.J.: Princeton University Press, 1990), chapter 3.

8. Robespierre, *Œuvres,* (speech delivered at the Society of the Friends of the Constitution, April 25, 1792), pp. 278–300.

9. In the Vendée, royalists and refractory priests were trying to exploit the religious feelings of the peasantry to stir them up against the Revolution; cf. Albert Soboul, *Histoire de la Révolution Française* (Paris: Gallimard, 1962), vol. 1, pp. 352–56.

10. Robespierre, *Œuvres,* National Convention, February 5, 1794, vol. 3, pp. 538–39 (my translation).

11. Ibid., National Convention, December 25, 1793, vol. 3, p. 512 (my translation).

12. Soboul, *Histoire de la Révolution Française,* vol. 2, p. 128–30.

13. Ibid., pp. 127–28.

14. Those who criticized Robespierre for lacking a class perspective failed to observe that his thought reflected the ideal of the French country laborer and of the as yet embryonic urban working class: the sans-culottes. In the *Études sur la Révolution Française,* Lefebvre commented that "the criticism made of the Revolution by the landless peasants was not that it had not created collective ownership, but that it had not distributed to each one of them a piece of land; what the workers complained about was not that the Revolution had failed to build large factories, but that in abolishing the guilds" it had made it impossible for them to become small owners (p. 95).

15. *Common Sense,* in *The Essential Thomas Paine,* ed. Sidney Hook (New York and Toronto: Mentor Books, 1969), p. 24.

16. Cited in Joseph Dorfman, "The Economic Philosophy of Thomas Paine," *Political Science Quarterly* 53 (1938), pp. 372–73.

17. "A Letter to Danton," Paris, April 20, 1793, in *Life and Writings of Paine,* ed. Daniel Edwin Wheeler (New York: Vincent Parke and Company, 1908), vol. 9, pp. 97–98.

18. Eric Foner, *Paine and Revolutionary America* (London: Oxford University Press, 1976), p. 249.

19. *The Agrarian Justice,* in Wheeler, ed., *Life and Writings of Paine,* vol. 10, p. 28.

20. Ibid., p. 30.

21. Paine, "A Letter to Danton," p. 99.

22. There was "one general principle that distinguished freedom from slavery, which is that all hereditary government over a people is to them a species of slavery, and representative government is freedom" (Paine, *The Rights of Man,* in Hook, ed., *The Essential Thomas Paine,* p. 259).

23. "Emancipation of Slaves," Preamble to act passed by the Pennsylvania Assembly, March 1770, in *Life and Writings of Thomas Paine,* pp. 117–19.

24. "Address to the People of France," in *Complete Writings of Paine,* ed. Philip Foner (New York: Citadel, 1969), p. 540.

25. *The Rights of Man,* in *The Essential Thomas Paine,* p. 267.

26. Abbé de Saint-Pierre, *Projet pour rendre la paix perpétuelle en Europe,* ed. Simone Goyard-Fabre (Paris: Garnier, 1981).

27. "We cannot say that men within a State have sacrificed a *part* of their inborn external freedom for a specific purpose, in order to find again their entire undiminished freedom in a state of lawful dependence (i.e., in state of right) for this dependence is created by their own legislative will" ("The Metaphysics of Morals," in *Kant's Political Writings,* ed. Hans Reiss, trans. H. B. Nisbet [Cambridge, Mass.: Cambridge University Press, repr. 1983], p. 140). See also "Justice," in *Kant's Political Philosophy,* ed. Patrick Riley (Totowa, N.J.: Rowman & Littlefield, 1983), p. 53; and Howard Williams, "Kant's Concept of Property," *Philosophical Quarterly* 27 (1977), pp. 32–40.

28. Immanuel Kant, *On the Old Saw: That May Be Right in Theory but It Won't Work in Practice,* trans. E. B. Ashton (Philadelphia: University of Pennsylvania Press, 1974), pp. 59–60.

29. "The Metaphysics of Morals," in *Kant's Political Writings,* p. 139.

30. Ibid., p. 140.

31. Cf. *Perpetual Peace,* in ibid., p. 99.

32. Kant, "Idea for a Universal History," in ibid., p. 50.

33. Harry van der Linden, *Kantian Ethics and Socialism* (Indianapolis and Cambridge, England: Hackett Publishing Company, 1988), pp. 210–11.

34. *The Contest of the Faculties,* in *Kant's Political Writings,* p. 182.

35. Immanuel Kant, "An Old Question Raised Again: Is the Human Progress Constantly Progressing?" in *On History,* Part II of *The Strife of the Faculties,* trans. Robert E. Anchor (Indianapolis and New York: Bobbs-Merrill, 1963), p. 146 n. 7.

36. Kant, *On the Old Saw,* p. 67.

37. *Perpetual Peace,* in *Kant's Political Writings,* pp. 94–96.

8. Europe and the Napoleonic Wars

1. A. J. Grant and Harold Temperley, *Europe in the Nineteenth Century (1789–1959)* (London, New York, and Toronto: Longman, 1952), pp. 73–78.

2. *The New Cambridge Modern History* (Cambridge: Cambridge University Press, 1957–79), vol. 8, p. 711; or Robert Roswell Palmer, *The World of the French Revolution* (New York: Harper & Row, 1967), pp. 149–62.

3. *The New Cambridge Modern History,* p. 713.

4. See R. C. Birch, *Britain and Europe 1789–1871* (Oxford and New York: Pergamon Press, 1969), p. 44.

5. Derek McKay and H. M. Scott, *The Rise of the Great Powers* (London and New York: Longman, 1983), pp. 280–338.

6. See Grant and Temperley, *Europe in the Nineteenth Century,* p. 197.

7. See Johann Gottfried von Herder, *Ideen zur Philosophie der Geschichte der Menschheit* (Berlin: Deutsche Buch-Gemeinshaft, 1924); Massimo d'Azeglio, *I miei ricordi* (Milan: Rizzolini, 1956).

8. Georges Louis Leclerc Buffon, *Histoire naturelle* (Paris: Martin Fabiani, 1942); Jean-Baptiste Antoine de Monet de Lamarck, *La Philosophie zoologique* (Paris: Union

Générale des Éditions, 1968); Erasmus Darwin, *The Golden Age: The Temple of Nature* (New York: Gallimard, 1978).

9. See also Stephen Jay Gould, *The Mismeasure of Man* (New York: W. W. Norton, 1981).

9. The Revolt against Universal Reason

1. See William Blake, *Works,* ed. Geoffrey Keynes (London and New York: Oxford University Press, 1966); William Wordsworth and Samuel Taylor Coleridge, *Lyrical Ballads* (New York: Barnes and Noble, 1963); Johann Wolfgang von Goethe, *Goethe's Werke* (Leipzig: Bibliographisches Institut, 1900–1908); Johann Gottfried von Herder, *Reflection on the Philosophy of the History of Mankind* (Chicago: University of Chicago Press, 1968); Alessandro Manzoni, *I promessi sposi,* trans. Danile J. Connor (New York: Macmillan, 1924); Giacomo Leopardi, *Opere* (Milan: Riccardo Riccardi, 1966); Joseph Marie de Maistre, *Œuvres complètes* (Geneva: Slatkine reprints, 1979); Louis-Gabriel-Ambroise, vicomte de Bonald, *Œuvres de M. de Bonald* (Paris: A. Leclerc, 1854); Aleksandr Sergeevich Pushkin, *Eugene Onegin,* trans. V Nabokov (New York: Pantheon Books, 1964); Adam Mickiewicz, *Œuvres poétiques complètes* (Paris: Frimin-Didot, 1859); and Ángel de Saavedra Rivas, *Obras Completas* (Madrid: M. Aguilar, 1956).

2. Edmund Burke, *Reflections on the Revolution in France,* ed., with introduction and notes, J. G. A. Pocock (Indianapolis and Cambridge: Hackett Publishing Company, 1978), p. 88.

3. Ibid.

4. Ibid., p. 223. The Euripus is a strait in the Aegean Sea with a marked rise and fall of the tide; the allusion is to the difference between landed property and paper money. Cf. editor's note (lv), p. 223.

5. "[The French clergy] was an old establishment, and not frequently revised. But I saw no crimes in the individuals that merited confiscation of their substance, nor those cruel insults and degradations, and that unnatural persecution which have been substituted in the place of meliorating regulation" (ibid., p. 123).

6. "Thoughts on the Cause of the Present Discontents" (1770), in *The Works of the Right and Honourable Edmund Burke* (London: Rivington Edition, 1803–27), vol. 2, p. 335. See also Francis Canevan, *The Political Reason of Edmund Burke* (Durham, N.C.: Duke University Press, 1960), pp. 5–6.

7. Burke, *Reflections on the Revolution in France,* p. 43. See also Alfred Cobban, *Edmund Burke and the Revolt against the Eighteenth Century* (New York: Macmillan, 1929), pp. 84–97.

8. De Maistre confessed in a letter to Henri Costa de Beauregard that the reading of Burke's *Reflections on the Revolution in France* did not convert him to antidemocratism or anti-Gallicanism but reinforced his prior opinions on the matter. Cf. Michel Fuchs, "Edmund Burke et Joseph de Maistre," *Revue de l'université d'Ottawa* 54, no. 3, pp. 50–53.

9. De Maistre, *Du Principe Générateur, Œuvres complètes,* vols. 1–2, book 2, chapter 8, p. 248 (my translation).

10. Ibid.

11. *Du Pape,* in ibid.

12. Cf. *De l'Église Gallicane,* in ibid., vols. 3–4, chapter 14. See also Charles Lombard, *Joseph de Maistre* (Boston: Twayne Publishers, 1976), p. 47; and Roger Henri

Soltau, *French Political Thought in the Nineteenth Century* (New York: Russell & Russell, 1959), p. 19.

13. De Maistre, *Œuvres complètes, De l'Église Gallicane*, in vols. 3–4, chapter 22, p. 22 (my translation).

14. Ibid. (my translation).

15. Ibid., pp. 22–23 (my translation).

16. *Considérations sur la France*, in de Maistre's *Œuvres complètes*, vols. 1–2, chapter 5, p. 55 (my translation). One has to remember also that de Maistre's *Considérations sur la France* (1796), published six years after Burke's *Reflections on the Revolution in France* (1790), could address more carefully the issue of the cult of the Goddess of Reason celebrated in 1793.

17. Ibid., p. 9 (my translation); see the section on the scientific revolution, Part I, chapter 2.

18. *Les Soirées de Saint-Petersbourg* (Fifth Dialogue), in ibid., vols. 3–4, p. 258 (my translation).

19. *Du Principe Générateur*, in ibid., vols. 1–2, p. 264 (my translation).

20. *Études sur la Souveraineté*, in ibid., vols. 1–2, chapter 8, p. 357 (my translation).

21. See Friedrich Karl von Savigny, *Das Recht des Besitzes* (Giessen: Bey Heyer, 1803); and Leopold von Ranke, *History of the Reformation in Germany*, ed. Robert A. Johnson, trans. Sarah Austin (New York: F. Unger, 1966).

22. De Maistre, *Études sur la Souveraineté*, in *Œuvres complètes*, vols. 1–2, chapter 10, p. 375 (my translation).

23. Ibid., p. 376 (my translation).

24. Ibid., p. 377 (my translation).

25. Johann Gottlieb Fichte, *Considérations destinées à rectifier les jugements du Public sur la Révolution Française*, trans. Jules Barni, intro. Marc Richir (Paris: Payot, 1974), pp. 229, 230, 250.

26. For a discussion of Fichte's critique of Kant, see Luigi Payerson, *Fichte: Il sistema della libertà* (Milan: U. Mursia, 1976), pp. 76–80.

27. See Fichte, *Considérations*, pp. 81, 89.

28. See Frederick Gentz's preface to Burke's *Reflections on the Revolution in France*, in Joël Lefebvre, ed., *La Révolution Française vue par les Allemands* (Lyon: Presses Universitaires de Lyon, 1987), pp. 77–78.

29. Fichte, *Considérations*, p. 102 (my translation).

30. For an interesting examination of the parallel between Kant and Fichte, see J. C. Goddard's preface in Johann Gottlieb Fichte, *Essai d'une Critique de toute Révélation* (Paris: Librairie Philosophique de Vrin, 1988), pp. 7–33. See also Alexis Philonenko, *Théorie et praxis dans la pensée morale et politique de Kant et de Fichte en 1793* (Paris: Librairie Philosophique de Vrin, 1976); and Russell Warren Stine, "The Doctrine of God in the Philosophy of Fichte" (Ph.D. diss. University of Pennsylvania, 1945), pp. 26–44.

31. Johann Gottlieb Fichte, *The Vocation of Man*, trans. William Smith, with a biographical introduction by E. Ritchie (Lasalle, Ill.: Open Court Publishing Company, 1965), p. 152.

10. Toward an Organic and Relativist Theory of the Nation

1. Edmund Burke, *Reflections on the Revolution in France*, ed., with introduction and notes, J. G. A. Pocock (Indianapolis and Cambridge: Hackett Publishing

Company, 1978), p. 216. See "Liberty is not an Abstract Principle," in *Burke's Politics,* ed. Ross J. S. Hoffmann and Paul Levack (New York: Alfred A. Knopf, 1949), pp. 65, 109–10; and, for a discussion of order and liberty, Alfred Cobban, *Edmund Burke and the Revolt against the Eighteenth Century* (New York: Macmillan, 1929), pp. 53–58.

2. Burke, *Reflections on the Revolution in France,* p. 28.

3. Burke, *Burke's Politics,* p. 69. In *The Rage of Edmund Burke* (New York: Basic Books, 1977), Isaac Kramnick showed that during the American Revolution, Burke, in his *Letter to the Sheriff of Bristol,* contrasted the upstart Americans with the English, who had experienced "a great change in the national character" (p. 119). In this letter, Burke compared the "unwielded haughtiness" of an England "pampered by enormous wealth, with the high spirit of free dependencies" (ibid.). Similarly, Kramnick observed that Burke admired the Irish national character, which enlivened the lethargic trend of the British spirit (p. 121).

4. Burke, *Reflections on the Revolution in France,* p. 44.

5. See Alexander Hamilton and James Madison, *The Federalist* (New York: Henry Holt and Company, 1898), nos. 1, 10, 49.

6. Burke, *Reflections on the Revolution in France,* p. 45.

7. Ibid.

8. Cf. *Burke's Politics,* p. 51.

9. Ibid., p. 121.

10. Ibid., p. 128 (Burke to Mr. Samuel Span, merchant adventurer of Bristol, April 1778).

11. Ibid.; see also pp. 126, 127. Reading these lines, one should not forget Burke's Irish origin.

12. For an interesting discussion of Burke's position on Hastings's policy in India, see Kramnick, *The Rage of Edmund Burke,* pp. 121, 128, 132.

13. Ibid., p. 193.

14. Burke, *Reflections on the Revolution in France,* p. 85.

15. For an interesting comparison of Rousseau and Burke, see David Cameron, *The Social Thought of Rousseau and Burke* (Toronto and Buffalo: University of Toronto Press, 1973), pp. 26–29, 82.

16. Burke, *Reflections on the Revolution in France,* p. 77.

17. Ibid., pp. 109–10.

18. Ibid., p. 124.

19. *Burke's Politics,* p. 116.

20. Burke, *Reflections on the Revolution in France,* pp. 116, 204. Referring to Necker's findings, Burke reported that "from the year 1726 to the year 1784, there was coined at the mint of France, in the species of gold and silver, to the amount of about one hundred millions of pounds sterling" ("De l'administration des finances de la France," par Monsieur Necker, in *Reflections on the Revolution in France,* p. 114 n. 31). However, Burke neglected to mention in his report that the national revenues obtained during these years were largely extracted by force from French colonies, and were so inequitably distributed within France as to retard economic growth. Furthermore, he failed to point out that from 1786 to 1789 Calonne, the controller-general of finances, reported that there was a national deficit of one hundred million livres in a total budget of 475 million. In short, Burke failed to consider that the National Assembly had inherited the financial crisis of the ancien régime. For an essential analysis of the political crisis of the late 1780s, see Jean Egret, *The French Pre-Revolution* (Chicago: University of Chicago Press, 1977).

21. De Maistre's *Considérations sur la France* was published in 1796, four years after the king had been put to death.

22. Joseph Marie de Maistre, *Considérations sur la France, Œuvres complètes,* (Geneva: Slatkine reprints, 1979), vols. 1–2, p. 135.

23. *Études sur la Souveraineté,* in ibid., p. 438 (my translation).

24. "Note à son Excellence M. de Gourief, Ministre des finances et du commerce," Saint Petersburg, July 24 (August 8), 1815, in ibid., vols. 13/14, pp. 107–9.

25. Johann Gottlieb Fichte, *Considérations destinées à rectifier les jugements du public sur la Révolution Française,* trans. Jules Barni, intro. Marc Richir (Paris: Payot, 1974), p. 138 (my translation).

26. Ibid., p. 140 (my translation).

27. Ibid., p. 144 (my translation).

28. Johann Gottlieb Fichte, *Gesamtausgabe der Bayerischen Akademie der Wissenschaft* (Stuttgart Bad Cannstat: Frommann, 1962), vol. 2, p. 117. See also Ernst Bloch, *Natural Law and Human Dignity,* trans. Dennis J. Schmidt (Cambridge, Mass., and London: MIT Press, 1986), p. 71.

29. Fichte, *Considérations,* p. 120 (my translation); H. C. Engelbrecht, *Johann Gottlieb Fichte: A Study of His Political Writings with Special Reference to His Nationalism* (New York: AMS Press, 1933), p. 36.

30. Rheinold Aris, *History of Political Thought in Germany* (London: Russell & Russell, 1936; repr. 1965), p. 182. Aris distinguished four periods in the evolution of Fichte's attitude toward the state. For the purpose of this study, Fichte's views can be divided into the pre- and post-Napoleonic periods: from 1789 to 1799 and from 1799 to 1815.

31. Cf. Otto Gierke, *Natural Law and the Theory of Society* (London: Cambridge University Press, 1934), p. 132.

32. Gierke observed that, in one way, Fichte went beyond Rousseau when he rejected the majority principle, opposing to it, with an eager advocacy, the principle of unanimity, and only making the limited concession that an overwhelming majority may be allowed in special cases to enjoy the right of declaring dissidents to be non-members (ibid., p. 133 n. 228).

33. Fichte, *Gesamtausgabe,* vol. 3, p. 477; Bloch, *Natural Law and Human Dignity,* p. 74.

34. Johann Gottlieb Fichte, *The Closed Commercial State,* in *The Political Thought of the German Romantics,* ed. and intro. Hans Reiss (Oxford: Basil Blackwell, 1955).

35. Cited in Eugene N. Anderson, *Nationalism and the Cultural Crisis in Prussia, 1806–1815* (New York: Octagon Press, 1966), p. 47.

36. Cf. Fichte, *Nachgelassene Werke,* vol. 3, p. 420 n. 2, cited in Aris, *History of Political Thought in Germany,* p. 355.

11. From Internationalism to Nationalism

1. *Annual Register* (1772), p. 34, cited in Alfred Cobban, *Edmund Burke and the Revolt against the Eighteenth Century* (New York: Macmillan, 1929), p. 115.

2. Cf. Charles Edwin Vaughan, *The Romantic Revolt* (New York: Scribner's, 1907), p. 133.

3. Burke, "The Regicide Peace," p. 214 n. 9, cited in Peter Stanlis, *Edmund Burke and the Natural Law* (Ann Arbor: University of Michigan Press, 1958), p. 89.

4. Edmund Burke, *Reflections on the Revolution in France,* ed., with an introduction and notes, J. G. A. Pocock (Indianapolis and Cambridge: Hackett Publishing

Company, 1976), p. 26. See editor's note 21, Livy, *History of Rome*, vol. 9, p. 1: "Wars are just when they are necessary."

5. Cf. Stanlis, *Edmund Burke and the Natural Law*, p. 95; or Cobban, *Edmund Burke and the Revolt against the Eighteenth Century*, p. 117.

6. *Annual Register* (1781), pp. 101–6, or quote 15 cited in Stanlis, *Edmund Burke and the Natural Law*, pp. 91–92.

7. *Burke's Politics*, ed. Ross J. S. Hoffmann and Paul Levack (New York: Alfred A. Knopf, 1949), p. 102.

8. Note 61, cited in Isaac Kramnick, *The Rage of Edmund Burke* (New York: Basic Books, 1977), p. 156; see also *Burke's Politics*, p. 77, where Burke explained why Englishmen are unfitted to be slaves.

9. Cf. *Reflections on the Revolution in France*, pp. 74–76, 78.

10. See Cobban, *Edmund Burke and the Revolt against the Eighteenth Century*, p. 129.

11. Cf. *The Works of the Right and Honourable Edmund Burke* (London: Rivington Edition, 1803–27), vol. 2, p. 467; Cobban, *Edmund Burke and the Revolt against the Eighteenth Century*, p. 99.

12. Joseph Marie de Maistre, *Considérations sur la France*, in *Œuvres complètes* (Geneva: Slatkine reprints, 1979), vols. 1–2, pp. 28, 33, 34 (my translation).

13. Cf. *Les Soirées de Saint-Pétersbourg* (Seventh Dialogue), in ibid., vols. 5–6, pp. 5–6 (my translation).

14. Ibid., p. 15.

15. *Considérations sur la France*, in ibid., vols. 1–2, chapter 3, p. 37 (my translation).

16. *Les Soirées de Saint-Pétersbourg* (Fifth Dialogue), in ibid., vols. 3–4, p. 285 (my translation).

17. Ibid. (Seventh Dialogue), vols. 5–6, p. 25 (my translation).

18. Ibid. (Fourth Dialogue), vols. 3–4, pp. 223–31.

19. Ibid., vols. 5–6, p. 13 (my translation).

20. *Considérations sur la France*, in ibid., vol. 1, pp. 74–75.

21. Ibid., p. 27; and *Fragments sur la France*, in *Œuvres complètes*, vols. 1–2, p. 197.

22. Ibid. (my translation).

23. Ibid., pp. 187–88 (my translation). For a discussion of the predetermined destination of nation, see also Vaughan, *The Romantic Revolt*, pp. 431–32.

24. Cf. *Études sur la Souveraineté*, in *Œuvres complètes*, vols. 1–2, p. 378.

25. Johann Gottlieb Fichte, *The Vocation of Man*, trans. William Smith (Lasalle, Ill.,: Open Court Publishing Company, 1965), pp. 123, 124.

26. Cf. Johann Gottlieb Fichte, *An Outline of International and Cosmopolitan Law*, Werke, vol. 3, pp. 369–81, cited in Hans Reiss, ed., *The Political Thought of the German Romantics* (Oxford: Basil Blackwell, 1955), pp. 77–81.

27. Ibid., p. 82.

28. Ibid., p. 85. See also H. C. Engelbrecht, *Johann Gottlieb Fichte: A Study of His Political Writings with Special Reference to His Nationalism* (New York: AMS Press, 1933), p. 69. One could note that Fichte's internationalist influence coincided with his active participation in the Free Masonic Lodge (see Engelbrecht, pp. 191–202).

29. Cited in Engelbrecht, *Johann Gottlieb Fichte*, p. 125.

30. See *The Closed Commercial State*, in Reiss, ed., *The Political Thought of the German Romantics*, pp. 96, 102.

31. *Philosophie der Maurerei* (Briefe an Konstant), 1800, cited in Engelbrecht, *Johann Gottlieb Fichte,* p. 74.

32. Cf. Johann Gottlieb Fichte, *Gesamtausgabe der Bayerischen Akademie der Wissenschaft* (Stuttgart Bad Canstatt: Frommann, 1962), vol. 3, p. 513; Engelbrecht, *Johann Gottlieb Fichte,* p. 94.

33. Johann Gottlieb Fichte, *Sämtliche Werke,* ed. Immanuel Hermann von Fichte (Berlin: Veitum Omp, 1845–46), vol. 11, p. 234; in Eugene N. Anderson, *Nationalism and the Cultural Crisis in Prussia, 1806–1815* (New York: Octagon Press, 1966), pp. 35–36.

Conclusion

1. See Karl R. Popper, *The Open Society and Its Enemies* (Princeton, N.J.: Princeton University Press, 1963); and Charles Taylor, *Hegel and Modern Society* (Cambridge: Cambridge University Press, 1979).

2. See Herbert Marcuse, *Reason and Revolution* (Atlantic Highlands, N.J.: Humanities Press, 1989); and Shlomo Avineri, *Hegel's Theory of the Modern State* (London and New York: Cambridge University Press, 1972).

3. Cf. Joachim Ritter, *Hegel et la Révolution Française* (Paris: Beauchesne, 1970), p. 40.

4. *Hegel's Philosophy of Right,* ed. T. M. Knox (Oxford and New York: Oxford University Press, 1967), section 270, p. 11.

5. Hegel wrote that "civil servants and the members of the executive constitute the greater part of the middle class, the class in which the consciousness of right and the developed intelligence of the mass of people is found" (ibid., section 297, p. 193).

6. Karl Marx, *Critique of Hegel's Philosophy of Right,* ed. Joseph O'Malley, trans. Annette Jollin and Joseph O'Malley (London and New York: Cambridge University Press, 1970), p. 49.

7. *Hegel's Philosophy of Right,* section 209, p. 134.

8. Ibid., section 258, pp. 156–57.

9. For a discussion on this issue, see Pierre Méthais, "Contrat et volonté générale selon Hegel et Rousseau," in *Hegel et le siècle des lumières,* ed. Jacques d'Hondt (France: Presses Universitaires de France, 1974); and Avineri, *Hegel's Theory of the Modern State,* p. 84.

10. *Hegel's Philosophy of Right,* section 279, p. 181.

11. For an interesting discussion of the liberal aspect of the state, see Karl Löwith, *From Hegel to Nietzsche: The Revolution in Nineteenth-Century Thought,* trans., from the German, David E. Green (New York, Chicago, and San Francisco: Holt, Rinehart and Winston, 1964), p. 242.

12. *Hegel's Philosophy of Right,* section 324, p. 209.

13. This topic will be the focus of a future book.

Bibliography

Adams, John. *The Works of John Adams*. 10 vols. Boston: Little, Brown, 1850–56.

Adamson, Robert. *Fichte*. Philadelphia: J. B. Lippincott, 1881.

Adamson, Walter L. *Hegemony and Revolution*. Berkeley, Los Angeles, and London: University of California Press, 1980.

Adorno, T. W., and H. Horkheimer. *Dialektik der Auflärung*. Frankfurt am Main: Fischer Taschenbuch Verlag, 1971.

Agnelli, A. "Motivi e sviluppi della costanza del diritto di Giambattista Vico." *Rivista internazionale di filosofia del diritto* 30 (1956).

Aldridge, Alfred Owen. *Man of Reason: The Life of Thomas Paine*. Philadelphia: J. B. Lippincott, 1959.

d'Alembert, Jean Le Rond. *Essai sur les éléments de philosophie*. Edited by Richard N. Schwab. Hildesheim, N.Y.: Ohms, 1965.

Alott, Philip. *Eunomia: New Order for a New World*. Oxford and New York: Oxford University Press, 1990.

Althusius, Johannes. *Politica Methodice Digesta of Johannes Althusius*. Cambridge, Mass.: Cambridge University Press, 1932.

Anderson, Benedict. *Imagined Communities*. London: Verso, 1986.

Anderson, Eugene N. *Nationalism and the Cultural Crisis in Prussia, 1806–1815*. New York: Octagon Press, 1966.

Anderson, M. S. *Europe in the Eighteenth Century*. Vol. 8. New York: Holt, Rinehart and Winston, 1961.

Anderson, Perry. *Passages from Antiquity to Feudalism*. London: Verso, 1974.

d'Anglas, François Antoine Boissy. *Loi qui rapporte celle du 27 Mars*. Microfilm. Woodbridge, Conn.: Research Publications, 1976.

Arendt Hannah. *On Revolution*. New York: Viking Press, 1963.

Aris, Rheinold. *History of Political Thought in Germany*. London: Russell & Russell, 1936; repr. 1965.

Avineri, Shlomo. *Hegel's Theory of the Modern State*. London and New York: Cambridge University Press, 1972.

Ayling, Stanley. *Edmund Burke: His Life and Opinions*. New York: St. Martin's Press, 1988.

d'Azeglio, Massimo. *I miei ricordi*. Milan: Rizzolini, 1956.

Bacon, Francis. *Great Instauration Prooemium Preface, Plan of the Work, and Novum Organum*. Garden City, N.Y.: Doubleday, 1937.

———. *Novum Organum*. Translated by M. D. London: University Microfilms International, printed for Thomas Lee, 1876.

Barber, Benjamin R. *Strong Democracy: Participatory Politics for a New Age*. Berkeley and London: University of California Press, 1984.

Barny, R. *Rousseau dans la Révolution: le personnage de Jean-Jacques et les débuts du culte révolutionnaire (1787–1791)*. Oxford: Voltaire Foundation, 1986.

Beccaria, Cesare di. *On Crimes and Punishments*. Translated by Henry Paolucci. Indianapolis: Bobbs-Merrill, 1963.

Becker, Carl L. *The Declaration of Independence: A Study of the History of Political Ideas*. New York: Vintage Books, 1942.

Berlin, Isaiah. *Against the Current: Essays in the History of Ideas*. London: Hogarth Press, 1979.

———. *Vico and Herder: Two Studies in the History of Ideas*. New York: Viking Press, 1976.

Betti, Franco. *Vittorio Alfieri*. Boston: Twayne Publishers, 1984.

Bevan, Ruth A. *Marx and Burke: A Revisionist View*. Lasalle, Ill.: Open Court Publishing Company, 1973.

Birch, R. C. *Britain and Europe 1789–1871*. Oxford and New York: Pergamon Press, 1969.

Birn, Raymond. *Crisis and Absolutism, Revolution: Europe, 1648, 1789/91*. Lasalle, Ill.: Dryden Press, 1977.

Black, Antony. *Political Thought in Europe 1250–1450*. Cambridge: Cambridge University Press, 1992.

Blackburn, Robin. "The French Revolution and New World Slavery." In *Socialism and the Limits of Liberalism,* edited by Peter Osborne. London and New York: Verso, 1991, pp. 73–90.

Blake, William. *Works*. Edited by Geoffrey Keynes. London and New York: Oxford University Press, 1966.

Bloch, Ernst. *Natural Law and Human Dignity*. Translated by Dennis J. Schmidt. Cambridge, Mass., and London: MIT Press, 1986.

Blum, Carol. *Rousseau and the Republic of Virtue*. Ithaca, N.Y.: Cornell University Press, 1986.

Bodin, Jean, *Les œuvres philosophiques*. Paris: Presses Universitaires de France, 1951–52.

Boehmer, Heinrich. *Luther and the Reformation in the Light of Modern Research*. Translated by E. S. G. Potter. New York: Dial Press, 1930.

Bolingbroke, Henry St. John, Viscount. *Letters of the Spirit of Patriotism*. London: Printed for A. M. Millar, 1752.

Bonald, Louis-Gabriel-Ambroise, vicomte de. *Œuvres de M. de Bonald*. Paris: A. Leclerc, 1854.

Bourne, Henry E. *The Revolutionary Period*. New York: Century, 1916.

Brancato, Francesco. *Vico nel Risorgimento*. Palermo: S. F. Flaccovio, 1969.

Breuning, Charles. *The Age of Revolution and Reaction: 1789–1850*. New York and London: W. W. Norton, 1977.

Bronner, Stephen E. *Socialism Unbound*. New York: Routledge, 1990.

Brown, Norman. *Closing Time*. New York: Random House, 1973.

Brunschwig, Henri. *Enlightenment and Romanticism in Eighteenth-Century Prussia*. Chicago: University of Chicago Press, 1974.

Bruun, Geoffrey. *Europe and the French Imperium, 1790–1814*. New York: Harper, 1938.

Buffon, Georges Louis Leclerc. *Histoire naturelle*. Paris: Martin Fabiani, 1942.

Burke, Edmund. *Burke's Politics*. Edited by Ross J. S. Hoffmann and Paul Levack. New York: Alfred A. Knopf, 1949.

———. *The Correspondence of Edmund Burke*. Vols. 8–9. Edited by R. B. McDowell. Chicago: University of Chicago Press, 1970.

———. *Edmund Burke on Government, Politics and Society*. Edited by B. W. Hill. Brighton: Harvester, 1975.

———. *Reflections on the Revolution in France*. Edited, with an introduction and notes, by J. G. A. Pocock. Indianapolis and Cambridge: Hackett Publishing Company, 1978.

———. *The Works of the Right and Honourable Edmund Burke*. 16 vols. London: Rivington Edition, 1803–27.

Butler, Charles. *The Life of Hugo Grotius*. London: John Murray, 1826.

Byron, George Gordon. *Childe Harold's Pilgrimage*. Boston: Crosby, Nichols, Lee and Company, 1860.

Calvin, Jean. *Institutes of the Christian Religion*. 6th American ed. Translated by John Allen. Philadelphia: Presbyterian Board of Publication and Sabbath-School Work, 1911.

Cambridge History of the British Empire. Edited by Holland Rose, A. P. Newton, and E. A. Benians. Vol. 8. Cambridge: Cambridge University Press, 1929–59.

Cameron, David. *The Social Thought of Rousseau and Burke*. Toronto and Buffalo: University of Toronto Press, 1973.

Canevan, Francis. *The Political Reason of Edmund Burke*. Durham, N.C.: Duke University Press, 1960.

Canning, Joseph. *The Political Thought of Baldus de Ubaldi*. Cambridge, England, and New York: Cambridge University Press, 1987.

Caponigri, A. Robert. *Time and Idea: The Theory of History of Giambattista Vico*. Chicago: Henry Regnery Company, 1953.

Carrington, C. E. *The British Overseas: Exploits of a Nation of Shopkeepers*. London: Cambridge University Press, 1950.

Cassirer, Ernst. *Kant's Life and Thought*. New Haven: Yale University Press, 1981.

———. *The Myth of the State*. New Haven: Yale University Press, 1946.

———. *The Philosophy of the Enlightenment*. Princeton, N.J.: Princeton University Press, 1951.

———. *The Question of Jean-Jacques Rousseau*. Edited and translated by Peter Gay. New York: Columbia University Press, 1954.

———. *Rousseau, Kant and Goethe*. New York and London: Harper & Row, 1963.

Chapman, Gerald. *Edmund Burke: The Practical Imagination*. Cambridge, Mass.: Harvard University Press, 1967.

Chateaubriand, François-René de. *Grands écrits politiques*. Edited by Jean-Paul Clément. Paris: Imprimerie Nationale, 1993.

Clayes, Gregory. *Thomas Paine: Social and Political Thought*. London and Boston: Unwin Hyman, 1989.

Cobban, Alfred. *Aspects of the French Revolution*. New York: George Braziller, 1968.

————. *Edmund Burke and the Revolt against the Eighteenth Century.* New York: Macmillan, 1929.

————. *Rousseau and the Modern State.* N.p.: George Allen and Unwin, reprint 1964.

————. *The Social Interpretation of the French Revolution.* Cambridge: Cambridge University Press, 1965.

Cohler, Anne M. *Rousseau and Nationalism.* New York: Basic Books, 1970.

Comminel, George C. *Rethinking the French Revolution.* London: Verso, 1987.

Condillac, Etienne Bonnot. *Essai sur l'origine des connaissances humaines.* Paris: Galilée, 1973.

Condorcet, Marquis de. *Œuvres de Condorcet.* Paris: Frimin-Didot, 1847–48.

Cone, Carl B. *The English Jacobins.* New York: Scribner's, 1968.

Conway, Moncure Daniel. *The Life of Thomas Paine.* New York: Benjamin Bloom, 1972.

————. *Thomas Paine: révolution dans les deux mondes.* Paris: Plon Nourrit, 1900.

Coolidge, Olivia. *Tom Paine, Revolutionary.* New York: Scribner's, 1969.

Copleston, Frederick. *A History of Philosophy: Fichte to Nietzsche.* Vol. 7. London: Search Press, 1963.

Cornell, Drucilla, Michel Rosenfeld, and David Gray Carlson. *Hegel and Legal Theory.* London: Routledge, 1991.

Croce, Benedetto. *La Filosofia di Giambattista Vico.* Bari: Laterza, 1962.

Crombie, Alistair C. *Augustine to Galileo.* Cambridge, Mass.: Harvard University Press, 1953.

————. *Medieval and Early Modern Science.* 2 vols. New York: Doubleday Anchor Books, 1959.

Crouzet, F. "England and France in the Eighteenth Century: A Comparative Analysis of Two Economic Growths." In *The Causes of the Industrial Revolution in England,* edited by Donald Maxwell Hartwell. London: Methuen, 1967.

Dante Alighieri. *The Divine Comedy.* Italian text and translation by Charles S. Singleton. Princeton, N.J.: Princeton University Press, 1970.

Danton, Georges Jacques. *Œuvres de Danton.* Edited by A. Vermorel. Paris: Cournel, 1866.

Darwin, Erasmus. *The Golden Age: The Temple of Nature.* New York: Gallimard, 1978.

Delumeau, Jean. *Naissance et Affirmation de la Réforme.* Paris: Presses Universitaires de France, 1965.

Derathé, Robert. *Jean-Jacques Rousseau et la science politique de son temps.* Geneva: Sklatine reprints, 1979.

————. *Le Rationalisme de Jean-Jacques Rousseau.* Paris: Presses Universitaires de France, 1948.

Descartes, René. *Discourse on Method.* Translated by Lawrence J. Lafleur. New York: Liberal Arts Press, 1956.

————. *Œuvres complètes.* Paris: Librairie Joseph Gibert, n.d.

Desmoulins, Camille. *Œuvres de Camille Desmoulins.* Published by Jules Claretie. Paris: Charpentier, 1874.

Deutsch, Karl. *Nationalism and Social Communication: An Inquiry into the Foundation of Nationality.* Cambridge, Mass.: Cambridge University Press, 1966.

Dide, Auguste. *J.-J. Rousseau: le Protestantisme et la Révolution Française.* Paris: Flammarion, n.d.

Diderot, Denis. *Le Rêve de d'Alembert.* Paris: L'Avant-scène, 1987.

Diderot, Denis, and Jean Le Rond d'Alembert. *Encyclopedia.* New York: Pergamon Press, 1985.

Diksterhuis, Eduard J. *The Mechanization of the World Picture.* London, Oxford, and New York: Oxford University Press, 1961.

Dorfman, Joseph. "The Economic Philosophy of Thomas Paine." *Political Science Quarterly* 53 (1938).

Dorn, W. L. *Competition for Empire, 1740–1763.* New York: Harper & Brothers, 1940.

Doyle, W. *The Old European Order 1600–1800.* New York: Oxford University Press, 1978.

Dreyer, Frederick A. *Burke's Politics: A Study in Whig Orthodoxy.* Waterloo, Ont.: Wilfrid Laurier University Press, 1979.

Droetto, Antonio. *Studi Groziani.* Turin: Edizioni Giappichelli, 1968.

Dumbauld, Edward. *The Life and Legal Writings of Hugo Grotius.* Norman: University of Oklahoma Press, 1969.

Durkheim, Émile. " 'Le contrat social' de Rousseau." *Revue de Métaphysique de la Morale* (January–February and March–April 1918).

Dyke, Ian, ed. *Citizen of the World: Essays on Thomas Paine.* New York: St. Martin's Press, 1988.

Edwards, Charles. *Hugo Grotius: The Miracle of Holland.* Chicago: Nelson-Hall, 1928.

Edwards, Samuel. *Rebel: A Biography of Thomas Paine.* New York: Praeger, 1974.

Egret, Jean. *The French Pre-Revolution.* Chicago: University of Chicago Press, 1977.

Einaudi, Mario. *The Early Rousseau.* Ithaca, N.Y.: Cornell University Press, 1967.

Eisenstein, Elizabeth. "Who Intervened in 1788? A Commentary on the Coming of the French Revolution." *American Historical Review* 71 (October 1965): 77–103.

Engelbrecht, H. C. *Johann Gottlieb Fichte: A Study of His Political Writings with Special Reference to His Nationalism.* New York: AMS Press, 1933.

Ergang, Robert R. *Herder and the Foundation of German Nationalism.* New York: Columbia University Press, 1931.

Esposito, Robert. *Vico e Rousseau, e il Moderno Stato Borghese.* Bari: De Donato, 1976.

Everett, C. C. *Fichte's Science of Knowledge: A Critical Exposition.* Chicago: Griggs & Company, 1884.

Fasel, George. *Edmund Burke.* Boston: Twayne Publishers, 1983.

Fasso, Guido. *Vico e Grozio.* Naples: Guida Editori, 1971.

Fauci, Dario. "Vico and Grotius: Jurisconsult of Mankind." In *Giambattista Vico: An International Symposium,* edited by Giorgio Tagliacozzo and Hayden V. White. Baltimore: Johns Hopkins University Press, 1969.

Fenessy, R. R. *Burke, Paine and the Rights of Man.* The Hague: Martin Nijhoff, 1963.

Fichte, Johann Gottlieb. *Address to the German Nation.* Edited with an introduction by G. Amstrong Kelly. New York: Harper Torchbooks, 1968.

———. *The Closed Commercial State.* In *The Political Thought of the German Romantics.* Edited and introduced by Hans Reiss. Oxford: Basil Blackwell, 1955.

———. *Considérations destinées à rectifier les jugements du public sur la Révolution Française.* Translated by Jules Barni, with an introduction by Marc Richir. Paris: Payot, 1974.

———. *Essai d'une Critique de toute Révélation.* Preface by J. C. Goddard. Paris: Librairie Philosophique de Vrin, 1988.

————. *Fichte's Early Philosophical Writings.* Translated and edited by Daniel Brezeale. Ithaca, N.Y., and London: Cornell University Press, 1988.

————. *Gesamtausgabe der Bayerischen Akademie der Wissenschaft.* 4 vols. Stuttgart Bad Cannstat: Frommann, 1962.

————. *Sämtliche Werke.* 8 vols. Edited by Immanuel Hermann von Fichte. Berlin: Veit um Omp, 1845–46.

————. *The Vocation of Man.* Translated by William Smith. Lasalle, Ill.: Open Court Publishing Company, 1965.

Figgis, John Neville. *Studies of Political Thought from Gerson to Grotius, 1414–1625.* Cambridge: Cambridge University Press, 1931.

Flint, Robert. *Vico.* Edinburgh: William Blackwood & Sons, 1884.

Foner, Eric. *Paine and Revolutionary America.* London: Oxford University Press, 1976.

Forster, J. G. *Ansichten vom Niederrhein, von Brabant, Flandern, Holland, England und Frankreich in April, Mai und Juni 1790.* 2 vols. Leipzig: n.p., 1790.

Frank, Andre Gunder. *Dependent Accumulation and Underdevelopment.* New York: Monthly Review Press, 1979.

Franklin, Benjamin. *The Works of Dr. Benjamin Franklin in Philosophy, Politics and Morals.* Philadelphia: W. Duane, 1808–18.

Freeman, Michael. *Edmund Burke and the Critique of Political Radicalism.* Chicago: University of Chicago Press, 1980.

Friedrich, Carl J., ed. *The Philosophy of Hegel.* New York: Modern Library, 1953.

Fuchs, Michel. "Edmund Burke et Joseph de Maistre." *Revue de l'Université d'Ottawa* 54, no. 3: 49–58.

Furet, François. *Penser la Révolution Française.* Paris: Gallimard, 1978.

Galilei, Galileo. *Dialogo sopra i due massimi sistemi del mondo.* Edited by F. Flora. Milan: Rizzoli, 1959.

Gay, Peter. *The Enlightenment.* New York: Alfred A. Knopf, 1967.

Gellner, Ernest. *Nation and Nationalism.* Ithaca, N.Y.: Cornell University Press, 1983.

Gentili, Alberico. *De jure belli tres.* Translation of the edition of 1612 by John C. Rolfe. Introduction by Coleman Phillipson. New York: Oceana, 1964.

Gentz, Frederick. "Preface to Burke's *Reflections on the Revolution in France.*" In *La Révolution Française vue par les Allemands,* edited by Joël Lefebvre. Lyon: Presses Universitaires de Lyon, 1987.

Gianturco, E. "Vico's Significance in the History of Legal Thought." In *Giambattista Vico: An International Symposium,* edited by Giorgio Tagliacozzo and Hayden V. White. Baltimore: John Hopkins University Press, 1969.

Gierke, Otto. *Johannes Althusius und die Entwicklung des naturrechtlichen Staatstheorien.* New York: H. Fertig, 1966.

————. *Natural Law and the Theory of Society.* London: Cambridge University Press, 1934.

————. *Political Theories of the Middle Age.* Cambridge: Cambridge University Press, 1968.

Gilbert, Alan. *Democratic Individuality.* Cambridge: Cambridge University Press, 1990.

————. "Must Global Politics Constrain Democracy?" *Political Theory* (February 1992): 8–37.

Gipson, L. H. *The British Empire before the American Revolution.* New York: Alfred A. Knopf, 1936.

Godwin, William. *Enquiry Concerning Political Justice, and Its Influence on Morals and Happiness.* Philadelphia: Bioren and Madan, 1796.

Goethe, Johann Wolfgang von. *Goethe's Werke.* Leipzig: Bibliographisches Institut, 1900–1908.

———. *On Art and Literature.* Edited by John Geary. New York: Suhrkamp, 1986.

Goldmann, Lucien. *The Human Sciences and Philosophy.* London: Chaucer Press, 1969.

———. *Immanuel Kant.* Bristol: Western Printing Service, 1971.

Goldstone, Jack. *Revolution and Rebellion in the Early Modern World.* Berkeley: University of California Press, 1991.

Gooch, G. P. *Germany and the French Revolution.* London: Longman, 1920.

Gould, Stephen Jay. *The Mismeasure of Man.* New York: W. W. Norton, 1981.

Gowan, Peter. "The Gulf War and Liberalism." *New Left Review* 187 (May–June 1991): 29–70.

Gramsci, Antonio. *Selections from the Prison Notebooks.* Edited and translated by Quintin Hoare and Geoffrey Nowell Smith. New York: International Publishers, 1971.

Grant, A. J., and Harold Temperley. *Europe in the Nineteenth Century (1789–1959).* London, New York, and Toronto: Longman, 1952.

Green, F. C. *Rousseau and the Idea of Progress.* Folcroft, Pa.: Folcroft University Press, 1950.

Greenfeld, Liah. *Nationalism: Five Roads to Modernity.* Cambridge, Mass.: Cambridge University Press, 1992.

Grimaldi, Alfonsina Albini. *The Universal Humanity of Giambattista Vico.* New York: S. F. Vanni, 1958.

Grotius, Hugo. *The Freedom of the Seas.* New York: Oxford University Press, 1916.

———. *Grotius's Jurisprudence of Holland.* 2 vols. Edited and translated by R. W. Lee. Oxford: Clarendon Press, 1936.

———. *The Law of War and Peace.* Edited by Walter J. Black. Translated by Louise R. Loomis, with an introduction by P. E. Corbett. New York: Published by W. J. Black for the Classics Club, 1949.

———. *The Law of War and Peace.* Translated by F. W. Keisley, with an introduction by J. B. Scott. New York: Bobbs-Merrill, 1925.

———. *Meletius Sive de IIs Quae Inter Christianos Conveniunt Epistola.* Edited and translated by G. H. M. Posthumus Meyjes. Leiden: E. J. Brill, 1988.

———. *The Rights of War and Peace.* Edited by A. C. Campbell, with an introduction by David J. Hill and M. Walster. New York: M. W. Dunne Publisher, 1901.

Gutman, Herbert G. ed. *Who Built America?* New York: Pantheon Books, 1989.

Hamilton, Alexander, and James Madison. *The Federalist.* New York: Henry Holt and Company, 1898.

Hamilton, Berenice. *Political Thought in Sixteenth-Century Spain.* Oxford: Clarendon Press, 1963.

Hardwick, Charles. *A History of the Christian Church during the Reformation.* London: Macmillan, 1877.

Hawke, David. *Paine.* New York: Harper & Row, 1974.

Hayes, Carlton. *Essays on Nationalism.* New York: Macmillan, 1933.

Hazard, Paul. *La Pensée Européenne au XVIIIème Siècle.* Paris: Fayard, 1963.

Hecksher, Eli F. *Mercantilism.* 2 vols. Translated by Mendel Shapiro. London: George Allen and Unwin, 1935.

Hegel, G. W. F. *The Difference between Fichte's and Schelling's System of Philosophy*. Translated by H. S. Harris and W. Cerf. Albany: State University of New York Press, 1977.

———. *Hegel's Philosophy of Right*. Edited by T. M. Knox. Oxford and New York: Oxford University Press, 1967.

———. *Hegel's Political Writings*. Translated by T. M. Knox. Oxford: Clarendon Press, 1964.

Helvétius, Claude Adrien. *De l'Esprit*. Paris: Durand, 1758.

Heranshaw, F. J. C., ed. *The Social & Political Ideas of Some of the Great Thinkers of the Sixteenth and Seventeenth Centuries*. Washington, D.C., and New York: Kennikat Press, 1926.

Herder, Johann Gottfried von. *Ideen zur Philosophie der Geschichte der Menschheit*. Berlin: Deutsche Buch-Gemeinshaft, 1924.

———. *Reflection on the Philosophy of the History of Mankind*. Chicago: University of Chicago Press, 1968.

Hirschman, Albert O. *Passions and Interests*. Princeton, N.J.: Princeton University Press, 1977.

Hobbes, Thomas. *The Leviathan*. Introduction by A. D. Lindsay. New York: Dutton, 1950.

Hobsbawm, E. J. *Echoes of the Marseillaise: Two Centuries Look Back on the French Revolution*. London: Verso, 1990.

———. *Nations and Nationalism since 1780: Programme, Myth, Reality*. Cambridge: Cambridge University Press, 1990.

Hoffmann, Stanley. *The State of War: Essays on the Theory and Practice of International Politics*. New York: Praeger, 1965.

Holbach, Baron von. *The System of Nature* or *Laws of the Moral and Physical World*. Translated by H. D. Robinson. Boston: J. P. Mendum, 1868.

Hölderin, Friedrich. *Gesammelte Werke*. Potsdam: G. Kiepenheuer, 1922.

d'Hondt, Jacques. *Hegel et le siècle des lumières*. Paris: Presses Universitaires de France, 1974.

Horkheimer, Max. *Anfänge der bürgerlichen Geschichtsphilosophie*. Stuttgart: Verlag von W. Kohlhammer, 1930.

Hubert, René. *Rousseau et l'Encyclopédie*. Paris: J. Gamber, Librairie Universitaire, n.d.

Hume, David. *Essays: Moral, Political and Literary*. London: Oxford University Press, 1963.

Illuminati, Augusto. *J.-J. Rousseau e la Fondazione dei Valori Borghesi*. Milan: Saggiatore, 1977.

Ishay, Micheline. "European Integration: The Enlightenment Legacy." *History of European Ideas*, no. 208, 1994.

Ishay, Micheline, and Omar Dahbour, eds. *The Nationalism Reader*. Atlantic Highlands, N.J.: Humanities Press, 1994.

Jefferson, Thomas. *The Declaration of Independence and the Constitution of the United States of America*. Introduction by Richard G. Stevens. Washington, D.C.: Georgetown University Press, 1984.

———. *The Writings of Thomas Jefferson*. Selected and edited by Saul K. Padover. New York: Heritage Press, 1967.

Johnson, James Turner. *Ideology, Reason, and the Limitation of War: Religious and Secular Concepts, 1200–1740*. Princeton, N.J.: Princeton University Press, 1975.

Kant, Immanuel. *Critique of Practical Reason.* Translated by Lewis White Beck. Indianapolis: Bobbs-Merrill, 1956; reprint 1982.

———. *Kant's Political Writings.* Edited by Hans Reiss and translated by H. B. Nisbet. Cambridge, Mass.: Cambridge University Press, reprint 1983.

———. *On the Old Saw: That May Be Right in Theory but It Won't Work in Practice.* Translated by E. B. Ashton. Philadelphia: University of Pennsylvania Press, 1974.

———. *Religion within the Limits of Reason.* Chicago: Open Court Publishing Company, 1934.

———. *The Strife of the Faculties.* Translated by Robert E. Anchor. Indianapolis and New York: Bobbs-Merrill, 1963.

Kaufman, Walter. *Hegel's Political Philosophy.* New York: Atherton Press, 1970.

Kedourie, Elie. *Nationalism.* London: Hutchinson, 1960.

Keohane, Robert, and Joseph Nye. *Power and Interdependence.* Boston: Little, Brown, 1977.

Kohn, Hans. *The Idea of Nationalism.* Toronto: Collier-Macmillan, 1969.

Kojève, Alexandre. *Kant.* Paris: Gallimard, 1973.

Krafft, Olivier. *La Politique de Jean-Jacques Rousseau: aspects méconnus.* Paris: Librairie générale de droit et de jurisprudence, 1958.

Kramnick, Isaac. *The Rage of Edmund Burke.* New York: Basic Books, 1977.

Kristeva, Julia. *Nations without Nationalism.* New York: Columbia University Press, 1993.

Kryger, Edna. *La notion de liberté chez Rousseau et ses répercussions sur Kant.* Paris: Librairie A. G. Nizet, 1979.

Lafayette, Marie Joseph Paul Yves. *Memoirs of General Lafayette.* Hartford, Conn.: Barber and Robinson, 1825.

Lamarck, Jean-Baptiste Antoine de Monet de. *La philosophie zoologique.* Paris: Union Générale des Éditions, 1968.

La Mettrie, Julien Offray de. *L'Homme machine.* Paris: Frereric Henry, 1865.

Lanjuinais, Jean-Denis. *French Revolution and Napoleonic Era Pamphlets on Nationalized Property, 1790–1814.* Ithaca, N.Y.: Cornell University Department of Rare Books.

Launay, Michel. *Jean-Jacques Rousseau et son temps.* Paris: Librairie A. G. Nizet, 1969.

Lebrun, Richard. *Joseph de Maistre: An Intellectual Militant.* Kingston and Montreal: McGill Queen's University Press, 1988.

Lefebvre, Georges. *The French Revolution.* 2 vols. Translated by Elizabeth Moss Evanson. London: Routledge and Kegan Paul/New York: Columbia University Press, 1962–64.

———. *Napoléon.* Translated by J. E. Anderson. New York: Columbia University Press, 1969.

———. *La Révolution Française.* Paris: Presses Universitaires de France, 1968.

———. "Sur la pensée de Robespierre." In *Études sur la Révolution Française.* Paris: Presses Universitaires de France, 1963.

Lefebvre, Joël, ed. *La Révolution Française vue par les Allemands.* Translated by Joël Lefebvre. Lyon: Presses Universitaires de Lyon, 1987.

Leibniz, Gottfried Wilhelm von. *Philosophische Schriften und Briefe.* Edited by Ursula Goldenbaum. Berlin: Akademie Verlag, 1922.

Lemaître, Jean. *Jean-Jacques Rousseau.* New York: Macluse Company, 1907.

Léon, Xavier. *Fichte et Son Temps.* 3 vols. Paris: Librairie Armand Collin, 1959.

Leopardi, Giacomo. *Opere.* Milan: Riccardo Riccardi, 1966.

Lessing, Gotthold Ephraim. *Education of the Human Race.* Edited by John D. Haney. New York: Teacher's College, Columbia University, 1908.

———. *Nathan der Weise.* Berlin: Wagenbach, 1977.

Levy, Darline, and Harriet Applewhite. "Women and Political Revolution in Paris." In *Becoming Visible: Women in European History,* edited by Renate Bridenthal and Claude Konz. Boston: Houghton Mifflin, 1987.

Lietzmann, Hans. *The Founding of the Universal Church.* Translated by Bertrand Lee Woolf. New York: Scribner's, 1938.

Linden, Harry van der. *Kantian Ethics and Socialism.* Indianapolis and Cambridge, England: Hackett Publishing Company, 1988.

Lock, F. P. *Burke's Reflections on the Revolution in France.* London: George Allen and Unwin, 1985.

Locke, John. *The Second Treatise of Government.* New York: Macmillan, 1956.

Lombard, Charles. *Joseph de Maistre.* Boston: Twayne Publishers, 1976.

Löwith, Karl. *From Hegel to Nietzsche: The Revolution in Nineteenth-Century Thought.* Translated from the German by David E. Green. New York, Chicago, and San Francisco: Holt, Rinehart and Winston, 1964.

Lukács, Georg. *The Young Hegel: Studies in the Relations between Dialectics and Economics.* London: Merlin Press, 1975.

Luther, Martin. *Ausgewählte Deutsche Schriften.* Edited by Hans Volz. Tübingen: Niemeyer, 1966.

Lyotard, Jean-François. *L'enthousiasme: La critique kantienne de l'histoire.* Paris: Galilée, 1986.

Maccunn, John. *The Political Philosophy of Burke.* London and New York: Longman, 1913.

Machiavelli, Niccolò. *Il principe.* Introduction and notes by Luigi Rosso. Florence: Sansoni, 1958.

MacIntyre, Alasdair, ed. *Hegel: A Collection of Critical Essays.* Notre Dame, Ind.: University of Notre Dame Press, 1976.

Maffei, Scipione. *Merope.* London: Sold by J. Chrichley et al.

Maistre, Joseph Marie de. *Œuvres complètes.* 14 vols. Geneva: Slatkine reprints, 1979.

———. *The Works of Joseph de Maistre.* Translated and edited by Jack Lively. New York and London: Macmillan, 1965.

Manfred, Alfred. *La grande Révolution Française.* Moscow: Foreign Language Edition, 1961.

———. *Rousseau, Mirabeau, Robespierre: Trois figures de la Révolution.* Moscow: Éditions du Progrès, 1986.

Mannheim, Karl. *An Essay on Sociology and Social Psychology.* Edited by P. Kecskemete. New York: Oxford University Press, 1953.

Manson, Richard. *The Theory of Knowledge of Giambattista Vico.* n.p.: Archon Books, 1969.

Manuel, Frank. *The Age of Reason.* Ithaca, N.Y.: Cornell University Press, 1951.

Manzoni, Alessandro. *I promessi sposi.* Translated by Danile J. Connor. New York: Macmillan, 1924.

Marat, Jean-Paul. *Textes choisis.* Edited by Lucien Scheler. Paris: Éditions de Minuit, 1945.

Marcuse, Herbert. *Hegel's Ontology and the Theory of Historicity*. Cambridge, Mass.: MIT Press, 1987.
———. *Reason and Revolution*. Atlantic Highlands, N.J: Humanities Press, 1989.
Marx, Karl. *Critique of Hegel's Philosophy of Right*. Edited by Joseph O'Malley and translated by Annette Jollin and Joseph O'Malley. London and New York: Cambridge University Press, 1970.
———. *The German Ideology*. New York: International Publishers, 1939.
Masson, Pierre Maurice. *La formation religieuse de Rousseau*. Paris: Hachette, 1916.
Master, Roger. *The Political Philosophy of Rousseau*. Princeton, N.J.: Princeton University Press, 1968.
Mathiez, Albert. *The Fall of Robespierre and Other Essays*. London: Hazell, 1927.
———. *The French Revolution*. New York: Russell & Russell, 1962.
Mazzarino, Santo. *Vico: l'annalistica e il diritto*. Naples: Guida Editori, 1971.
McDonald, Joan. *Rousseau and the French Revolution, 1762–1791*. London: Athlone Press, 1965.
McGrath, Alistair. *Reformation Thought: An Introduction*. Oxford and New York: Basil Blackwell, 1988.
McKay, Derek, and H. M. Scott. *The Rise of the Great Powers*. London and New York: Longman, 1983.
McWilliams, W. Carey. "Civil Religion, in the Age of Reason: Thomas Paine on Liberalism, Redemption, and Revolution." *Social Research* 54, no. 3 (autumn 1987): 447–90.
Mehta, V. R. *Hegel and the Modern State: An Introduction to Hegel's Political Thought*. New Delhi: Associated Publishing House, 1968.
Mendelssohn, Moses. *Selections, Moses Mendelssohn: Eine Auswahl aus seinen Schriften und Briefen*. Frankfurt am Main: Kauffman, 1929.
Merriam, C. E. *History of the Theory of Sovereignty since Rousseau*. New York: AMS Press, 1968.
Méthais, Pierre. "Contrat et volonté générale selon Hegel et Rousseau." In *Hegel et le siècle des lumières*, edited by Jacques d'Hondt. Paris: Presses Universitaires de France, 1974.
Meynier, Albert. *Jean-Jacques Rousseau, revolutionnaire*. Paris: Schleicher Frères, 1911.
Mickiewicz, Adam. *Œuvres poétiques complètes*. Paris: Frimin-Didot, 1859.
Mirabeau, Honoré-Gabriel Riqueti. *Discours*. Edited by François Furet. Paris: n.p., 1973.
Molière, Jean-Baptiste Poquelin. *Le bourgeois gentilhomme*. Paris: Librairie générale Française, 1985.
Morely, John. *Burke*. London: Macmillan, 1882.
Muratori, Ludovico. *Opere*. Milan: Riccardo Riccardi, 1964.
Nevins, Allan, and Henry Steele Commager. *A Pocket History of the United States*. New York: Simon & Schuster, 1976.
New Cambridge Modern History. 14 vols. Cambridge: Cambridge University Press, 1957–79.
Newman, Gerard. *The Rise of English Nationalism: A Cultural History 1740–1830*. New York: St. Martin's Press, 1987.
Newton, Isaac. *The Mathematical Principles of Natural Philosophy*. London: Sherwood, Neely and Jones, 1819.
Nicholson, Peter. "Kant on the Duty to Resist the Sovereign." *Ethics* 86 (1976): 214–30.

Nicolini, Fausto. *Commento storico alla seconda scienza nuova*. Rome: Edizioni di Storia e Letteratura, 1949.

Nicolini, Fausto. *La filosofia di Giambattista Vico*. Florence: Sansoni, 1963.

———. *La religiosità di Giambattista Vico*. Bari: Laterza, 1949.

Noether, Emiliana Pasca. *Seeds of Italian Nationalism, 1700–1815*. New York: Columbia University Press, 1951.

Novalis (Friedrich von Hardenberg). *Weltanschauung der Frühromantik*. Edited by Paul Kluckhohm. Leipzig: P. Redam, 1932.

O'Gorman, Frank. *Edmund Burke: His Political Philosophy*. London: George Allen and Unwin, 1973.

Ogg, David. *Europe of the Ancien Régime, 1715–1783*. New York: Harper & Row, 1965.

Packard, Laurence B. *The Commercial Revolution*. New York: Henry Holt and Company, 1927.

Paine, Thomas. *Complete Writings of Paine*. Edited by Philip Foner. New York: Citadel, 1969.

———. *The Essential Thomas Paine*. Edited by Sidney Hook. New York and Toronto: Mentor Books, 1969.

———. *Life and Writings of Paine*. 10 vols. Edited by Daniel Edwin Wheeler. New York: Vincent Parke and Company, 1908.

———. *The Writings of Thomas Paine*. 4 vols. Edited by Moncure D. Conway. New York: AMS Press, 1967.

Palmer, Robert Roswell. *The Age of the Democratic Revolution: A Political History of Europe and America*. Princeton, N.J.: Princeton University Press, 1959.

———. *The World of the French Revolution*. New York: Harper & Row, 1967.

Palmer, Robert Roswell, and Joel Colton. *History of the Modern World*. New York: Alfred A. Knopf, 1965.

Pasini, Dino. *Diritto società e stato in Vico*. Naples: Editore Jovene, 1970.

Payerson, Luigi. *Fichte: Il sistema della libertà*. Milan: U. Mursia, 1976.

Philonenko, Alexis. *Théorie et praxis dans la pensée morale et politique de Kant et de Fichte en 1793*. Paris: Librairie Philosophique de Vrin, 1976.

Pickman, Edward M. *The Mind of Christendom*. London, New York, and Toronto: Oxford University Press, 1937.

Plan, Pierre-Paul. *J.-J. Rousseau raconté par les gazettes de son temps*. New York: Lenox Hill Publishers, 1912.

Pocock, J. G. A. *Virtue, Commerce, and History*. New York: Cambridge University Press, 1985.

Pompa, Leon. *Vico: A Study of the "New Science."* Cambridge: Cambridge University Press, 1975.

Popper, Karl R. *The Open Society and Its Enemies*. Princeton, N.J.: Princeton University Press, 1963.

Pufendorf, Samuel. *De officio hominis et civis juxta legem naturalem*. Cantalorigiae: Ex Officiana Joan Hayes ... Impensis Joan Creed, 1682.

Pushkin, Aleksandr Sergeevich. *Eugene Onegin*. Translated by V. Nabokov. New York: Pantheon Books, 1964.

Ranke, Leopold von. *History of the Reformation in Germany*. Edited by Robert A. Johnson and translated by Sarah Austin. New York: F. Unger, 1966.

Reiss, Hans, ed. *The Political Thought of the German Romantics*. Oxford: Basil Blackwell, 1955.

Remec, Peter R. *The Position of the Individual in International Law according to Grotius and Vattel.* The Hague: Martinus Nijhoff, 1960.

Riley, Patrick, ed. *Kant's Political Philosophy.* Totowa, N.J.: Rowman & Littlefield, 1983.

Ritter, Joachim. *Hegel et la Révolution Française.* Paris: Beauchesne, 1970.

Rivas, Ángel de Saavedra. *Obras Completas.* Madrid: M. Aguilar, 1956.

Robespierre, Maximilien. *Discours et rapports de Robespierre.* Edited by Charles Vellay. Paris: Fasquelles, 1908.

———. *Œuvres.* 3 vols. Edited by Laponneraye. New York: Burt Franklin, 1970.

———. *Œuvres complètes de Maximilien Robespierre.* 10 vols. Edited by Marc Bouloiseau and Albert Soboul, Société des Études Robespierristes. Paris: E. Leroux, 1910.

Rose, Richard. *The Postmodern President: George Bush Meets the World.* 2d ed. Chatham, N.J.: Chatham House, 1991.

Rousseau, Jean-Jacques. *Œuvres complètes.* Edited by Bernard Gagnebin and Marcel Raymond. Paris: Gallimard, 1964.

———. *Œuvres et correspondance inédites de J.-J. Rousseau.* Edited by M. G. Streckeisen-Moultou. Paris: Michel Lévy, 1864.

———. *The Political Writings of Jean-Jacques Rousseau.* Edited from the original MSS and authentic edition with introduction and notes by C. E. Vaughan. 2 vols. Oxford: Basil Blackwell, 1962.

———. *Rousseau's Religious Writing.* Edited by Ronald Grimsley. Oxford: Clarendon Press, 1970.

Rudé, George. *Robespierre: Portrait of a Revolutionary Democrat.* New York: Viking Press, 1975.

———, ed. *Robespierre.* Englewood Cliffs, N.J.: Prentice Hall, 1967.

Sa'adah, Anne. *The Shaping of Liberal Politics in Revolutionary France.* Princeton, N.J.: Princeton University Press, 1990.

Sabine, George. *History of Political Theory.* 3d edition. New York: Holt, Rinehart and Winston, 1966.

Saint-Just, Louis-Antoine-Leon de. *Œuvres complètes de Saint-Just.* Edited by Charles Vellay. Paris: Charpentier et Fasquelle, 1908.

Saint-Pierre, Abbé de. *Projet pour rendre la paix perpétuelle en Europe.* Introduction by Simone Goyard-Fabre. Paris: Garnier, 1981.

Sassoferrato, Bartolo da. *La tiberiade.* Rome: G. Gigliotto, 1587.

Satrobinski, Jean. *Jean-Jacques Rousseau: La Transparence et l'Obstacle.* Paris: Gallimard, 1971.

Savigny, Friedrich Karl von. *Das Recht des Besitzes.* Giessen: Bey Heyer, 1803.

Schama, Simon. *Citizens.* New York: Alfred A. Knopf, 1989.

Schelling, Friedrich Wilhem von. *Introduction à la philosophie de la mythologie.* Translated by S. Jankelevitch. Paris: Aubier, Éditions Montaigne, 1945.

Schlegel, August Wilhelm von. *Neue philosophische Schriften.* Edited by Joseph Körner. Frankfurt am Main: Schulte-Bulmke, 1935.

Schlereth, Thomas J. *The Cosmopolitan Ideal in the Enlightenment.* Notre Dame, Ind.: University of Notre Dame Press, 1977.

Scott, Sir Walter. *The Political Writings of Walter Scott.* Edited by B. J. Legie Robertson. London: Oxford University Press, 1964.

Seidel, George J. *Activity and Ground: Fichte, Schelling, and Hegel.* Hildesheim, N.Y.: Olms, 1976.

Selden, John. *Mare Clausum of the Dominium or Ownership of the Sea*. London: Printed by William Dugard, 1652.

———. *Two Treatises*. London: Printed for Thomas Basset and Richard Chismell, 1683.

Seth, Andrew. *The Development from Kant to Hegel with Chapters on the Philosophy of Religion*. London: Williams and Northgate, 1882.

Shklar, Judith. *Men and Citizens: A Study of Rousseau's Social Theory*. Cambridge: Cambridge University Press, 1969.

Sieyès, Emmanuel Joseph. *Qu'est-ce que le Tiers État?* Edited critically by Roberto Zapperi. Geneva: Droz, 1976.

Simons, Walter. *The Evolution of International Public Laws in Europe since Grotius*. New Haven: Yale University Press, 1931.

Skocpol, Theda. *States and Social Revolutions: A Comparative Analysis of France, Russia and China*. Cambridge, England, and New York: Cambridge University Press, 1979.

Smith, Adam. *The Wealth of Nations*. Edited, with an introduction, by Edwin Cannan. New York: Modern Library, 1937.

Smith, Anthony. *Theories of Nationalism*. New York: Holmes and Meier, 1983.

Smith, Frank. *Thomas Paine: Liberator*. New York: Frederick Strock Company, 1938.

Soboul, Albert. *Comprendre la révolution*. Paris: François Maspero, 1981.

———. *The French Revolution 1787–1789: From the Jacobin Dictatorship to Napoleon*. 2 vols. Bristol: Western Printing Services, 1974.

———. *Histoire de la Révolution Française*. 2 vols. Paris: Gallimard, 1962.

Société des Études Robespierristes. *Jean-Jacques Rousseau, 1712–1778*. Paris: Gap, Imprimerie Louis-Jean, n.d.

Soltau, Roger Henri. *French Political Thought in the Nineteenth Century*. New York: Russell & Russell, 1959.

Stanlis, Peter. *Edmund Burke and the Natural Law*. Ann Arbor: University of Michigan Press, 1958.

Sternhell, Zeev. *La Droite Révolutionnaire: 1885–1914*. Paris: Éditions du Seuil, 1978.

———. *Ni Droite, ni Gauche: L'idéologie fasciste en France*. Éditions du Seuil, 1983.

Stine, Russell Warren. "The Doctrine of God in the Philosophy of Fichte." Ph.D. dissertation, University of Pennsylvania, 1945.

Tagliacozzo, Giorgio, ed. *Vico and Marx: Affinities and Contrasts*. London: Macmillan, 1983.

Tagliacozzo, Giorgio, and Hayden V. White, eds. *Giambattista Vico: An International Symposium*. Baltimore: Johns Hopkins University Press, 1969.

Tagliacozzo, Giorgio, and Donald Phillip Verene, eds. *Giambattista Vico's Science of Humanity*. Baltimore: Johns Hopkins University Press, 1976.

Talmon, J. L. *The Origins of Totalitarian Democracy*. New York: Praeger, 1960.

Taylor, Charles. *Hegel*. Cambridge: Cambridge University Press, 1975.

———. *Hegel and Modern Society*. Cambridge: Cambridge University Press, 1979.

———. *Multiculturalism and the "Politics of Recognition."* Edited by Amy Gutman. Princeton, N.J.: Princeton University Press, 1993.

Thompson, E. P. *The Making of the English Working Class*. New York: Pantheon Books, 1963.

Thompson, J. M. *Robespierre*. New York: Appleton-Century, 1936.

Tooke, Joan D. *The Just War in Aquinas and Grotius*. London: S. P. C. K., 1965.

Treadgold, Donald W. *A History of Christianity.* Belmont, Mass.: Nordland Publishing Company, 1979.

Tuck, Richard. *Natural Rights Theories: Their Origin and Development.* Cambridge: Cambridge University Press, 1979.

Van der Linden, Harry. *Kantian Ethics and Socialism.* Indianapolis and Cambridge, England: Hackett Publishing Company, 1988.

Vattel, Emmerich de. *The Law of Nations.* London: W. Clark and Sons, 1811.

Vaughan, Charles Edwin. *The Romantic Revolt.* New York: Scribner's, 1907.

Vergniaud, Pierre Victurnien. *Œuvres de Vergniaud.* Edited by A. Vermorel. Paris: A. Faure, 1867.

Verri, Pietro. *Basta con la tortura.* Rome: Organizzazione editoriale topografica, 1944.

————. *Reflections on Political Economy.* Translated by B. McGilvray and P. Groenewegen. Fairfield, N.J.: A. M. Kelley, 1993.

Vico, Giambattista. *The Autobiography of Giambattista Vico.* Translated by Max H. Fisher and Thomas Goddard Bergin. New York: Great Seal Books, 1963.

————. *The New Science of Giambattista Vico.* Translated and revised by Thomas G. Bergin and Max H. Fisher. New York: Anchor Books, 1961.

————. *On the Study of Our Time.* Translated with an introduction by Elio Gianturco. New York: Bobbs-Merrill, 1965.

————. *Opere.* Edited by Fausto Nicolini. Milan and Naples: Riccardo Riccardi, 1953.

Vitoria, Francisco de. *Political Writings.* Edited by Anthony Pagden and Jeremy Lawrance. New York: Cambridge University Press, 1991.

————. *Relecciones sobre los indios y el derecho de guerra.* Buenos Aires: Espasa-Calpe Argentina, 1946.

Volpe, Galvano della. *Rousseau and Marx.* London: Lawrence and Wishart, 1978.

Voltaire, François-Marie Arouet de. *Œuvres complètes.* 13 vols. Paris: chez Th. Desoer, 1817.

Vreeland, Hamilton. *Hugo Grotius.* New York: Oxford University Press, 1917.

Vullemin, Jules. *L'héritage Kantien et la révolution Copernicienne.* Paris: Presses Universitaires de France, 1954.

Wallerstein, Immanuel. *The Modern World System.* New York: Academic Press, 1980.

Walzer, Michael. *Just and Unjust War.* New York: Basic Books, 1977.

Weber, Max. *The Protestant Ethic and the Spirit of Capitalism.* Translated by Talcott Parsons, with a foreword by R. T. Tawney. London: George Allen and Unwin, 1930.

White, Andrew D. *Seven Great Statesmen: In the Warfare of Humanity with Reason.* New York: Century City Company, 1915.

Wieland, Christoph Martin. *Geschichte des Agathon.* Munich: Goldman, 1965.

Wilkins, Burleigh Taylor. *The Problem of Burke's Political Philosophy.* Oxford: Clarendon Press, 1967.

Williams, Howard. "Kant's Concept of Property." *Philosophical Quarterly* 27 (1977): 32–40.

————. *Kant's Political Philosophy.* Oxford: Basil Blackwell, 1983.

Williamson, Audrey. *Thomas Paine: His Life, Work and Times.* New York: St. Martin's Press, 1973.

Winfree, Arthur T. *The Geometry of Biological Time.* New York: Springer Verlag, 1980.

Wolff, Christian von. *Gesammelte kleine philosophische Schriften*. Hildesheim, N.Y.: Olms, 1981.

Wollaston, William. *Religion of Nature Delineated*. Delmar, N.Y.: Scholars' Facsimiles and Reprints, 1974.

Wood, Allen W. *Kant's Moral Religion*. Ithaca, N.Y., and London: Cornell University Press, 1970.

Woodward, W. E. *Tom Paine: America's Godfather, 1737–1809*. New York: Dutton, 1945.

Woolf, Cecil Nathan Sidney. *Bartolus of Sassoferrato: His Position in the History of Medieval Political Thought*. Cambridge: Cambridge University Press, 1913.

Wordsworth, William. *A Wordsworth Selection*. Edited by Edith C. Batho. London: University of London, Athlone Press, 1962.

Wordsworth, William, and Samuel Taylor Coleridge. *Lyrical Ballads*. New York: Barnes and Noble, 1963.

Zeno, Apostolo. *Euristeo*. Printed by G. Wood Fall, 1757.

Zouche, Richard. *Juris et Judicii Fecialis*. Edited by Thomas E. Holland. Washington, D.C.: Carnegie Institution of Washington, 1911.

Zweig, Arnulft. *Kant's Philosophical Correspondance*. Chicago: University of Chicago Press, 1967.

Index

Compiled by Eileen Quam and Theresa Wolner

Micheline R. Ishay was born in Tel Aviv and raised in Israel, Luxemburg, and Brussels, Belgium. She is currently assistant professor at the Graduate School of International Studies at the University of Denver, where she is also serving as director of the human rights program and the executive director of the Center on Rights Development. She is coeditor of *The Nationalism Reader*.